Understanding
C

HOWARD W. SAMS & COMPANY
HAYDEN BOOKS

Related Titles

For the retailer nearest you, or to order directly from the publisher, call 800-428-SAMS. In Indiana, Alaska, and Hawaii call 317-298-5699.

Sams
Understanding
Series

Understanding C

Carl Townsend

HOWARD W. SAMS & COMPANY

A Division of Macmillan, Inc.
4300 West 62nd Street
Indianapolis, Indiana 46268 USA

FIRST EDITION
SECOND PRINTING — 1988

International Standard Book Number: 0-672-27278-4
Library of Congress Catalog Card Number: 88-61548

Acquisitions Editor: James S. Hill
Development Editor: James Rounds
Interior Design: Positive Identification, Inc.
Cover Art: DGS&D Advertising, Inc.
Cover Photography: Cassell Productions, Inc.
Illustrator: Don Clemons
Indexer: Ted Laux
Technical Reviewer: Michael P. Maurice
Compositor: Shepard Poorman Communications, Indianapolis

Printed in the United States of America

Cover graphic components are courtesy of ComputerLand®, Indianapolis, and B. Dalton Bookseller, Castleton.

Appendixes B, C, D, and E are reproduced with permission of the publisher, Howard W. Sams & Company, Indianapolis, *QuickC™ Programming for the IBM* by Carl Townsend, Copyright 1988.

Trademark Acknowledgments

Contents

Chapter 7

Introduction to Pointers 107

Chapter 8

Using Functions and Macros 129

Chapter 9

Variable Storage and Memory Models 155

Chapter

14

Using BIOS Services   287

Chapter

15

Introduction to Structured Development   303

Appendix

A

Turbo C and QuickC Comparison   319

Appendix

B

ASCII Character Set   323

Appendix

C

C Operators   331

Preface

C is a simple yet sophisticated programming language that is the choice of many professional programmers. This book is designed as a tutorial introduction to programming with the C language. Two implementations of the language are emphasized—Turbo C and QuickC. These low-cost compilers offer new features that have never been part of any previous C compiler—an integrated developmental environment and graphics support.

Understanding C includes many examples that you can use later as components of your larger programs. Unless otherwise noted, each example will work with both QuickC and Turbo C. Use your compiler to execute these examples. Then experiment with them to see what happens.

Like other books in this series, this book builds understanding of the subject matter in a step-by-step manner. Each chapter builds on the previous one and follows the same format. The chapter begins with a preview of the topics to be discussed. Tutorial examples and drawings illustrate the basic principles set forth in the discussion. The chapter ends with a review of important points and a multiple-choice quiz. Answers to the quiz are provided at the end of the book.

Seven appendixes contain a variety of useful information, including an ASCII table, tips for C users, and resources of books and products. A glossary of computer terms is also included.

Acknowledgments

The author gratefully acknowledges the help of Mike Maurice for his technical support in authoring this book. A special thanks also to Creative Computer (Vitamin C) and FairCom (c-tree and r-tree products).

1 | Introduction to C

About This Chapter

This book is about the C language. It is written for programmers and also those who wish to learn programming. This chapter will introduce the C language and describe its advantages and disadvantages as compared with other languages.

The Computer

A *computer* is a system that solves a problem by processing information.

Until recently, the computer was considered a data processor; that is, it primarily performed operations on numeric values. With the advent of the information age, however, the computer's role suddenly expanded and became even more important: today the computer is an *information processor* capable of handling both data and text. The computer solves a problem by processing information.

A computer has no internal intelligence, except that given to it by a human. The processing that a computer does in solving a problem is controlled by a *program*, a series of instructions designed to accomplish a specific procedure or task.

The programmer generally begins by

For most computer applications, the first step in solving a problem is to define the procedure, or *algorithm*, that can be used to solve the

1

defining a procedure, or *algorithm*, for solving the problem.

problem. This procedure, then, is translated to a computer program and the computer can execute the program (and the procedure) any number of times. The only exceptions to this rule are applications in the area of artificial intelligence. Here, the programmer does not know the procedure, but the programmer can define rules that the computer can use in finding a procedure to solve the problem.

What Is a Programming Language?

Programming languages are used to communicate the problem to a computer in a language that the programmer and computer can understand.

Computers use a specialized language of bits and bytes that is difficult for anyone but a professional programmer to understand. For computers to be useful to lay persons, there must be some way of translating a specific problem into language that the computer can understand. Languages intended for this purpose are called *programming languages*. Once the problem has been translated into a language that the machine can understand, the computer can follow instructions and solve the problem (figure 1.1). A *program* is therefore a set of instructions that a computer can use to solve a problem.

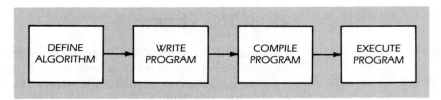

Figure 1.1 Steps for solving a problem

Machine Language

A *machine language* is a language that uses the internal binary codes of the computer's processor. For example, assume that you have the simple problem of solving for z when x has a value of 2 and z is the value of *x + 1*. You could express this problem in simple algebra as:

```
x = 2
z = x + 1
```

In the machine language of an IBM-compatible computer, this set of instructions would be (in hexadecimal notation):

```
C746FE0200 8B46FE
40
8946FC
```

If you try to program the computer using machine language, you will encounter several difficulties:

- The language and the coding are obscure and are difficult to read and interpret.

- The instructions refer to specific memory locations, which could change as the program changes. The programmer must manage the memory locations for storing the data.

- The coding is very machine-dependent. To be executed on a computer different from that for which the program was written, the program must be completely rewritten.

- Most programs comprise many lines of machine-coded instructions.

Assembly Language

You can make machine language easier to understand by using meaningful mnemonics rather than hexadecimal notation. In the previous example, the program becomes:

```
MOV Word Ptr [x],0002
MOV AX,Word Ptr [x]
INC AX
MOV Word Ptr [z],AX
```

The program can be translated into the machine language of the computer by using an *assembler*.

Using assembly language improves the readability of the program, reduces programming errors, and makes the program less dependent on specific memory locations. Even so, assembly language still has the disadvantages of being more a machine-like language than a human language, being processor-dependent, and requiring many lines of code for even a simple program.

In low-level languages, one instruction line written by the programmer translates into one computer instruction.

Machine language and assembly language are both *low-level languages*; that is, a single line of instruction written by the programmer translates into a single instruction in the computer.

High-Level Languages

A *high-level language* is a computer language that is more human-like than a low-level machine language. It uses a single instruction line to represent many lines of assembly-language or machine-language code. This reduces the program development time and makes the program less dependent on the specific processor. High-level languages are bridges, permitting a programmer to write programs quickly with relatively few instructions to solve complex problems (figure 1.2).

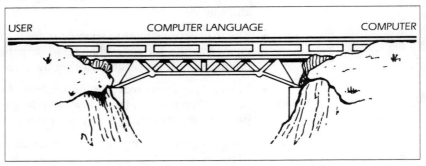

Figure 1.2 Computer languages are bridges

In a high-level language, one instruction written by the programmer translates to several computer instructions.

In a high-level language, one instruction generally translates into several machine-level instructions. This reduces the length of the program that the programmer has to write. Programs written in high-level languages, however, generally require more memory and execute more slowly than programs written in assembly language. High-level language compilers are not as efficient in translating procedures to machine language as a human being is. They do not use the system resources as effectively as programs written in assembly language. Often, some features of the processor are unavailable to the language. High-level languages are generally designed to support a specific type of application and may be inefficient with other types of applications. For example, COBOL is best at financial processing; FORTRAN, at floating point and math applications.

Although almost 200 high-level languages exist today, fewer than a dozen of these languages are in common use by programmers. Here is a quick overview of the most popular high-level languages:

FORTRAN and *COBOL*, two of the earliest computer languages, were developed for mainframe systems. Both are still popular today, with FORTRAN used for many scientific applications and COBOL for commercial business applications (general ledger, accounts receivable, accounts payable). The fact that so much software already exists in these languages ensures that they will be around for a long while. It's often easier to use an old program in one of the older languages, modifying it slightly to solve a new problem, than to write a new program in one of the more recent languages.

BASIC was developed to resemble the English language and to simplify the use of computers. BASIC is easy to learn, and modern BASIC compilers enable inexperienced programmers to quickly write productive and practical programs. BASIC programs, however, are generally inefficient, and the language encourages the use of poor programming practices.

Pascal is a general-purpose language named after the French philosopher and mathematician Blaise Pascal. It was designed to teach good programming techniques. Although very popular in the educational environment, it is not often used to develop commercial products.

dBASE III is a very high-level language that is primarily designed for supporting database management applications.

LISP, SmallTalk, and *Prolog* are used for artificial intelligence applications. In such applications the procedure to solve a problem is poorly defined or not available, but it is possible to define rules for finding the procedure.

Medium-Level Languages

C is a medium-level language that has some of the advantages of both low- and high-level languages.

A *medium-level language* is somewhere between a low-level and a high-level language in the number of instructions required to represent a single machine instruction (see table 1.1). It has many advantages of a machine language, yet gives the developer some of the advantages of a high-level language. C and FORTH are examples of medium-level languages.

C is a general-purpose language that is rapidly gaining popularity for developing application, system, and utility programs for computers. The remainder of this chapter will address its advantages and disadvantages as compared with other languages.

Written in C, the program of the previous section would be

```
main()
{
    int x, z;
    x = 2;
    z = ++x;
}
```

A Short History of C

The C language was created in 1972 as a tool for developing the UNIX operating system.

The C language is a relatively modern language. It was developed by Dennis Ritchie of Bell Laboratories in 1972 as a tool for developing the UNIX operating system. It evolved from an earlier B language developed by Ken Thompson, who also helped to develop this same operating system. Unlike other languages of the time, C was developed for professional programmers and designed to support their specific needs.

The original language was simple, but elegant. Serious programmers quickly recognized the extensive capabilities of the language, and C eventually migrated to the early microcomputers. Application products developed in C were almost always faster than competing products. Moreover, products could be developed on larger machines and then "ported," or converted, to the personal computer.

Table 1.1 Comparison of Low-, Medium-, and High-Level Languages

	Low-Level Language	Medium-Level Language	High-Level Language
Example	Assembly	C	BASIC
Pros	Efficient use of computer resources	Good use of computer resources	Good portability
	Fast execution time Access to all of the computer's resources	Good execution time Good access to the computer's resources	Fast development time Standard language (in most cases)
		Fair readability	Good readability
		Supports structured programming	
Cons	Slow development time	Often slow development time	Slow execution
	Nonstandard language	Nonstandard implementations	Poor use of computer resources
	Poor readability		Limited access to computer resources
	Poor portability Nonstructured		

Today, almost all major application products are developed with the C language.

Today, almost all major application products for the personal computer are developed by using the C language. Ashton-Tate, Microsoft, and Lotus Corporation have chosen this language as the primary vehicle for their product development. During the rest of this chapter, you will see why.

The introduction of low-cost compilers such as QuickC and Borland International's Turbo C has introduced a new dimension in the development of application software. For the first time, developers have an integrated compiler and editor that can produce executable code in seconds.

QuickC and Turbo C have introduced a new dimension in programming, making it possible to develop high-quality executable code in a very short time.

Why are most applications written today developed in C? The answer is simple. The C language offers a versatility, power, and efficiency that is unsurpassed by any other language.

What Is C Used for?

Because C uses computer resources so efficiently and permits access to virtually every feature of the computer system, programmers use it for almost every type of application. Here are a few examples of products that can be developed in C:

- Operating systems
- Application programs
- Artificial intelligence programs (expert systems, robotics, etc.)
- Communication, control, and real-time applications
- System utilities

Features of C

Now let's look at C's specific advantages (all of these are also true of Turbo C and QuickC):

C offers the advantage of very efficient code, standardization, portability, flexibility in data structures, and structured programming support.

- C is one of the most efficient languages available for procedural applications. Programs developed in C will often run faster than those developed in any other language except assembly language. Developers generally write their original program in C and then identify the portions of the program that still cause bottlenecks (loss of speed). These portions are then converted to assembly language, leaving the primary portion in C.

- C has become a significant language by producing the fastest executable code of any language compiler (except assembly).

- For most applications, C makes better use of system resources (such as memory) than other languages.

- C is a standard language. Most compiler writers adhere closely to the ANSI standard, which means source programs can be compiled with any version of C. The difference is primarily in the extended features, such as the graphics support.

- C is portable. Programs developed in C can generally be moved to other systems with a minimum of change. Personal computer programs can be moved up to minicomputers and mainframes, and those on the larger systems can be converted to run on personal computers. Programs can even be moved to other operating systems with a minimum of change, such as from MS-DOS to UNIX. Portability has suffered over the years, however, as extensions to the language have been developed for the various compilers.

- C provides access to virtually every computer feature available to software. You can use it to write operating systems, other language compilers, modem programs, or artificial intelligence tools.

- C is a modern language and supports the new programming techniques that have become popular today: structured programming, top-down planning, recursion, and modular design.

- C is low in cost, with a large number of optional support tools available (at additional cost) for menu design, database management, communications, windowing, and graphics. (The source code for many of these tools is available to the user.) The market for C tools and libraries is large, competition is keen, and consequently prices are low and the variety large.

- C supports a wide variety of data structures, permitting extensive flexibility in representing information. Data structures can be designed to fit the problem, rather than vice-versa.

Limitations of C

It would not be fair to praise the language without also mentioning its limitations:

- C is a lower-level language in comparison with high-level languages, requiring many lines of code for a typical application. For most applications, the user will need to purchase additional libraries to support the specific application. Purchasing commercial libraries reduces the development time and the amount of code that the developer has to write, but it adds to the cost of the original language tool.

- C is a procedural language. Before you can use it, you need to know the procedure to solve the problem. It is difficult to apply C to artificial intelligence applications in which the procedure is not known. Prolog and LISP are often more efficient in these areas. (You can, however, write a Prolog or LISP compiler in C.)

- C is not as readable as high-level languages, and its extensive features make it more difficult to master in comparison with many other languages.

- Although the C language is defined by a standard that has been adopted by most implementations, there is considerable variation between different implementations. For example, although both Turbo C and QuickC (two C implementations) support the ANSI standard, there are important differences between the two.

The Operating System

The *operating system* is a special type of computer program that manages, or supervises, the execution of programs on a computer. At the request of a user, the operating system loads programs from an external memory system (disk, tape, etc.) to the computer's memory and executes them. In the case of the MS-DOS operating system, the operating system releases control of the system to the program once the program is loaded. When the program has completed its task, the program returns control to the operating system. Certain parts of the operating system remain in the computer's memory during the program's execution and may be used by the user's program.

MS-DOS is one of the most popular computer operating systems ever developed.

Operating systems for microcomputers are generally written in assembly language or C. The primary operating system for IBM-compatible microcomputers is known as PC-DOS (for IBM systems) or MS-DOS. MS-DOS is the more generic form, and either operating system supports the use of Turbo C and QuickC.

Introduction to Programming

Before exploring the C language, let's take a few minutes to explore some basic concepts of programming.

Compilers versus Interpreters

When a program is written in assembly language or a high-level language, the code written by the programmer is said to be the *source code*. Once translated by the computer to machine language, it becomes the *executable code*. There are two basic ways of accomplishing this conversion: using a compiler or using an interpreter.

Any computer language can be implemented as either a compiler or an interpreter (table 1.2). If the language is an *interpreter*, it remains in memory with the source code as the program executes. Each time the program is executed, the interpreter reads each line, interprets it, and then executes it. For this reason, using an interpreter is slower than executing a compiled program. The second disadvantage is that the interpreter always remains in memory, occupying critical memory space.

Third, the user must have a copy of the interpreter to run the application program. Finally, the source code is difficult to protect. The user must have the source code to execute the program. Anyone who can read the source code can easily see the procedure, or algorithm, that was used to solve the problem, and the programmer may wish to keep that proprietary.

Table 1.2 The Compiler and Interpreter

Compiler	Interpreter
Fast execution	Slow execution
Minimum use of memory	Extensive use of memory
Source code protected	Source code not protected
Program execution unmanaged	Execution managed under interpreter
Difficult to debug	Easy to debug

Interpreters do have a distinct advantage, however. The interpreter is always in control of the program execution. The execution can be stopped at any point, variables examined or altered, and the execution resumed at the same point or at another point in the program. For this reason, interpreters are popular with developers. BASICA is an example of a computer language interpreter.

A *compiler*, in contrast, is used as part of a process that converts the source code to a machine language program that can then be run without any additional language support. The source code is created with an editor or any word processor in a nondocument mode. A compiler is then used to convert the program to an OBJ file. A *linker* is used to convert the OBJ file to an EXE file (figure 1.3).

A *compiler* converts the source code written by the programmer to an object module. A *linker* is used to convert the object module to a final executable program.

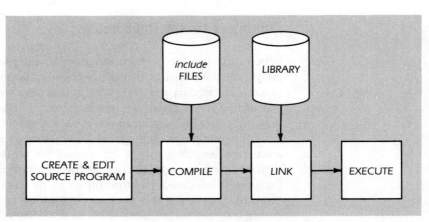

Figure 1.3 The compiling process

You can execute an EXE file as many times as desired. It runs quickly, since it is already in the computer's language and no interpreting is necessary. Moreover, it is very difficult for the user to work backwards to discover the original source code.

The compiler alternative also offers another advantage: frequently used code can be compiled and kept in a library. This library can be used with many source programs. Finally, large programs can be broken down into several smaller programs and each compiled separately, even by different programmers. The linker can then combine all of the compiled OBJ files with any necessary library files, producing a final large EXE file. Both Turbo C and QuickC are compilers, yet contain an editor and many features of an interpreter.

Procedural versus Data-Driven Languages

C is a *procedural language*; that is, before you can write a program you must define a procedure. A *procedure* is a set of steps that, when followed, produces a desired result. The set of steps is known as the *algorithm* for solving a particular problem. Once the program is compiled, it executes one step of the procedure at a time. If the procedure and program are correct and the input data is correct, the output will be correct. BASIC, Pascal, and FORTRAN are other examples of procedural languages.

Sometimes the procedure may be unknown, but basic rules may exist that can be used in an attempt to find a solution for a problem. For example, a physician in making a diagnosis uses his or her experience, intuition, procedures, and other information to arrive at a conclusion that has only a certain probability of being correct. If you were writing a program to help a physician make a medical diagnosis, you would not be able to define a specific procedure that would always work. In this case the program must use the input data to define its own procedure, and the results have only a limited certainty of being correct. Languages used in these types of applications are known as data-driven languages and are used in applications such as robotics, expert systems, and natural language processing. C can be used in such applications, but it is more commonly used to develop higher-level language compilers for these applications. The predominant languages for data-driven applications include Prolog, LISP, and FORTH.

A Simple Example

Before leaving this chapter, try compiling a program to gain some experience with the process of writing, editing, and compiling a program. Here is a simple example you could try:

```
/* FIRST - your first program */

#include <stdio.h>
main()
{
     int x;

     x = 5;
     printf("The value of x is %d.\n", x);
}
```

The four parts of a C source program are the comments, directives, declarations, and body.

Don't worry about how the program works just now, but do examine the basic program components as shown in figure 1.4.

```
/* FIRST - your first program */          Comments

#include <stdio.h>                        Compiler Directive
main()
{
    int x;                                Declaration

    x = 5;
    printf("The value of x is %d.\n",x);  Body
}
```

Figure 1.4 Components of a C program

Note that the program begins with a ***comment***. Comments are statements that aren't executed, but could be used to communicate information to someone reading the source code. They can be placed anywhere in the program. Typical purposes for comments at the beginning of the program include describing the purpose of the program, the author's name, and other details. Comments at other places in the program describe the purpose of a section of code or provide information for debugging. Comments always begin with a forward slash and an asterisk (/*) and end with an asterisk and forward slash (*/).

After the comments are one or more ***compiler directives***. These are directions to the compiler about other files that will be needed during compiling or about definitions that are assumed. Directives have no terminating semicolon and always begin with a pound sign (#). In our program in figure 1.4, the compiler directive is in the form of an *#include* statement. This will be explained in chapter 3, but here the *#include* statement specifies a file that the compiler should read in compiling. You might also add some *#define* directives here that instruct the compiler to make some substitutions in the source code file.

The `main()` name follows the compiler directives and defines the actual beginning of the program. All C programs begin with this `main()` name, regardless of the name of the program.

After the compiler directives and the name of the program come the *declarations*. These are used to associate identifiers in the program with C objects, such as variables, functions, or types. Each declaration is terminated by a semicolon. (Declarations will be discussed more in chapter 2.)

The *body* of the program consists of statements that implement the desired procedure and produce the desired action or output. Each statement is terminated with a semicolon. Statements control the order and flow of the program execution.

Braces are used to set off the body. A *block* is a sequence of declarations and statements enclosed by a set of curly braces. Braces always occur in pairs. A program always consists of at least one block, but braces may be used to define other blocks within the main block.

After you enter the program with the editor and compile it, you should see the following line displayed:

```
The value of x is 5.
```

Review

This chapter has covered the following points:

1 | A computer is an information processor.

2 | A program is a sequence of instructions that enables a computer to solve a problem.

3 | The operating system supervises the execution of programs on the computer.

4 | C is a medium-level language that can be used to develop almost any type of program.

5 | C supports the development of programs that have fast execution speed and make good use of the computer's resources.

6 | The primary parts of a C program are the comments, directives, declarations, and body.

This chapter has also provided an opportunity to compile and execute a simple program.

Quiz for Chapter 1

1 | If the same program is written in each of the following languages, which language will probably produce the fastest execution?
    a | BASIC
    b | FORTRAN
    c | Pascal
    d | C

2 | If the same program is written in each of the following languages, which language will probably produce the fastest execution?
    a | Pascal
    b | COBOL
    c | C
    d | Assembly language

3 | If the same program is written in each of the following languages, which language will probably translate to the shortest executable file?
    a | BASIC
    b | FORTRAN
    c | Pascal
    d | C

4 | If the same program is written in each of the following languages, which version will probably have the fewest number of source code lines?
    a | Assembly language
    b | Turbo C
    c | QuickC
    d | BASIC

5 | Give one reason why programmers use the C language.
    a | All C implementations are standard.
    b | Development time is much less than with other languages.
    c | Programs developed in C generally execute faster than those developed in high-level languages.
    d | C is easy to learn and use.

6 | What is one advantage of a compiler over an interpreter?
    a | A compiled program usually executes faster than an interpreted program.
    b | Most compilers cost less than an interpreter.
    c | Programs can be developed faster with a compiler than with an interpreter.
    d | The compiler is easier to use.

7 | Which of the following is not a procedural language?
    a | C

      b | BASIC
      c | Assembly language
      d | LISP

8 | Which of the following is the most recent language?
      a | COBOL
      b | FORTRAN
      c | BASIC
      d | C

9 | What is one characteristic difference of a program written in a low-level language as compared with a program written in a high-level language?
      a | It has more lines of source code.
      b | It executes slower.
      c | It is easier to read and modify.
      d | None of the above

10 | C has its roots in which operating system?
      a | MS-DOS
      b | PC-DOS
      c | UNIX
      d | None of the above

11 | What type of character(s) is used to indicate the beginning of a comment?
      a | Pound sign
      b | No character
      c | Slash-asterisk
      d | Asterisk-slash

12 | What part of the C program contains the statements that implement the desired procedure?
      a | Declarations
      b | Directives
      c | Body
      d | None of the above

13 | What is the first statement in a C program after the compiler directives?
      a | Declaration
      b | A comment
      c | `main()`
      d | The name of the executable file

14 | Which is the favored language of most professional program developers?
      a | Pascal
      b | BASIC
      c | COBOL
      d | C

15 | Which of the following is not a compiler?
   a | Assembler
   b | Turbo C
   c | QuickC
   d | BASICA

2 | Representing Data

About This Chapter

This chapter will explain the fundamentals of representing data in a C program. You will learn which types of variables and constants can be used in C, how to declare variables, and what techniques to use in initializing variables and constants.

Variables and Constants

The data in a computer is a symbol of something in the real world.

A computer program uses two types of data: constants and variables.

When you use a computer, information about the real world is abstracted to data. The program processes the data (figure 2.1). Data is always an abstraction of reality, a symbol of something in the real world.

A computer program uses two types of data: constants and variables. *Variables* are data that can change during the program's execution. *Constants* are variables that do not change in value during the execution of the program. Variables always have names. Constants may or may not have names.

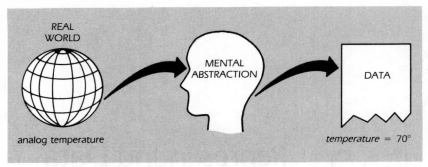

Figure 2.1 From the real world to data

Declaring Variables

In a C program all variables and identifiers must be declared before they can be used. Declaring a variable means associating the variable with some type of C object.

In any C program all variables and other identifiers must be declared before you can use them. *Declaring a variable* means to associate the variable with some kind of C object, such as a variable, function, or type, for example:

```
int x;
```

In this case the variable x is identified as an *int* type. (*Int* types and other data types are discussed in the section "Data Types.") The declaring of identifiers is generally done at the beginning of the program.

Using your C compiler, try to compile the following program both with and without the declaration line. What happens when you omit the declaration line?

```
main()
{
        int x; /* declaration line */

        x = 3;
}
```

With QuickC or Turbo C, if the variable x is not declared, you will get an error message that x is undefined.

Declaring a variable also indirectly defines how much space the variable will use, names the storage location for the variable, and limits the type and range of values that the variable can have. The amount of storage space required for a variable and the range that can be associated with a numeric data type vary with the compiler (C implementation).

You can use multiple declaration statements, such as

```
int x;
int y;
```

or you can use

```
int x, y;
```

The C language, by forcing you to declare all variables, has several advantages over languages that do not declare variables (such as BASIC):

Because C forces the programmer to declare variables, C provides better control of the environment than languages that do not support declarations.

- Having all variables declared in one place (at the beginning of a program or function) makes it easier to see what the program is doing and to add appropriate comments.

- It is easier to add, edit, and delete variable names when they are declared in a single location. It is also easier to prevent the duplication of variable names.

- You have better control of the environment during compiling and execution.

- Declaring variables forces you to think ahead and plan what the program will do.

- Declaring variables helps you to find variable names that are misspelled in the program.

Naming Variables

An *identifier* is a name that you give a variable.

With C, you have a lot of flexibility in naming variables. The name that you give a variable is called an *identifier*. The general rules for creating identifiers in Turbo C and QuickC are as follows:

1 | Identifiers must start with a letter or an underscore.

2 | The remainder of the identifier can consist of letters, underscores, or digits. No other special characters are allowed. To use a two-word name, separate the two words with an underscore:

   `last_name`

3 | Only the first 31 characters of the identifier are significant in QuickC; the first 32 in Turbo C.

4 | Identifiers are case-sensitive; for example, the identifier `Initial` is not the same as `initial`.

5 | It is illegal to use keywords as variable names. For C, the keywords are:

auto	do	fortran	register	switch
break	double	goto	return	typedef
case	else	huge	short	union
cdel	enum	if	signed	unsigned
char	extern	int	sizeof	void
const	far	long	static	volatile
continue	float	near	struct	while
default	for	pascal		

6 | Avoid beginning an identifier with an underscore. Identifiers beginning with an underscore are reserved for system variables.

Tip | In naming variables in your program, choose names that are meaningful in the context of the program. This will dramatically improve the readability of the program.

Data Types

In an earlier section you learned that to declare a variable means to associate it with some type of C object. A *type* is both a set of values and a set of operations performed on these values. In the previous examples you used the *int*, *float*, and *char* types. Assigning a variable to the *int* type constrains the variable to the *domain* of *int*; that is, the value of the variable must be within a specified range and only those operations permitted by that type are permitted.

The C language provides a wide range of built-in types to support almost any data structure that you need to represent.

The C language provides a wide range of built-in types, including the three already used, as well as pointers, enumerations, arrays, structures, unions, and functions. In later chapters you will use examples of each of these. Figure 2.2 shows the basic relationships of the various types. These relationships give C a lot of flexibility in managing data.

This section will introduce some of the more common data types used by the C language. These are divided into two categories: integral types and floating point types. Other types will be introduced in subsequent chapters.

Integral Types

The integral data types are used to store integers and characters.

Integral data types are used to store integers and characters. An *integer* is a whole number such as 123, 1, or −12. For numeric data processing, you should use integer data types as much as possible. Processing is much faster and more accurate than with floating-point data types. Integers also require less memory space than floating point types do.

HOWARD W. SAMS & COMPANY
HAYDEN BOOKS

The Waite Group's Advanced C Primer ++
Stephen Prata
ISBN: 0-672-22486-0, $24.95

The Waite Group's C Primer Plus, Revised Edition
Mitchell Waite, Stephen Prata, and Donald Martin
ISBN: 0-672-22582-4, $23.95

The Waite Group's Microsoft® C Programming for the IBM®
Robert Lafore
ISBN: 0-672-22515-8, $24.95

The Waite Group's Turbo C Programming for the IBM®
Robert Lafore
ISBN: 0-672-22614-6, $22.95

The Waite Group's Inside the Amiga with C, Second Edition
John Berry
ISBN: 0-672-22625-1, $24.95

Hayden Books C Library Programming in C, Revised Edition
Stephen G. Kochan
ISBN: 0-672-48429-X, $24.95

Programming in ANSI C
Stephen G. Kochan
ISBN: 0-672-48408-0, $24.95

Advanced C: Tips and Techniques
Paul Anderson and Gail Anderson
ISBN: 0-672-48417-X, $24.95

(more titles on the back)

To order, return the card below, or call 1-800-428-SAMS. In Indiana call (317) 298-5699.

Please send me the books listed below.

Title	Quantity	ISBN #	Price

☐ Please add my name to your mailing list to receive more information on related titles.

Name (please print) _____

Company _____

City _____

State/Zip _____

Signature _____
(required for credit card purchase)

Telephone # _____

Subtotal _____

Standard Postage and Handling **$2.50**

All States Add Appropriate Sales Tax _____

TOTAL _____

Enclosed is My Check or Money Order for $_____

Charge my Credit Card: ☐ VISA ☐ MC ☐ AE

Account No. ☐☐☐☐ ☐☐☐☐ ☐☐☐☐ ☐☐☐☐

Expiration Date _____

27278

**Hayden Books UNIX® System
Library
Topics in C Programming**
Stephen G. Kochan, Patrick H. Wood
ISBN: 0-672-46290-7, $24.95

**Miscellaneous
C Programmer's Guide to
Serial Communications**
Joe Campbell
ISBN: 0-672-22584-0, $26.95

**C with Excellence:
Programming Proverbs**
Henry Ledgard with John Tauer
ISBN: 0-672-46294-X, $18.95

**QuickC Programming for the
IBM®**
Carl Townsend
ISBN: 0-672-22622-7, $22.95

**Portability and the C
Language (forthcoming)**
Rex Jaeschke
ISBN: 0-672-48428-5, $24.95

**The Waite Group's Microsoft®
C Bible (forthcoming)**
Naba Barkakati
ISBN: 0-672-22620-0, $24.95

**The Waite Group's Turbo C
Bible (forthcoming)**
Naba Barkakati
ISBN: 0-672-22631-6, $24.95

Place
Postage
Here

HOWARD W. SAMS & COMPANY

Dept. DM
4300 West 62nd Street
Indianapolis, IN 46268-2589

|.|..|.||....|.|.||..|.|..|..|.|.|.|.|..|.|.|..||..|

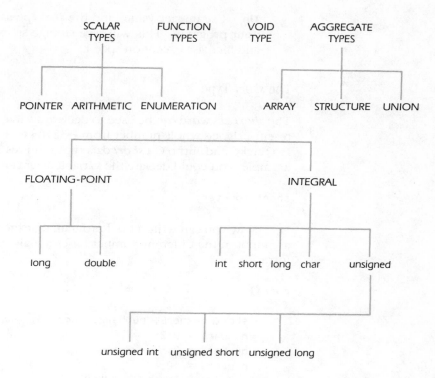

Figure 2.2 Categories of types for C

You can express variable values for integers in decimal, octal, or hexadecimal numbering. To indicate the appropriate numbering system, use the following rules:

1 | Prefix the number with *0x* or *0X* to indicate a hexadecimal value.

2 | Prefix the number with *0* to indicate an octal value.

3 | Do not use any prefix for decimal values. If no prefix is used, the number is assumed to be decimal.

All of the following expressions are equivalent:

```
012 = 0XA = 0xA = 10
```

Any input value, regardless of the way it is entered, is stored as the same binary value. You will see an example of this in the next section.

The four types of integer variable keywords are *short*, *int*, *long*, and *char*.

There are four basic types of integer variable keywords: *short*, *int*, *long*, and *char*. There is also another keyword, *unsigned*, that you can use to extend the positive range of any other keyword. For example, *unsigned int* permits the storage of positive values up to twice as large as the values stored with an *int* type.

Tip | Use integer values and the *int* type as much as possible in your programs. This will save storage space, improve accuracy, and increase execution speed.

The *short* Type

The *short* keyword can be used to declare a variable that is used to represent a signed whole number from −32768 to +32767 on an IBM PC. In QuickC and Turbo C a *short* data type requires 2 bytes of storage. For example, you could declare the variable `counter` as

```
short counter;
```

Now you can write a brief program that shows how numbers that are input in the different number bases are all stored in an equivalent form:

```
main()
{
      short number1, number2, number3;
      number1 = 012;
      number2 = OXA;
      number3 = 10;
      printf("Number1 is %d\n",number1);
      printf("Number2 is %d\n",number2);
      printf("Number3 is %d\n",number3);
}
```

What is the output when you execute this program? Note that *printf( )* is a standard C function that will be explained fully in chapter 4. For this chapter and the next one, you need only understand certain basic aspects of *printf( )*. Its form is

```
printf(control string[,item₁,item₂,itemᵢ,...itemₙ]);
```

The `control string` represents what is written, and contains text and format identifiers. The format identifiers begin with a percent sign, for example:

```
printf("Number1 is %d\n",number1);
```

The *items* are the variables associated with the respective format identifier. If `number1` is 5, the preceding statement will produce

```
Number1 is 5
```

The \n is a backslash code that initiates the writing of a new line on the output device. For now, you should note the following format identifier codes:

%d   Integer decimal value

%f   Floating point value

%c   Character value

%s   String value

For more information on identifier codes, see chapter 4.

Although the *short* type may seem the best alternative for the programmer, most compilers are designed to produce their most efficient code with the *int* type, and it is the preferred alternative.

The *int* Type

For any given C implementation, *int* is generally the most efficient data type.

In the standard C language, the *int* keyword defines an integer type that has a limited numeric range. In QuickC, for a PC, XT, AT, or PS/2 compatible computer, the numeric range of an *int* variable is the same as that for a *short* variable. For most computers, the *int* type is the most efficient for calculations, and it should be used whenever possible in your program.

With any given C implementation, the representation of a *short* variable is generally 16 bits and a *long* variable is 32 bits. QuickC and Turbo C use this same representation. The representation of an *int* variable, however, is implementation dependent. With QuickC and Turbo C, it is 16 bits (the same as a *short* variable). The DEC PDP-11 also uses 16 bits. A DEC VAX, however, uses a 32-bit *int* variable.

The *long* Type

In the standard C language, the *long* keyword defines an integer (whole number) type that has an extended numeric range. With QuickC and Turbo C, a variable declared as *long* requires 32 bits (4 bytes) of storage, twice as much as a *short* variable. It can be used to represent any integer from −2,147,482,648 to +2,147,482,647.

As with a *short* variable, the declaration may or may not contain the *int* keyword. The following declarations are both the same type:

```
long quantity1;
long int quantity2;
```

When constants are used in a program, QuickC and Turbo C automatically pick the proper storage type for the numeric value. For example, 900,000 would be stored as a *long* integer. If you have a *short* integer constant and wish to store it as a *long* integer, the value must be terminated with an uppercase *L* to indicate that it is *long*, for example, 0X1AL or 23L.

Note | A lowercase *l* is legal, but not recommended.

Unsigned Integers

You can use the *unsigned* keyword with *int*, *short*, or *long* to extend the positive range of a variable if negative values are excluded, for example:

```
unsigned int counter1;
unsigned counter2;
unsigned long int counter3;
unsigned long counter4;
```

Notice that if an unsigned keyword is used with no additional keywords, *int* is assumed. In this example, `counter1` has the same positive range as `counter3`, a *long* integer (approximately 64,000). The variable `counter1`, however, cannot be used with negative numbers.

The *unsigned short* type has a range of 0 to 65,535. The *unsigned long* type has a range of 0 to 4,294,967,295.

The *char* Type

Variables declared as *char* can be used to store any valid single character.

You can declare a variable as a *char* type when you want to store a single character. Character variable values can be any valid character, including special and nonprintable characters. The character must be enclosed in single quotes. Only 1 byte of storage is used. In the following example the character **C** is enclosed in single quotes.

```
main()
{
    char ch;

    ch = 'C';
    :
    :
}
```

Like other integral types, the *char* type is simply a form of integer storage. The C program stores a character by using an integer value. The program converts the input character to an integer, stores it, and then converts it back to a character when writing.

The numeric codes used to represent characters have been standardized by the American National Standards Institute and are referred to as the *ASCII Code*. The Code consists of 94 printable characters and 34 nonprintable control characters. On the IBM PC systems, this range has been extended by a group of graphics characters.

You can also declare an *unsigned char* type. The signed *char* type has a range from −128 to +127. The unsigned *char* type has a range from 0 to 255.

You might think that a *char* type is a good way to store a small integer, since it uses only 1 byte of storage. In practice, however, the opposite is true. The *char* type is generally a poor choice for storing even single characters. Compilers are designed to be most efficient with the *int* type. In addition, the *char* type may sometimes introduce unusual errors. Use the *int* type to store character constants. Here is an example using an *int* type to store a character:

```
/* CHAR.C */

main()
{
    int ch;

    ch = 's';
    printf("The character is %c.",ch);
}
```

Use the *char* type primarily for character strings (arrays).

Floating Point Numbers

Floating point numbers are numbers with a fractional part. They are stored by Turbo C and QuickC as binary numbers.

A *floating point number* is a number that can contain a fractional part, such as 123.23 or −34.5. Floating point numbers are roughly equivalent to the real numbers used by mathematicians.

Floating point numbers in Turbo C and QuickC are stored as binary numbers, not as decimal numbers. The base part and exponent are stored separately. This permits you to represent decimal fractions and to store a far greater numeric range than is possible with integer values.

Floating-point variable values and floating point constants can be expressed in either of two ways: *numeric values* or *exponential notation*. For example, both of the following are acceptable and represent the same value:

```
3.248E2
324.8
```

You cannot use octal or hexadecimal floating point numbers.

You can use either decimal or exponential notation:

- The decimal notation contains a decimal point, such as 10.23. This is the most common notation for most people.

- The exponential notation consists of two parts separated by an *e* or *E*, such as 1023E −2. The first part (1023) is the mantissa. The second part (2) is the exponent and represents a power of ten. The notation 10.23, then, is the decimal equivalent of 1023E−2.

> **Note** | Floating point numbers are subject to round-off errors and other problems if you are not careful. Use integers whenever possible to improve accuracy. Use floating point numbers when decimal values or extended numeric ranges are necessary.

In exponential notation Turbo C and QuickC provide two methods of declaring floating point numbers: *float* and *double*.

The *float* Type

The *float* keyword is used as the most general type of floating point declaration.

The *float* keyword is used for the most general form of floating point declaration. For Turbo C and QuickC, this requires 32 bits of storage (4 bytes), which is the same amount of storage used for a *long* integer. The numeric range that can be stored, however, is much larger: −3.4E−38 to +3.4E+38 in either implementation.

> **Note** | Be careful to distinguish between the *precision* of a number and its *range*. Try the following example to understand the difference between precision and range. You will see that the output is not the exact value of x. Turbo C and QuickC use only 2 bytes to store the mantissa, and if a number is too precise, some digits will get lost. In the following program, why doesn't the output match the value of x exactly?

```
/* FLOAT example */

main()
{
    float x;

    x =123456789.0;
    printf("%f",x);
}
```

Turbo C and QuickC can handle the range in this example, but not at the precision of the variable x. To declare a floating point number, use the *float* keyword with the name of one or more variables, such as:

```
float centigrade, fahrenheit;
```

The *double* Type

Declaring a variable as *double* permits you to allocate twice as much storage space to the variable, or 64 bits (8 bytes). This gives you a higher precision and greater range for floating number types. Try the previous example again with x declared as *double*. What happens now? The full precision is maintained.

To declare a floating point number as *double*, use the *double* keyword with the name of one or more variables, such as

```
double centigrade, fahrenheit;
```

The range for a Turbo C or QuickC *double* type is $-1.7E-308$ to $+1.7E+308$.

Initializing Variables

You can use the declaration statement to initialize a variable.

You can use the declaration statement to initialize a variable to any specific value. For example, you could simplify the program in figure 1.4 of chapter 1 as

```
main()
{
    int x = 5;

    printf("The value of x is %d.\n", x);
}
```

Notice that the variable is declared and initialized in one statement.

Representing Character Strings

A *character string* is a series of one or more characters, for example,

```
"My favorite ice cream is vanilla."
```

The quote marks are not considered part of the character string and are not stored with it. Quote marks are used to define a string in a source program, just as single quotes are used to define a character.

Storing Character Strings

Character strings are stored as character arrays.

C has no special variable type for storing strings. To store a string, an array of the *char* type is used. An *array* is an ordered sequence of data elements of the same type. You could think of the characters as being stored in a series of adjacent memory locations, with 1 character in each byte. The resulting memory space looks much like figure 2.3. Notice that the last character of the array is \0, which is the *null character*. The null character is used to mark the end of a string.

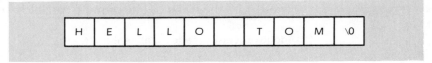

Figure 2.3 Storing a character string

An array of characters is defined by putting the number of cells in the array in brackets after the variable name. For example, to declare an array of 20 characters for the variable **msg**, you would use

```
char msg[20 + 1];
```

A "pad" of 1 character is used for the terminating null character. The variable **msg** contains the address of the first character of the string. Remember that you must save enough space for the string and the null character. For example, to save the 5-character string **"Hello"** as the maximum size in **msg**, you need to define the array as

```
char msg[6];
```

Now try an example program using a character string:

```
#include <stdio.h>
main()
{
        char msg[20];

        printf("What is your favorite flower? ");
        fgets(msg,20,stdin);
        printf("Your favorite flower is the %s",msg);
}
```

The *char* declaration saves an array space of 20 characters for **msg**. The first *printf( )* function displays a prompt for the user. The *fgets( )* function saves whatever the user enters in **msg**. The *printf( )* function then writes the array to the output device. Chapter 4 will explain these functions. The *#include* compiler directive will be explained in chapter 3.

After you have entered, compiled, and executed this program with your C compiler, try the following experiments:

1 | Enter a number as the input string. What does the program write to the screen?

2 | Change the declaration to declare msg as an array of 4 characters:

```
char msg[4];
```

3 | Now enter a 5-character input string. What does the program write to the screen?

Since the text string is stored as an array (or string) of characters, you could also access any particular character in the string. The following program returns the first character of the input string:

```
#include <stdio.h>
main()
{
      char msg[20];

      printf("What is your favorite flower? ");
      fgets(msg,20,stdin);
      printf("The first character of your favorite flower is
            %c\n",msg[0]);
}
```

As a final experiment, try to enter and compile this program:

```
#include <stdio.h>
main()
{
      char msg[20];

      msg = "Hello out there!";
      printf("The computer's message is %s",msg);
}
```

This program won't even compile correctly and return an error message. What's wrong? You have declared an array for the text, and then it appears that you tried to assign a text string to this array. The problem is that the variable msg is the storage location for the address starting point of the array. This is a fixed location, and the compiler will not let you change this value with an assignment statement (see chapter 3). An array name is a storage location for the address of the starting character of an array. It is a constant that can't be modified or assigned a value. The correct form is

```
#include <stdio.h>
main()
{
      char msg[20];

      strcpy(msg,"Hello out there!");
      printf("The computer's message is %s\n",msg);
}
```

In this example the function *strcpy( )* is used to copy the string value to the array.

Initializing a Character Array

Character string arrays can be initialized when declared, just as numeric variables can.

Arrays can be initialized when they are declared, just as numeric values can. There are two additional factors, however, that must be considered. The first is that when an array is initialized at the same time as it is declared, you must also use the *static* keyword. The second is that the size of the array does not need to be specified. Here are three ways you could initialize a starting array to contain the value "Hello":

```
static char msg1[] = "Hello";
static char msg2[] = {'H','e','l','l','o','\0'};
static char msg3[6] = "Hello";
```

The *static* keyword forces the compiler to allocate space for the array when it is compiled (it actually does even more than this, and you will learn more about its role in chapter 10). You don't need to specify the array size because when the program is compiled the compiler can determine the array size from the size of the initializing string. How large would the array be in the preceding example?

Again, you would not be able to change the value of **msg** in the program, but you could change the characters stored in the **msg** buffer. The following would work perfectly:

```
#include <stdio.h>
main()
{
      static char msg[]="Hello";

      strcpy(msg,"ABCDE");
      puts(msg);
}
```

The screen would display the value `ABCDE`.

Other Data Types

C provides you with the capability to define your own data types and structures. Boolean variables, complex structures, and other variations are possible. You will see more of this in other examples, particularly in chapter 11.

Review

In this chapter you have learned how to name, declare, and initialize variables. Specifically, you have learned:

1 | That variables must be declared before they are used.

2 | Why identifiers are declared in C.

3 | How to name an identifier.

4 | What the C data types are: *int*, *short*, *long*, *unsigned*, *char*, *float*, and *double*.

5 | What the most efficient type of identifier for most C operations in most C compilers is: the *int*.

6 | How to store a text string using a character array.

7 | How to initialize variables and character arrays.

Quiz for Chapter 2

1 | Which of the following is not a valid identifier in C?
  a | currency$value
  b | part_no
  c | 2Able
  d | Able2

2 | Which of the following are not valid integer values in QuickC and Turbo C?
  a | 1A
  b | 038
  c | 0x2F
  d | None of the above

3 | To save a name having a maximum of 20 characters, which of the following declarations is correct?
  a | char name[19];
  b | char name[20];
  c | char name[21];
  d | None of the above

4 | What is the output of the following program?

```
main()
{
        static char msg[] = "Hello";

        printf("%c",msg[1]);
}
```

  a | H
  b | e
  c | It will not compile.
  d | None of the above

5 | What is the output when rose is entered?

```
#include <stdio.h>
main()
{
        char msg[4 + 2];

        printf("What is your favorite flower? ");
        fgets(msg,6,stdin);
        printf("Your favorite flower is the %s.\n",msg);
}
```

  a | rose
  b | ros

    c | It will not compile.

    d | None of the above

6 | Which of the following declarations is incorrect?

    a | unsigned int x;

    b | float y = 4.1;

    c | char message[ ] = "This is a test";

    d | char answer[3];

7 | Which of the following declarations is incorrect?

    a | short abc;

    b | unsigned char 'c';

    c | unsigned int 'c';

    d | char "a"

8 | Which of the following is the most efficient data type for storing a single character in most C implementations?

    a | short

    b | char

    c | int

    d | long

9 | How many bytes are needed to store the string "Writing C programs is fun!"?

    a | 26

    b | 27

    c | 28

    d | None of the above

10 | Which of the following declarations is incorrect?

    a | char ch = "s";

    b | float x, y, z = 3.2;

    c | int ch = 'c';

    d | None of the above

11 | Which of the following is invalid:

    a | int union=2;

    b | short ch = 1;

    c | float temperature;

    d | char msg[2] = "a";

12 | Which of the following is false?

    a | C has more data types than most other languages.

    b | C stores strings as an array of characters.

    c | char ch = '\007' is illegal as a declaration.

    d | Using a *double* type instead of *float* can improve the precision of an answer.

13 | Which of the following is not a valid identifier name?

    a | Near

    b | Near_stuff

      c | near

      d | None of the above

14 | How many characters are unique in a Turbo C name?

      a | 8

      b | 5

      c | 31

      d | 15

15 | Which of the following characters are not allowed in an identifier name?

      a | Space

      b | Period

      c | Exclamation point

      d | Comma

3 | Arithmetic Operations and Expressions

About This Chapter

Operators define actions
to be performed on one
or more operands.

This chapter will examine the use of operators in statements. C uses operators to perform actions. Operators are the verbs in a C statement. An *operator* defines the action that is to be performed on one or more operands.

The following C statement contains four operators:

```
centigrade = (5.0/9.0) * (fahrenheit - 32.0);
```

The four operators in this statement are: /, *, -, and =. C has about 40 operators available to the programmer. Some, of course, are used far more than others.

Types of Operators

C provides six types of operators: assignment, arithmetic, bitwise, relational, logical, and special. The following sections will examine each type.

The Assignment Operator

The *assignment operator* is perhaps the most basic of operators. It is represented by an equal sign, for example:

```
x = 34.5/2.0;
```

The assignment operator assigns a value to a variable.

This statement results in x being assigned the value of **34.5** divided by **2.0**, or 17.25. In reality x is the name of a storage location. The result of the division is placed in that storage location.

With C, you can do multiple assignments in a single statement. The following is perfectly valid if both variables are *ints*:

```
age = previous_age = 12;
```

This assigns the value of **12** to **age** and **previous_age**.

> **Note** | It is important to recognize that the assignment operator changes the value of the variable to the left of the operator. Do not use it to check for equality. Use a relational operator for that purpose (see "Relational Operators").

Arithmetic Operators

Arithmetic operators permit C to do numeric operations on variables.

C provides five *arithmetic operators*:

Arithmetic Operators

+	Plus (addition)
–	Minus (subtraction)
*	Times (multiplication)
/	Divided by (division)
%	Modulo (integer remainder)

Each operator performs an action with two operands. You can use them with constants or variables, and they can be part of a function argument. For example,

```
age = first_age + 3;
```

assigns the value of **3** plus **first_age** to **age**. The next example shows an arithmetic operator used as part of a function argument:

```
printf("%d",10+12);
```

This produces the value 22.

In any expression, spaces are nulls and can be used as necessary for clarity. The preceding expression is the same as:

```
printf("%d", 10 + 12);
```

The minus sign can be used to represent both subtraction and negative numbers:

```
temperature = (-30);
printf("%d", 40 - 12);
```

The modulus operator can be used only for integer arithmetic. It gives the remainder that results when the left operand is divided by the right operand. For example,

```
x = 25 % 3;
```

reads as "25 modulo 3" and produces a value of 1 (25 divided by 3 is 8, with a remainder of 1). For *float* or *double* type, use the *fmod( )* function. For example, the following program returns a value of 4 to z:

```
main()
{
        double x,y,z;

        x = 24;
        y = 5;
        z = fmod(x,y);
        .
        .
        .
}
```

Note | To facilitate portability, C arithmetic should be written in the following style:

```
x = add(a,b)
```

in which **add( )** is a function or macro. This permits more consistent control of the operation, for example, when you are checking for errors.

Bitwise Operators

Bitwise operators permit operations at the bit level.

Bitwise operators allow you to perform operations at the bit level. The following six bitwise operators are available in C:

Bitwise Operators

&	AND
¦	OR
^	XOR
~	NOT
<<	Shift left one bit
>>	Shift right one bit

Now let's look at examples of these operators.

The NOT Operator

The *NOT operator* changes each 0 to 1 and 1 to 0:

```
~(10110) == 01001
```

The AND Operator

The *AND operator* produces a 1 in the corresponding output bit position only if both of the input bits in that position are 1. There is no carry.

```
(10110) & (01011) == 00010
```

The OR Operator

The *OR operator* produces a 1 in the corresponding output bit position if either of the input bits in that position is 1:

```
(10110) ¦ (01011) == 11111
```

The EXCLUSIVE OR Operator

The *EXCLUSIVE OR operator* produces a 1 in the corresponding bit position if either of the input bits in that position is 1, but not both:

```
(10110) ^ (01011) == 11101
```

Shift Operators

The *left shift operator* shifts the bits of the left operand to the left by the number of places specified by the right operand:

```
101010 << 2 == 101000
```

The left bits are lost, and the right bits that are moved in are filled with zeros.

The *right shift operator* shifts the bits of the left operand to the right by the number of places specified by the right operand:

```
1010 >> 2 == 0010
```

The bits moved past the right end are lost. For unsigned data types, the bits vacated at the left are replaced by zeros.

> **Note** | Use the shift operators with unsigned integer types only. The behavior of the right shift with signed types is very compiler dependent.

Using Bitwise Operators

Bitwise operators can be used to extract information from flag variables by means of masks.

One use of the bitwise operators is to extract information from flag variables by means of masks. A *mask* is a pattern of bits that is used to select bits from a variable. The bits of the flag variable represent on/off states, and a mask is ANDed with the variable to obtain the desired bit. This bit is then tested to see if the state is on or off.

For example, assume that you have an adventure game in which each room has a variable `condition(room)` associated with it of 8 bits. The rightmost bit indicates whether the room has light or whether it is dark. If dark, of course, the adventurer would need a light to see any objects in the room or to move. You could then test to see if the room had light by using the mask `LIGHTMASK(00000001)` as:

```
(condition(room) & LIGHTMASK)
```

This would mask off the right bit, which could then be tested by using an *if* statement (see chapter 5) to determine whether the room had light. Table 3.1 shows the rules for using bitwise operators. A left shift (`<<`) multiplies the number by two; a right shift (`>>`) divides it by two.

Table 3.1 *Rules for Using Bitwise Operators*

First Operand	Second Operand	AND &	OR ¦	XOR ^
0	0	0	0	0
0	1	0	1	1
1	0	0	1	1
1	1	1	1	0

Relational Operators

Relational operators are used for comparing two quantities.

Relational operators are used in conditional statements (chapter 5) to compare two quantities. There are six relational operators in C:

Relational Operators

>	Greater than
>=	Greater than or equal to
<	Less than
<=	Less than or equal to
==	Equal to
!=	Not equal to

These operators will be introduced more completely in chapter 5, but notice two facts:

- The result of an expression with relational operators is either 1 (true) or 0 (false).

- In comparing for equality, a double equal sign (==) rather than a single equal sign is used. The double equal sign tests for equality. The single equal sign assigns a value to a variable.

Logical Operators

Expressions with logical operators always produce a value of 0 or 1.

Logical operators, like relational operators, are used in conditional statements (chapter 5). Expressions with logical operators always produce a value of 1 or 0. Any nonzero value is accepted as true. Logical operators are used with relational and other operators to create expressions. For example, x = 4 + (x < y) is a legal C expression.

Logical Operators

&&	AND
¦¦	OR
!	NOT

The && and ¦¦ operators require two operands. The ! operator requires only one.

```
if ('0' <= x && c <='9')
     printf("x is the digit %c\n");
else
     printf("x is not a digit.\n");
```

Note | Avoid trying to test a floating point variable for equality with a constant. The test will usually fail unless it is made after the variable has been initialized.

Type Conversions

Data types can be mixed in a C expression.

Turbo C and QuickC permit you to mix data types in a C expression. The following program, for example, works properly and creates no error message:

```
main()
{
     int x = 2;
     float y = 3;
     float z;

     z = x + y;
}
```

This extensive flexibility can also create problems. When data types are mixed in an expression, the compiler converts the data variables to compatible types before carrying out the operation. In the previous example, the result is a *float*, and the integer would be converted to a *float* before performing the operation.

In converting downward, you must use caution, for example:

```
main()
{
     int x = 20000;
     float y = 30000;
     int z;

     z = x + y;
}
```

In this case the calculation is performed by converting the *int* to a *float*, adding the values, and then converting the *float* result to an *int*. Here, the result (*float*) is too large to fit in the data type for which it is intended (*int*), and the value will be corrupted.

To avoid problems, try to minimize your data conversions, particularly converting from larger to smaller integer types, from an integer to a character, or between signed and unsigned types.

Special Operators

C has several special operators. This section covers the following special operators: increment and decrement, pointer-related, comma, cast, and *sizeof*.

The Increment and Decrement Operators

The increment and decrement operators can often simplify addition or subtraction.

The addition of unit quantities can be simplified by using increment or decrement operators. These operators are valuable for loop counters and related functions.

In its simplest form, the *increment operator* in a statement works like this:

```
aa = a++;
bb = ++b;
```

In the first statement, **a** is incremented by 1 *after* the assignment takes place. In the second statement, **b** is incremented by 1 *before* the assignment takes place. The result is that if **a** and **b** were equal on starting, **bb** now has a value 1 higher than **aa**, and **a** and **b** both equal **bb**.

Try the following program:

```
/* Program to test increment operator */

main()
{
        int a = b = 7;
        int aa, bb;

        aa = a++;
        bb = ++b;
        printf("a = %d\n",a);
        printf("b = %d\n",b);
        printf("aa = %d\n",aa);
        printf("bb = %d\n",bb);
}
```

The result will show **bb** with a value of 8 and **aa** with a value of 7. Both **a** and **b** are now 8.

The *decrement operator* works in the same way:

```
aa = a--;
bb = --b;
```

In the first statement, the **a** variable is decremented *after* the assignment; in the second, the **b** variable is decremented *before* the assignment.

The increment and decrement operators produce very efficient code. The **a++;** statement, for example, reduces to a single machine instruction. Use these operators whenever possible.

The Pointer-Related Operators

C supports two pointer-related operators. One of these is the *ampersand* (**&**); the other is the *asterisk* (*****). Chapter 7 will discuss both.

The Comma Operator

The *comma operator* (**,**) is used in a loop expression to control loop initialization. For example, two loop variables could be initialized in a *for* statement by separating them with commas.

The Cast Operator

Casting can be used to force a change in a data type.

You can force a change in the data type of a variable by *casting* it, or putting the type name in parentheses before the variable in the expression. Casting can be explicit or implicit, for example:

```
main()
{
        int x = 3;
        float y = 5.2;
        float z;

        z = x + y;
}
```

This program converts the integer value of **x** to a *float* value, adds it to **y**, and then assigns **z** to the *float* result. This is an example of *implicit* *casting*; that is, the casting follows the internal rules of the C compiler. It may or may not be what you wish.

When casting is necessary, it is generally better to do explicit casting. With *explicit casting*, you place the type name of the result in parentheses before the variable in the expression:

```
x = (int) 3.6 + (int) 4.7;
```

The preceding statement assigns the value of 7 to x. Both values to the right of the assignment operator are truncated before they are added.

Try the following program to see how C conversions work:

```
/* Basic conversion examples */

main()
{
     float f1=107.73, f2;
     int      i1=25, i2;

     /* convert a float to an integer */
     i2 = (int) f1;
     printf("%f converted to an integer produces %d\n",f1,
          i2);

     /* convert an integer to a float */
     f2 = (float) i1;
     printf("%d converted to float produces %f\n",i1,f2);

     /* divide an integer by an integer */
     i2 = i1/2;
     printf("%d divided by two produces %d\n",i1,i2);

     /* divide a float by an integer */
     f2 = f1/ (float) i1;
     printf("%f divided by %d produces %f\n",f1,i1,f2);

     /* divide an integer by a float */
     f2 = (float) i1/f1;
     printf("%d divided by %f produces %f\n",i1,f1,f2);

     /* divide a float by a float */
     f2  = f1/25.0000;
     printf("%f divided by 25.0000 produces %f\n",f1,f2);
}
```

This will produce the following output:

```
107.730000 converted to an integer produces 107
25 converted to float produces 25.000000
25 divided by 2 produces 12
107.730003 divided by 25 produces 4.309200
25 divided by 107.730003 produces 0.232062
107.730003 divided by 25.0000 produces 4.309200
```

The *sizeof* Operator

The *sizeof* operator returns the size of the operand to its right. It can be used with a variable or a constant:

```
x = sizeof(float);
y = sizeof(temperature);
```

As an example, the following program returns the size of each numeric type:

```
main()
{
        int a = 3;
        float b = 5.0;
        short c = 3;
        long d = 4;
        double e = 5.0;

        printf("The integer size is %d\n",sizeof(a));
        printf("The short size is %d\n", sizeof(c));
        printf("The long size is %d\n",sizeof(d));
        printf("The float size is %d\n",sizeof(b));
        printf("The double size is %d\n",sizeof(e));
}
```

The output of this program will be:

```
The integer size is 2
The short size is 2
The long size is 4
The float size is 4
The double size is 8
```

Expressions and Statements

An *expression* is a combination of operands and operators.

In an *expression* is any combination of operands and operators, for example:

```
centigrade = (5.0/9.0) * (fahrenheit - 32.0);
```

A C *statement* is an expression followed by a semicolon. The preceding expression is also a statement. Another example of a statement is

```
printf("%6.2f",price);
```

Tip | Keep your expressions simple. If you need to use a complex expression, break it down into multiple statements. With some compilers, this will increase the compiled program's execution speed. Optimizing compilers should permit you to break down multiple expressions into several simple expressions and still maintain the same execution speed. QuickC is not an optimizing compiler, but Turbo C is.

In creating expressions, you can use a shorthand notation to combine operations. Note the following equivalencies in C:

Long Form	Shorthand
counter = counter + 3;	counter +=3;
price = price * (old+1.00);	price *= oldprice+1.00;
a = a & b;	a &= b;

Use the shorthand notation as often as possible because it simplifies the expression and improves the reliability of the code. You can use shorthand expressions with either arithmetic or bitwise operations.

The Precedence of Operations

With C, operators are evaluated in the following order:

Operator	Type
! -	Unary, logical NOT, arithmetic minus
* / %	Arithmetic (multiplication, division)
+ -	Arithmetic (addition, subtraction)
< > <= >=	Relational (inequality)
== !=	Relational (equality)

&& ¦¦	Logical
= += -= *= /= %=	Assignment

As in most languages, you can use double parentheses to group expressions.

Overflow and Underflow

The result of an underflow or overflow is not defined in the C language.

In a numeric calculation, if a final or intermediate result exceeds the range of a data type, you will get an incorrect answer. For example, try the following program:

```
#include <stdio.h>
main()
{
        int a = 18000;
        int b = 2;
        int c;

        c = (a * b) / 6;
        printf("The result is %d\n",c);
}
```

This program will execute with most compilers but will not give the correct answer. Although all individual values are within the range of the data type for the value, intermediate results exceed the range of the integer data type, and the final value for **c** will be incorrect.

If the result of an expression is too small for the data type, an *underflow* condition is said to result. If the result is too large, an *overflow* condition is said to result. In either case, the C language does not specify the consequence. The result varies with the compiler and is not predictable. What actually happens depends on the compiler, the data types involved, and the type of error.

As an example, try the following program:

```
main()
{
        int x = 5;
        int y = 0;
        int z;

        z = x/y;
}
```

For Turbo C and QuickC with MS-DOS, there is an overflow error from an integer operation. The error is trapped by the operating system (not the program), and the error message is returned by the operating system.

With *float* types, the error trapping is different. Try this:

```
main()
{
        float x = 5.0;
        float y = 0.0;
        float z;

        z = x/y;
}
```

In this case you will still get an error message, but it is returned by the program from the floating point functions linked by the linker instead of from the operating system. The result is highly compiler dependent.

For all error operations, you may wish to write your own procedures to trap errors, keeping them as functions or macros (see chapter 8). This method reduces the problem of compiler dependency.

Defining Substitutions and Preprocessor Directives

Certain instructions for the compiler can be placed at the beginning of a C program.

C compilers recognize certain instructions that can be placed at the beginning of the program. These are called *preprocessor directives*, and their keywords are preceded by a # sign. The most common directives are *#define* and *#include*.

The *#define* Directive

The *#define* directive can be used to define a substitution that is used for each occurrence of an expression in the program.

The *#define* directive permits you to define a substitution that will be used for an expression each time it occurs in the program. With this directive you can define a value or expression for any name, after which the value or expression is substituted for the name wherever it appears in the program. No semicolon is used after the *#define* directive. (If a semicolon is used, it is considered part of the definition and can have undesirable effects.)

The advantage of the *#define* directive is that a complex expression can be defined once at the beginning of the program and given a name that is meaningful in the context of the program. After the expression is defined, it can be referenced as many times as necessary in the body of the program. The result is a shorter source code program and better readability. The *#define* statement, however, does not reduce the size of the final executable program, since the compiler will expand the program by substitution before compiling.

The following program is an example of using a *#define:*

```
#define FIVE 5
main()
{
    double x, y, z;

    x = 24;
    y = FIVE;
    z = fmod(x,y);
    .
    .
    .

}
```

In the next example, an expression is defined for substitution by using the *#define* directive. (Note that some of the standard C functions in this example also require the use of *#include* files—see chapter 8.)

```
#define CONSTANT (5.0/9.0)

/* Fahrenheit to centigrade converter*/

#include <math.h>
#include <stdio.h>
main()
{
    double fahrenheit, centigrade;
    char fahrena[10];

    printf("What is the temperature in Fahrenheit? ");
    fgets(fahrena,10,stdin);
    fahrenheit = atof(fahrena);
    centigrade = CONSTANT * (fahrenheit - 32.0);
    printf("The temperature is %6.1f degrees
    Centigrade\n", centigrade);
}
```

This example uses several functions and *#include* files, and will be better understood after a few more chapters. The basic concept of using substitutions for expressions, however, should be easy to follow. Notice that constants defined in this way are generally written in uppercase to distinguish them from variables. No declaration statement is needed.

The *#define* directive can be used with any type of constant, including strings:

```
#define MESSAGE "This is a test."
```

The *#include* Directive

The *#include* directive
can be used to define
additional files that are
read by the compiler.

The *#include* directive can be used to specify additional files that should be read by the compiler. The additional files are considered part of the source file. In most cases, for example, you would put *#define* directives in a separate *#include* file and name that file at the beginning of the program:

```
#include "const.h"
```

In this case the `const.h` file would contain:

```
#define CONSTANT (5.0/9.0)
```

This technique makes it easy to add, edit, or change constant values as necessary and have the change affect the entire program:

```
#include "const.h"
#include <math.h>
#include <stdio.h>
/* Fahrenheit to centigrade converter */

#include <stdio.h>
main()
{
      double fahrenheit, centigrade;
      char fahrena[10];

      printf("What is the temperature in Fahrenheit? ");
      fgets(fahrena,10,stdin);
      fahrenheit = atof(fahrena);
      centigrade = CONSTANT * (fahrenheit - 32.0);
      printf("The temperature is %6.1f Centigrade.\n",
            centigrade);
}
```

The name of the *#include* file can be referenced by using either quotation marks or left and right arrows. If quotation marks are used, the search begins in the current directory and then follows the currently specified path. If the left and right arrows are used, there is no search in the current directory and only the currently specified path is used. Normally you would want to use quotation marks with *#include* files that were created in the current directory, and left and right arrows for *#in-*

clude files that were provided with your C compiler. The previous example illustrated both types.

Review

This chapter introduced the basic concepts of C operators, expressions, and statements. Here are the important points that you should have learned:

1 | Operators are the verbs in a C statement. They define an action that is to be performed on one or more operands.

2 | C has six types of operators: assignment, arithmetic, bitwise, relational, logical, and special.

3 | The assignment operator assigns a value to a variable. It is represented by the equal sign (=).

4 | Arithmetic operators perform mathematical operations on the specified operands. There are five arithmetic operators: +, -, *, /, and %.

5 | Bitwise operators perform operations at the bit level with one or two operands. There are six bitwise operators: &, ¦, ^, ~, <<, and >>.

6 | Relational operators are used for comparing two qualities, and the expression returns a value of true (1) or false (0). There are six relational operators: >, >=, <, <=, ==, and !=.

7 | Logical operators are used in conditional expressions and, as with relational operators, the expressions return a value of true (1) or false (0). There are three logical operators: &&, ¦¦, and !.

8 | Special operators include the increment and decrement operators, the pointer-related operators, the comma operator, the cast operator, and the *sizeof* operator.

9 | An expression is any combination of operands and operators.

10 | A C statement is an expression followed by a semicolon.

11 | Data types can be mixed in a C expression by implicit or explicit casting.

12 | The *#define* directive permits a substitution to be defined that will be applied for each instance in the program.

13 | The *#include* directive permits external files to be identified that will be included as part of the source program at compile time.

Quiz for Chapter 3

1 | What is the value of z?

```
int x = 5;
float y = 9.0;
float z;

z = y/x;
```

  a | 1
  b | 1.8
  c | 2
  d | None of the above

2 | What is the value of z?

```
float z;

z = (int) 3.0 + (int) 3.8;
```

  a | 6.8
  b | 6.0
  c | 7.0
  d | None of the above

3 | What is the value of z?

```
int x;
float y = 6.0;
float z;

x = 5.7;
z = x + y;
```

  a | 11.7
  b | 12
  c | 11
  d | None of the above

4 | On starting, all four values of x, y, xx, and yy are equal. After the following execution, what is true?

```
xx = x++;
yy = ++y;
```

  a | xx and yy are each one higher than x and y.
  b | x, y, and yy are equal and all are one higher than xx.
  c | All four values are still equal.
  d | None of the above

5 | What is the result of the following operation?

(101) ¦ (101)

   a | 110
   b | 101
   c | 010
   d | None of the above

6 | What is the result of the following operation?

(101) & (101)

   a | 110
   b | 101
   c | 010
   d | None of the above

7 | Which operator changes the value of the variable to the left of the operator?
   a | ==
   b | =
   c | %
   d | <

8 | What is the result of the expression **23 % 3**?
   a | 7
   b | 2
   c | 21
   d | None of the above

9 | What type of operators are used in conditional statements?
   a | Conditional operators
   b | Logical operators
   c | Relational operators
   d | b and c

10 | What type of operator is used to compare for equality?
   a | =
   b | ==
   c | =!
   d | :=

11 | Which of the following is not true?
   a | Using a *#define* directive generally reduces the size of the source code.
   b | The *#define* directive can be used to improve readability of the program.
   c | Using a *#define* directive generally reduces the size of the executable file.
   d | The *#define* directive has no semicolon at the end.

12 | Which of the following is not true?
    a | There are two types of casting: implicit and explicit.
    b | The *sizeof* operator can be used with a variable or a constant.
    c | Data types can be mixed in an expression.
    d | For a more robust program, use implicit casting.

13 | Which of the following is not an assignment operator?
    a | =
    b | +=
    c | !=
    d | b and c

14 | Which of the following is not a logical operator?
    a | &&
    b | &
    c | ¦¦
    d | a and c

15 | Which of the following is not a relational operator?
    a | <
    b | =
    c | >=
    d | <<

4 | Basic Input and Output

About This Chapter

Input and output
functions are an integral
part of almost every
program that you write.

Almost any program that you write must include some provision for writing and reading data. In the previous chapter, examples of both reading and writing data were included. In each case you used a function that was an integral part of the C language, such as *printf( )* or *fgets( )*. The C language provides several other functions that can be used for input and output (I/O). In each case, the functions occur in pairs; that is, an output function corresponds to another input function. This chapter will introduce these basic I/O functions: *printf( )/scanf( )*, *puts( )/gets( )*, and *getchar( )/putchar( )*. In addition, you will find an introduction to the *fgets( )* function.

Before discussing these functions, however, let's look at what a function is and at the concept of buffering input and output.

Introduction to Functions

A *function* is a part of a
program that performs a
single operation.

Functions are parts of programs that perform a single operation. Most C compilers provide certain standard functions that are included in a library with the compiler. These have the same names in any compiler.

The *printf( )* and *fgets( )* functions that you have used in the preceding chapters are examples of these.

In any program, it is necessary for the user to pass data to functions and, in return, to obtain data that is passed back. Information is passed to the function as an argument. Information is returned as either a value or an argument. For example, in the following function call:

```
printf("%s",msg)
```

the function inputs are the two arguments: the control string and the pointer to the character string. With Turbo C and QuickC, as with many other C compilers, the function can return a value if you use the form:

```
no_of_characters = printf("%s",msg)
```

in which case it returns the number of characters written.

For more extensive information on functions, refer to chapter 8. For now, let's move on to how the input and output functions are used.

Arguments can be used to pass data to or from a function.

The *#include* Directive

Many C functions require the use of files that must be read at compile time with the #include directive.

Many of the C functions that are part of the library included with your C compiler require certain definitions to work properly. These are designated as *#include*, or .H files, with your compiler. When using that particular function, you should always use any *#include* files that the function requires. To find out which *#include* files are necessary for a function with Turbo C, use the reference manual and check the keyword prototype under the function listing. For QuickC, you need only place the cursor on any character in the function name on the screen and press the Shift and F1 keys. A help screen will define the *#include* files needed for that function. For the examples in this and subsequent chapters, the proper *#include* files will always be shown.

Buffers

Most of the C input and output functions use buffering to improve their efficiency.

Buffering is a technique that improves the efficiency of input and output functions. With any computer system, reading and writing is generally the slowest part of the program execution. By using buffering techniques, the speed of both reading and writing is improved. Basically, buffering involves setting aside a storage place to hold data until the output device is ready for it (when writing) or the computer is ready for it (when inputting).

The buffer becomes even more important in file operations (chapter 12), but for now you should simply be aware that buffers are used for most input and output. Buffers are used with all functions in this chapter. The *stdio.h* file should always be included in any program that uses these functions, since it defines the buffer size. In chapter 12 you will learn how to use the buffer for file operations, as well as how to bypass this buffer if necessary.

Formatted Output and Input: *printf( )* and *scanf( )*

You have already been introduced to the formatted output function: *printf( )*. There is also a formatted input function, *scanf( )*. Let's look more closely at each of these.

The *printf( )* Function

Formatted output is done with the *printf( )* function.

The example of the previous chapter had an output statement:

```
printf("Your favorite flower is the %s",msg);
```

The *printf( )* is a C function name. It is a standard C output function (available in any C compiler) and has the general form:

```
printf(control string[,item₁,item₂,itemᵢ,...itemₙ]);
```

The first argument is the *control* (or format) *string*. It determines the format for writing the data or data variables. The remaining arguments are the data or data variables to be written:

```
printf("This is test %d\n",test);
```

The Control String for *printf( )*

The first argument of the *printf( )* function, the control string, has one or more of three components: text, identifiers, and escape sequences.

The control string has three components: text, identifiers, and escape sequences. You can use any text and any number of escape sequences. The number of identifiers should match the number of variables or values to be written.

Identifiers in the format string determine how each of the other arguments will be written:

```
printf("Your favorite flower is the %s",msg);
```

There should be one identifier for each of the remaining arguments. Each identifier begins with a percent sign (%) and a code to indicate the output format of the variable. In this case the **%s** indicates a character string.

C provides the user with the following identifier codes:

Identifier	Format
%d	Decimal integer
%c	Single character
%s	Character string
%f	Floating point (decimal)
%e	Floating point (exponential notation)
%g	%e or %f, whichever is shorter
%u	Unsigned decimal integer
%o	Unsigned octal integer
%x	Unsigned hexadecimal integer

The first four codes will serve almost all of your basic needs. The number is written right-justified. In a later section you will learn how to write with center- or left-justification. With QuickC, this table is provided on a help screen, which is only an F1 keystroke away.

Escape characters are used for control purposes. They always begin with a backslash.

```
printf("Your favorite flower is the %s\n",msg);
```

Historically, escape characters refer to control codes sent to the printer to do carriage returns, form feeds, and such. In reality, the escape characters are far more powerful; in fact, by using them you can send almost any code to the output device that the device can recognize.

Backslash codes can be used to send a control character to a display device or printer.

There are special backslash codes that can be used for controlling the output device during writing:

Code	Meaning
\a	Bell
\b	Backspace
\f	Form feed
\n	Line feed (LF)
\r	Carriage return (CR)
\t	Horizontal tab
\v	Vertical tab
\\	Backslash
\'	Single quote
\"	Double quote

\xhhh	The character *hhh*, where *hhh* is hexadecimal
\ooo	The character *ooo*, where *ooo* is octal

For example, to print a backslash you could use \010 or \x008. Although not necessary, it is wise to use prefix zeros (as in this example) to prevent the compiler from assuming subsequent characters as part of the value. For example, \x08 will work, but if the next character after the backslash code is a zero, you will have \x080, and it will not work.

> **Tip** | Always represent nonprinting characters with a backslash sequence to prevent the compiler from being confused.

The following usages are invalid for the reasons indicated:

'\9'	Only octal values are permitted
'\A'	Undefined special value
'XYZ'	More than one character between quotes
\f	Single quotes missing
''	No character between the single quotes

You can mix backslash codes, using multiple escape sequences as desired:

```
printf("This is printed\nas two lines\n");
```

> **Note** | Be careful not to confuse the backslash escape character with the forward slash used for comments and division. Remember: backslash for escape characters, forward slash for comments and division.

Any constant characters, text strings, or data can be printed directly from the format string:

```
printf("The temperature is %f degrees Centigrade\n",
    centigrade);
```

Text in the format string will be printed exactly as shown.

You can add modifiers to the identifier to control the alignment or format. The following identifiers are accepted:

Identifiers	Meaning
-	Left-justify item
NNNNN	Minimum field width

.*NNNN*	Formatting control; indicates digits to display to the right of the decimal
L	The data item is *long* instead of *int*

The following example will display `centigrade` as left-justified, and having a field width of 6 characters, with 1 digit to the right of the decimal.

```
printf("The temperature is %-6.1f degrees Centigrade\n",
    centigrade);
```

Output formatting can be controlled dynamically by using an asterisk.

You can also control the format dynamically by using an asterisk. However, you must add an argument to specify the field width.

```
width=6;
qty=34;
printf("The quantity on hand is %*d\n),width,qty);
```

If you need to use a percent sign in writing a number, use a double percent sign in the format string:

```
growth = 12;
printf("Your investment has grown by %d%%\n",growth);
```

> **Tip** | If you want the decimal points to align in a table of decimal numbers, use a modifier to output the numbers. Specify a width larger than any of the numbers.

An Example Using *printf( )*

Before continuing, try entering and using the following program to experiment with the *printf( )* function:

```
/* Test program for printf function  */

#include <stdio.h>
#define TEST "This is a test string"
main()
{
    static char surname[] = "Mr.";
    static char name[] = "Jones";
    int letter;
    float amount;
    int width, value;

    /* printing a constant string */
```

```
printf("This is a test\n");

/* printing a constant */
printf("%d\n",234);

/* printing a constant, defining a small field */
printf("%2d\n",234);

/* writing a string, defining a small field */
printf("%3s\n",TEST);

/* multiple value output */
amount=5000;
printf("%s %s, you have just won $%6.2f dollars!\n",
surname,name,amount);

/* dynamically controlling the field format */
width=4;
value=233;
printf("The number is %*d\n",width,value);

/* printing the ASCII value of a letter */
letter = 'c';
printf("The equivalent ASCII for %c is %d\n",letter,
       letter);
}
```

Reading with the *scanf( )* Function

Formatted input can be read with the *scanf( )* function.

The *scanf( )* function is the formatted input function. This function can be used to enter machine-formatted numbers, characters, or character strings to a program, for example:

```
scanf("%f",&fahrenheit);
```

The appearance of *scanf( )* is similar to the *printf( )* function, but there is a distinct difference. The general form of the *scanf( )* function is a format string and one or more input variable item pointers:

```
scanf(control string,item1 pointer,item2 pointer,itemn
      pointer,...itemn pointer);
```

Notice the difference. With the *printf( )* function, the actual variables are listed. With the *scanf( )* function, the address of the variables is used as the argument. In the previous example, the ampersand with the variable name in the argument indicated that the address of the variable was used rather than the variable.

For a string variable, the variable name is the address of the first character. In this case the ampersand is not used:

```
char name[20];

scanf("%s",name);
```

> **Note** | You should avoid, unless necessary, the use of the *scanf( )* function for keyboard input. The *scanf( )* function should be used only for machine-formatted input. For user input, it is considered more portable to use the *gets( )* or *fgets( )* functions (see the next sections) and then to use the appropriate conversion routine to convert any numbers entered.

The Control String for *scanf( )*

The control string for the *scanf( )* function consists only of identifiers. Most of the same identifiers used for writing data can also be used for reading data:

Identifier	Format
%d	Decimal integer
%c	Single character
%s	Character string
%f	Floating point
%e	Floating point
%u	Unsigned decimal integer
%o	Unsigned octal integer
%x	Unsigned hexadecimal integer
&h	Short integer

Compare this list of identifier codes with those given for *printf( )*. Notice that there is no **%g** option, the **%h** option for short integers is added, and the **%f** and **%e** are equivalent, each accepting decimal or exponential input numbers.

The function returns the number of fields read. The returned value can be used as a check in a program to determine if all of the fields were read.

Using the *scanf( )* Function

The *scanf( )* function can be used for entering multiple values by using additional format codes in the control string. For example, the following lines of code might appear in a program reading preformatted addresses from an input device:

```
printf("Enter City and State: ");
scanf("%s %s",city,state);
```

Note that entered strings cannot have any white space, since a white space terminates the input reading. For the preceding example, New Orleans would be an illegal city input.

In our example, `city` and `state` are pointers to character arrays, and no ampersand is necessary. For numeric variables, the ampersand would have to be used.

Text strings cannot be part of the *scanf( )* control string. Prompts should be written from a separate statement using the *printf( )* or *puts( )* functions.

The *scanf( )* Function and User Input

In general, the *scanf( )* function should not be used for keyboard input.

Since the *printf( )* function is quite useful for formatted input, you might expect the *scanf( )* function to be useful for input, particularly for numeric values. From a practical viewpoint, however, it is best not to use the function for user input. You can see why by trying the following program:

```
/* This is an example of improper scanf() use */

#include <stdio.h>
main()
{
        int   address_no;
        char name[40+1];
        char street[40+1];
        char city[20+1];
        char state[2+1];
        char zip[5+1];

        printf("Address Number: ");
        scanf("%d",&address_no);
        printf("Name: ");
        gets(name);
        printf("Address: ");
        scanf("%s",street);
        printf("City, State, Zip: ");
        scanf("%s %s %s",city,state,zip);
}
```

There are three problems with this example:

1 | The *scanf( )* function reads up to, but not including, the newline character. The *gets( )* function for the name reads the newline character. The result of the program execution is:

```
Address Number: 3
Name: Address:
```

In other words, the program doesn't wait for you to enter the name. The *scanf( )* function for the address number reads up to, but not including, the newline character. After the next prompt for the name, the *gets( )* function reads the newline character still in the buffer. Since this function reads through the next newline, *gets( )* thinks it has input and the program moves ahead to the address prompt.

2 | With the *scanf( )* function, you cannot have any white space in the input string. Once a space is read, the program assumes that all of the input string is read. You would not be able to use an address that contained any spaces.

3 | The behavior of the *scanf( )* function is extremely compiler dependent.

With a little programming work and with the use of a few Turbo C or QuickC functions, you could make the program work with the *scanf( )* function. It would be far better, however, to use the *fgets( )* function for all input, and later sections will show better ways of doing this same program.

String Output and Input: *puts( )* and *gets( )*

If you are reading and writing character strings, the easiest method is to use the *gets( )* and *puts( )* functions.

String Output

String output can be written with a *puts( )* function and read with a *gets( )* function.

The *puts( )* function can be used to output a simple character string. The general form is

```
puts(text_ptr)
```

where `text_ptr` is a pointer to the character string or to an array. You must also have an `#include <stdio.h>` line at the beginning of the program to enable C to find the *defines* for the function. Here is a simple example:

```
#include <stdio.h>
main()
{
      static char array[] = "This is an array text string.";

      puts(array);
      puts(&array[2]);
}
```

The result is:

```
This is an array text string.
i
```

The *puts( )* function is simple to use, but it can be used only with character strings. With a character string, *puts( )* takes less typing than the *printf( )* function. The *puts( )* function also automatically adds a newline character at the end of the output string, forcing a carriage return and linefeed. The *puts( )* function is also faster than *printf( )*.

One question you might have is this: how does *puts( )* know when the end of the character string is reached? The answer is that *puts( )* reads to the next null character. This can lead to some interesting and frustrating problems if you forget to include the null character. For example, DON'T try this:

```
main()
{
      static char bad_news[]={'H','E','L','L','O','!'};

      puts(bad_news);
}
```

Since there is no null character at the end of the string, the output function will continue to output until it can find one somewhere in memory. That could take a while and could send some very interesting codes to the screen.

String Input

You can use the complement of the *puts( )* function, the *gets( )* function, for the input of character strings. As with the *puts( )* function, you must include the *stdio.h* file. The general form is

```
gets(text_ptr)
```

Here is a simple example:

```
#include <stdio.h>
main()
{
        char name[80];

        puts("What is your name?");
        gets(name);
        printf("Your name is %s\n",name);
}
```

Notice that you can mix *puts( )* and *printf( )* functions as desired in a program.

Now here is a better form of the example given earlier (see "The *scanf( )* Function and User Input"):

```
#include <stdio.h>
main()
{
        int address_no;
        char address_noa[4];
        char name[40+1];
        char street[40+1];
        char city[20+1];
        char state[2+1];
        char zip[5+1];

        printf("Address Number: ");
        gets(address_noa);
        address_no = atoi(address_noa);
        printf("Name: ");
        gets(name);
        printf("Address: ");
        gets(street);
        printf("City: ");
        gets(city);
        printf("State: ");
        gets(state);
        printf("Zip: ");
        gets(zip);
}
```

Using the *gets( )* function for input can overflow the storage allocated for the string variable if the input entry is too long.

This version receives the input number as a character string and then uses the *atoi( )* function (see chapter 8) to convert the character string to an integer. (The *atof( )* function is similar, converting an input character string to a *float*.)

This program still has a problem, however. It would be quite possible for a user to enter a name, address, city, state, or zip code that was

For better input security, check the length of the input string or use the *fgets( )* function.

too long and overflowed the storage allocated for that variable. This could create execution problems. An even better program form would be to use the *fgets( )* function, which will be discussed later.

Single Character I/O

Use the *getchar( )* function to read a single input character. Use *putchar( )* to output the character.

The *getchar( )* function reads the next character from the input and returns its value. The character is echoed at the output. The function has no argument.

The *putchar( )* function prints a single character on the standard output device. It has a single argument, which is the output character or variable for the output character.

With both of these functions, you must include the *stdio.h* file. Now we can put *getchar( )* and *putchar( )* together in a simple example:

```
/* GETCHAR routine */

#include <stdio.h>
main()
{
    char c;
    printf("Please enter a character: ");
    c = getchar();
    putchar(c);
}
```

If you try to execute this program and enter a *b*, you will get:

```
Please enter a character: b        ←press Enter
b
```

The character you enter is echoed, and then, because of the *putchar( )* function, it is displayed again after the carriage return.

You can simplify this program with:

```
/* GETCHAR routine */

#include <stdio.h>
main()
{
    printf("Please enter a character: ");
    putchar(getchar());
}
```

This will work in an identical manner to the first example. Now enter several characters and press carriage return. What happens? Only the first character is returned.

Two other character input routines are also useful. The *getche( )* routine returns the input character without waiting for a carriage return, echoing it. The *getch( )* routine returns the input character without waiting for a carriage return and does not echo it.

As an example, you could use either of these routines to capture an option from a menu routine. Both routines require the program to include the *conio.h* file. (The *getchar( )* will wait for the user to enter a carriage return after the character is entered.)

The *fgets( )* Function

The *fgets( )* function checks the length of the input string and ensures that it does not overflow the allocated storage.

One of the best methods of keyboard input is the use of the *fgets( )* function to read an input character string. Use the appropriate function to convert the input if necessary. The *fgets( )* function has three arguments: the identifier for the character string, the number of characters read, and a stream, which is the source of the data and can be a file or a physical device. The general form for *fgets( )* is

```
fgets(string,n,stream)
```

The C language has certain previously defined external variables for standard streams:

Identifier	Device
stdin	Keyboard
stdout	Display
stdprn	Printer port
stderr	Output device for error messages
stdaux	Auxiliary port

To read text (up to 80 characters) from the keyboard to a variable name, then, you would use

```
char name[80+2];

fgets(name,82,stdin);
```

Now you can write a better form of the previous program:

```
#include <stdio.h>
```

```
main()
{
        int address_no;
        char address_noa[4];
        char name[40+2];
        char street[40+2];
        char city[20+2];
        char state[2+2];
        char zip[5+2];

        printf("Address Number: ");
        fgets(address_noa,4,stdin);
        address_no = atoi(address_noa);
        printf("Name: ");
        fgets(name,sizeof(name),stdin);
        printf("Address: ");
        fgets(street,sizeof(street),stdin);
        printf("City: ");
        fgets(city,sizeof(city),stdin);
        printf("State: ");
        fgets(state,sizeof(state),stdin);
        printf("Zip: ");
        fgets(zip,sizeof(zip),stdin);
}
```

Notice that a pad of 2 characters is used for each variable to permit room
in the buffer for the newline and null characters.

Review

This chapter has discussed three input and output function pairs for C
programs. All of them use standard input (*stdin*) or standard output
(*stdout*). Here is a summary of when to use each pair:

getchar( ) and *putchar( )*	Use for the input and output of single characters.
gets( ) and *puts( )*	Use for the input and output of character strings.
scanf( )	Use for machine-formatted input.
printf( )	Use for versatile output control of strings or numeric values.
getche( ) and *getch( )*	Use for entering single characters when you don't want to wait for a carriage return.

In addition, another input function has been introduced that can read from any type of input stream:

fgets( )   Use for entering character streams from the keyboard.

For more information on input and output functions, refer to chapter 12.

Quiz for Chapter 4

1 | Enter and compile the following program. What is the output?

```
/* Test program for printf function */

#include <stdio.h>
main()
{
      static char surname[] = "Mr."
      static char name[] = "Jones";
      float amount;

      amount=5000;
      printf("%s %s, you have just won $%6.2f
             dollars!\n",surname,name,amount);
}
```

   a | Mr. Jones, you have just won $5000.00 dollars!
   b | Mr. Jones, you have just won $5000 dollars!
   c | surname name, you have just won $amount dollars!
   d | , you have just won $ dollars.

2 | What is the output of the following program?

```
#include <stdio.h>
main()
{
      int width, value;

      /* dynamically controlling the field format */
      width = 4;
      value = 233;
      printf("The number is %*d\n",width,value);
}
```

   a | The number is 2 33
   b | The number is 233
   c | The number is 4
   d | The number is 4 233

3 | What is the output of the following program?

```
#include <stdio.h>
main()
{
      int letter;

      /* printing the ASCII value of a letter */
      letter = 'e';
```

```
        printf("The equivalent ASCII for %c is %d\n",
            letter,letter);
}
```

     a | The equivalent ASCII for e is 101
     b | The equivalent ASCII for e is e
     c | The equivalent ASCII for 101 is 101
     d | The equivalent ASCII for e is 0

4 | Which of the following is not a function?
     a | *scanf*
     b | *puts*
     c | *sizeof*
     d | All are functions.

5 | What is the minimum number of arguments that should be used with *printf( )*?
     a | 0
     b | 1
     c | 2
     d | 3

6 | Why is the *gets( )* function preferred over *scanf( )* for keyboard input?
     a | It is easier to use.
     b | It is more portable between C implementations.
     c | It produces a shorter executable file.
     d | It is part of more C libraries.

7 | Why is *fgets( )* preferred for input over *gets( )*?
     a | It is easier to use.
     b | It is more portable between C implementations.
     c | It produces a shorter executable file.
     d | An error check is performed on the length of the input string to be sure that it does not overflow the size of the input buffer.

8 | If the *fgets( )* function is used, how many extra buffer spaces are needed in addition to the length of the input string?
     a | 0
     b | 1
     c | 2
     d | 3

9 | What is wrong with this program?

```
main()
{
        char weird[]={'H','E','L','L','O','!'};

        puts(weird);
}
```

    a | The array should be static.
    b | There should be a terminating null character in the initializing string.
    c | The array size is not defined.
    d | a and b

10 | Which of the following is not a component of the control string in the *printf( )* function?
    a | Text
    b | Identifiers
    c | Escape sequences
    d | Variables to be written

11 | What is the return value from the *printf( )* function?
    a | An error value
    b | The number of characters written
    c | 0
    d | There is no return value.

12 | Which of the following is not true?
    a | Functions perform one or more operations.
    b | The library with your C compiler contains many functions.
    c | Data can be passed to functions.
    d | Data can be received from functions.

13 | Which of the following is not true?
    a | With most I/O functions, you must use the *#include* directive to include the *defines* for the function.
    b | All of the functions introduced in this chapter use buffered input or output.
    c | Identifier codes always begin with a percent sign.
    d | Every use of the *printf( )* function has at least one identifier code.

14 | How many identifiers should be in the control string of a *printf( )* function?
    a | 1
    b | 0
    c | One for each variable or value to be written
    d | 2

15 | How should control characters for a printer be represented in a *printf( )* control string?
    a | As character values using **%c**
    b | With a backslash code
    c | As integer values
    d | Control characters are not permitted in the control string.

5 | Program Control: If and Switch Structures

About This Chapter

Control structures are used to alter the sequence in which the program statements are executed.
In a *conditional structure* the program chooses one of several groups of statements to execute, based on the value of the control expression.

Up to now your programs have contained a series of statements that were executed in a specified order. In reality, with most programs you will wish to alter the sequence in which the instructions are executed, based on specified conditions. *Control structures* permit a program to alter its procedure dynamically, based on any specified condition.

There are two basic types of control structures: conditional and repetition. This chapter will introduce you to conditional types of structures. A *conditional structure* is one in which the program chooses one of several groups of statements to execute, based on the value of a control expression.

Control Expressions

The program determines which statements are executed at execution time, based on the value of a control expression. A *control expression* is any expression that evaluates to 0 or nonzero and that is used to determine which statements are executed or the order of the statement execution.

A *control expression* is any expression that evaluates to 0 or nonzero and that is used to determine which statements are executed or the order of statement execution.

The most common type of control structure is the *if* structure. As an example, examine the following statement group:

```
if (x==3)
        printf("The value of x is 3.\n");
```

In this case the *printf( )* statement is executed only if the value of x is **3**. The expression **(x==3)** is the control expression, and it determines whether the *printf( )* statement is executed.

Now try the following statements:

```
if (100)
        printf("Any nonzero number is true.\n");
if (-25)
        printf("This is true, too.\n");
```

In this example both *printf( )* statements are executed, since in each case the control expressions evaluate to a nonzero value.

Types of Conditional Control Structures

There are three types of conditional control: one-way, two-way, and multiway.

There are three types of conditional controls: one-way, two-way, and multiway.

One-Way

The simplest type of conditional control is that in which one or more statements are executed based on whether or not a specified expression is nonzero:

```
if (control expression)
        statements;
```

In a one-way conditional-control structure, one or more statements are executed if the value of a control expression is nonzero.

If *control expression* is nonzero, then *statements* is executed. If *control expression* is zero, then execution skips to the next statement after the *if*-statement semicolon and *statements* is not executed (see figure 5.1).

Look at this example:

```
if (temperature<=32)
        printf("It is freezing.\n");
```

Notice the following features of this C structure:

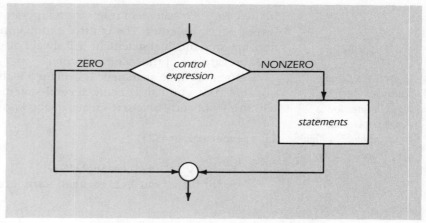

Figure 5.1 The one-way selection structure

- The conditional expression (condition for the test) is enclosed in parentheses after the *if*.

- There is no semicolon after the *if* component; there is only one semicolon and it is at the end of the statement.

- For readability, the statements that are to be executed if the control expression is nonzero are indented from the main program body.

In a control expression designed to test for equality, be sure to use the double equal sign:

```
if (temperature==32)
    printf("It is right at freezing.\n");
```

The double equal sign forces a test for equality. If you use the assignment operator instead (a single equal sign), you will discover a real problem. For example, try this program with its error:

```
main()
{
    int temperature;
    char tempa[10];

    printf("What is the temperature?");
    fgets(tempa,10,stdin);
    temperature = atoi(tempa);
    if (temperature=32)
        printf("It is right at freezing.\n");
    printf("The temperature is %d.\n",temperature);
}
```

In this case the *if* statement resets the temperature variable to **32**, regardless of what you enter. The control expression will always evaluate as nonzero, and the final statement will always display a temperature value of **32**, regardless of the value you enter.

To execute a group of statements when a control expression is nonzero, place the group, or block, within curly braces.

Often, a single statement is executed if the control expression is nonzero, but you can execute several statements if they are placed within a set of curly braces to create what is known as a *statement block*.

```
if (temperature<=32)
    {
    printf("It is freezing\n");
    printf"and you better wear warm clothes");
    }
```

All of the expressions within the braces will be executed if the control expression is nonzero.

Two-Way

In a two-way selection structure, the control expression determines which of two alternative statement groups is executed.

In the two-way selection structure, the control expression determines which of two alternative sets of statements is executed:

```
if (control expression)
    statements-1;
else
    statements-2;
```

In this case if the control expression is not zero, **statements-1** is executed. If the control expression is zero, **statements-2** is executed (see figure 5.2).

With C, there are two ways to create this selection structure: the *if . . . else* expression and the conditional operator, and they will be discussed next.

The *if . . . else* Expression

The most conventional *if* structure is the *if . . . else* expression, for example:

```
if (temperature<=32)
    printf("It is freezing.\n");
else
    printf("It is not freezing.\n");
```

In this case if **temperature** is equal to or below freezing, **It is freezing**

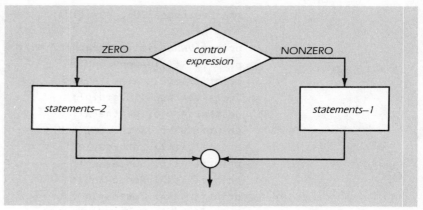

Figure 5.2 The two-way selection structure

is displayed. If not, **It is not freezing** is displayed. At least one of the two sets of statements must be executed.

Notice the general form: neither the *if* nor the *else* line contains a semicolon. There is one semicolon at the end of the expressions for each path; that is, there are two statements. The two statement groups are indented from the main body of the program.

If there is a statement block in a path, enclose the group of statements in braces, using semicolons to terminate each statement:

```
if (temperature<=32)
    {
    printf("It is freezing\n");
    printf("and you better wear warm clothes");
    }
else {
    printf("It is not freezing\n");
    printf("but watch for rain.\n");
    }
```

You can nest *if . . . else* clauses to any practical level, testing for additional conditions after an initial condition has been met. If there are several *else* clauses, you may find it difficult to decide which *else* goes with which *if*. The general rule is that the *else* always goes with the most recent *if* unless braces dictate otherwise. There should always be a matching *if* for each *else*. All *ifs*, however, may not have an *else*. Suppose, for example, you have the following program:

```
/* Illustration of poor program style */

main()
{
    int weather,day;
```

```
        char weathera[10], daya[10];

        printf("What is the weather?\n");
        printf("\t(1) sunny \n");
        printf("\t(2) rainy \n");
        fgets(weathera,10,stdin);
        weather = atoi(weathera);
        printf("What is the day?\n");
        printf("\t(1) Saturday\n");
        printf("\t(2) Sunday\n");
        printf("\t(3) Monday\n");
        printf("\t(4) Tuesday\n");
        printf("\t(5) Wednesday\n");
        printf("\t(6) Thursday\n");
        printf("\t(7) Friday\n");
        fgets(daya,10,stdin);
        day = atoi(daya);
        if (day == 1)
                if (weather == 1)
                        printf("Wash and wax car\n");
        else
                printf("Go to library\n");
}
```

In this case the *else* clause really goes with the second *if*. The text string
Go to library will be executed only if it is Saturday and the weather is
not sunny. If the day is Sunday, neither *printf( )* expression will be executed. How the program is indented has no effect. This means that you,
as a programmer, must indent properly to ensure that the program is
readable:

```
if (day == 1)
        if (weather == 1)
                printf("Wash and wax car\n");
        else
                printf("Go to library\n");
```

You could improve this program even more by using:

```
if (day == 1 && weather == 1)
        printf("Wash and wax car\n");
else
        printf("Go to library\n");
```

The Conditional Operator

As an alternative, a two-way structure can often be written by using a conditional operator.

There is yet another way to write an *if . . . else* structure. C has a conditional operator that can be used with short expressions. For example,

```
cost = (cost>10.00) ? 15.00 : 10.00;
```

is equivalent to

```
if (cost>10.00)
        cost = 15.00;
else
        cost = 10.00;
```

The expression immediately after the equal sign is the control expression. If the control expression is nonzero, the value to the left of the colon is assigned to the variable to the left of the equal sign. If the control expression is zero, the value to the right of the colon is assigned to the variable.

Notice that three operands are used with the conditional operator: the control expression and two additional expressions. The general form is

```
control expression ? expression-1 : expression-2
```

Multiway

Multiway structures permit you to choose from three or more alternative sets of statement groups. Multiway structures can be mutually exclusive or exclusive.

Sometimes you may wish to choose from three or more alternative sets of statement groups. There are two ways of accomplishing multiway structures: using multiple *if . . . else* structures and using a switch structure.

The execution of the statement groups may be mutually exclusive or inclusive. If only one condition can be met and only one of the statement groups can be executed, the structure is said to be *mutually exclusive*. If two or more conditions or statement groups can be executed, the structure is *inclusive*.

Using Nested *ifs*

You can nest *if . . . else* statements to create a multiway structure. The general form is

```
if control-expression-1
     statements-1;
else if control-expression-2
```

```
        statements-2;
else if control-expression-3
        statements-3;
    .
    .
    .
else if control-expression-n
        statements-n;
else
        statements-4;
```

Figure 5.3 shows the flow for this type of structure.

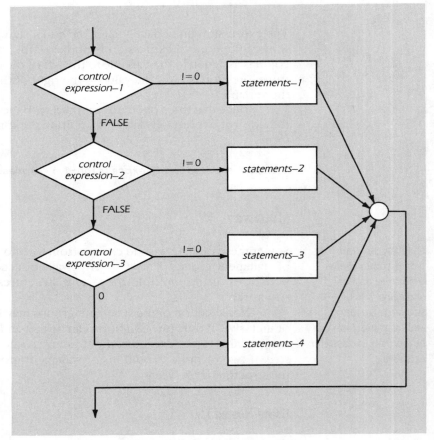

Figure 5.3 The multiway structure

You can always create complex multiway structures by using nested *if . . . else* expressions. The conditions can involve different variables in the testing or can have other complex relationships. Here is an example of a mutually exclusive structure:

```
main()
{
      int score;
      char grade;
      char scorea[10];

      printf("What is the score? ");
      fgets(scorea,10,stdin);
      score = atoi(scorea);
      if (score>=90)
            grade='A';
      else if (score>=80 && score<90)
            grade='B';
      else if (score>=70 && score<80)
            grade='C';
      else if (score>=69 && score<70)
            grade='D';
      else
            grade='F';
      printf("The grade is %c\n",grade);
}
```

In this example only one condition can be met and one statement group executed, so the structure is mutually exclusive.

For even one statement in multiway structures, many programmers prefer adding braces to improve the readability and to make it easier to add multiple statements in the block later:

```
if (score>=90)
    {
    grade='A';
    }
else if (score>=80 && score<90)
    {
    grade='B';
    }
```

In other cases you may wish to make the statement groups inclusive. Here is a simple program to calculate a utility rate based on a variable rate structure:

```
#include <math.h>
#include <stdio.h>
#define HIGH = 950
#define LOW = 300
#define RATE1(pwr) (.05*pwr)   /* rate for <= LOW kwhrs */
#define RATE2(pwr) (.06*pwr)   /* rate for HIGH-LOW kwhrs */
```

```
#define RATE3(pwr) (.07*pwr)  /* rate for >HIGH kwhrs */
main()
{
        double kwh,cost,x;
        char kwha[10];

        cost = 0;
        printf("What is the power usage in kwh? ");
        fgets(kwha,10,stdin);
        kwh = atof(kwha);
        if (kwh<=LOW)
                cost = RATE1(kwh);
        else {
                cost = RATE1(LOW);
                if (kwh<=HIGH) {
                        x = kwh-LOW;
                        cost = cost + RATE2(x);
                }
                else {
                        x = HIGH-LOW;
                        cost = cost + RATE2(x);
                        x = kwh-950;
                        cost = cost + RATE3(x);
                }
        }
        printf("The total cost is %6.2f \n",cost);
}
```

In this example the conditions are inclusive; that is, one or more conditions may be true.

The *switch* Structure

You can use the C *switch* structure to accomplish multiway branching.

Multiway branching is accomplished in C with a *switch* structure. Here is a simple menu program using a *switch* multiway structure (we will further develop this menu program later on):

```
#include <stdio.h>
main()
{
        char option;

        printf("MAIN MENU\n\n");
        printf("\t(1) Add a name\n");
        printf("\t(2) Edit a name\n");
```

```
printf("\t(3) List names\n");
printf("\t(4) Exit to DOS\n\n");
printf("Please enter desired option: ");
option = getchar();
switch(option)
{
    case '1' :
        printf("Option 1 selected\n");
        break;
    case '2' :
        printf("Option 2 selected\n");
        break;
    case '3' :
        printf("Option 3 selected\n");
        break;
    case '4' :
        exit(0);
    default :
        printf("Illegal option selected\n");
}
}
```

There are several points about this structure that you should be aware of:

- The *switch* statement consists of the keyword *switch*, with the control expression in parentheses, followed by a statement.

- The *case* keyword is used to check the control expression for a value. The expression is terminated by a colon.

- The *break* statements force an exit from the structure once any condition is met.

- A *default* test is optional and can be used to trap conditions not meeting any case condition.

Tip | Since both nested *ifs* and *switch* structures can be used for multiway, the user is faced with a choice between the two. With the C *switch* structure, the control expression must evaluate to an *int*, *short*, *long*, or *char* type. Pointers and floats are not allowed. The *case* keyword must be followed by a constant expression; that is, the expression must evaluate to a value that is constant at compile time.

Comparing Strings

To compare text strings by means of conditional tests, a special C function must be used. C provides several functions for this purpose.

The most general function is the *strcmp( )* function, which compares two strings and returns a zero if the strings are equal, for example:

```
main()
{
    char weather[10];

    printf("What is the weather? ");
    fgets(weather,10,stdin);
    if (0 == strcmp(weather,"sunny"))
        printf("Wash and wax the car.\n");
    else
        printf("Go to library.\n");
}
```

For more information on comparing strings, see chapter 7.

Guidelines for Writing Control Code

Here are a few guidelines to help you avoid common mistakes that could plague your early C programming:

- Do NOT use a semicolon after the control expression of an *if* structure. If the semicolon is used after the control expression, the next statement will always be executed regardless of the value of the control expression.

- Remember to use the double equal sign to test for equality. A single equal sign is an assignment operator in C.

- Use proper indention to control the readability of the structure.

- Use braces in a consistent way. One method is to try to keep the closing brace under the opening brace. Using this rule makes it easier to see which braces match.

- There is a *goto* in C, but you should seldom, if ever, need to use it. If you think you need to use it, evaluate why you believe it is necessary and see if you can use an alternative.

The following expression is incorrect:

```
if (a == 2 || 5 || 7)...
```

The correct form is

```
if (a == 2 || a == 5 || a == 7)...
```

In the former case, the control expression also evaluates to nonzero, regardless of the value of a.

Review

Here are the important points you should know from this chapter:

1 | The two basic types of control structures are the conditional and loop structures.

2 | The three basic types of conditional control structures are the one-way, two-way, and multiway structures.

3 | You can create one-way and two-way control structures with the *if . . . else* or *?* structures.

4 | The two types of multiway structures are the mutually exclusive and inclusive structures.

5 | You can use *if . . . else* or the *switch* keywords to create multiway structures.

This chapter has also provided you with opportunities to practice writing programs having *if* and *switch* structures.

Quiz for Chapter 5

1 | Which of the following is zero?
   a | 'a' < 'f'
   b | 3 < 20
   c | 'a' < 'A'
   d | 50 > 7 ¦¦ 8 > 9

2 | Which of the following is zero?
   a | 50 > 7 && 8 > 9
   b | 23
   c | −2
   d | !15

3 | What is the value of the expression (a==2 ¦¦ 5 ¦¦ 7) if *a* is 5?
   a | 2
   b | 5
   c | 0
   d | 1

4 | In which of the following conditions is *num* not between 1 and 9?
   a | num > 1 ¦¦ num < 9
   b | num < 1 ¦¦ num > 9
   c | !(num > 1 && num < 9)
   d | None of the above

5 | What is the numerical value of this expression: 'Z' > 'Y' ? 10 : 4;
   a | 4
   b | 10
   c | 0
   d | 1

6 | What is the value of this expression: a > b ? b > a : a > b
   a | 0
   b | 1
   c | a
   d | b

7 | What is the output of the following program:

```
main()
{
        int i = 0;

        switch(i++)
            {
            case 0 : "Merry "
            case 1 : "Christmas "
            case 2 : "to "
```

```
                    default : "you!"
                    }
    }
```

a | Merry
b | Merry Christmas to you
c | Nothing is printed.
d | Christmas

8 | What is the output of the following program:

```
main()
{
        int i = 0;

        switch(i++)
            {
            case 0 : "Merry "
                    break;
            case 1 : "Christmas "
                    break;
            case 2 : "to "
                    break;
            default : "you!"
            }
}
```

a | Merry
b | Merry Christmas to you
c | Christmas
d | The program will not compile.

9 | You need a program that permits you to enter two numbers and then states whether or not the first is evenly divided by the second. If the following program is used and the numbers 4 and 3 are entered, what is the output?

```
main()
{
        int one, two;
        char onea[10], twoa[10];

        printf("Please enter two numbers: ");
        gets(onea);
        gets(twoa);
        one = atoi(onea);
        two = atoi(twoa);;
        if (one % two = 0)
                printf("Evenly divided\n");
        else
```

```
                     printf("Not evenly divided\n");
    }
```

  a | Evenly divided
  b | Not evenly divided
  c | Execution terminates with an error message.
  d | Program does not compile.

10 | What is the output of the following program?

```
main()
{
        int ctr = 2;

        if ((ctr += 5) == 7)
                printf("Prog 1");
        else if (ctr == 5)
                printf("Prog 2");
        else
                printf("Prog 3");
}
```

  a | Prog 1
  b | Prog 2
  c | Prog 3
  d | No output

11 | If *x* is 2, what is the value of this expression: $((x -= 6) == 2)$
  a | 2
  b | 1
  c | 0
  d | None of the above

12 | What is the value of this expression: $(3 > 5) ? 3 : 2$
  a | 1
  b | 0
  c | 3
  d | 2

13 | Which of the following statements evaluates *min*, the minimum of
     a and *b*?
  a | min = (a < b) ? a : b
  b | min = (a > b) ? b : a
  c | Both are correct.
  d | Neither is correct.

14 | Which expression is nonzero?
  a | 100 > 3 || 'a' > 'd'
  b | !(100 > 50)
  c | Both are nonzero.
  d | Neither is nonzero.

15 | Which expression is zero?

    a | 'a' > 'f'

    b | 50 > 3 && 'a' > 'e'

    c | Both are zero.

    d | Neither is zero.

6 | Program Control: Iteration Structures

About This Chapter

Iteration structures
permit the program to
execute a group of
statements a specified
number of times, based
on a certain condition.

This chapter describes a second type of control structure: the loop or iteration structure. *Iteration structures* permit the program to execute a group of statements a specified number of times, based on a certain condition. Each execution of the group of statements is called an *iteration*, or loop.

There are two types of iterations, depending on when the condition is tested. The *while* iteration checks a control expression before executing the loop. The *for* structure is an alternative to the *while* loop. The *do . . . while* checks a control expression at the end of the loop.

The *while* Structure

A *while* structure
executes a group of
statements as long as a
control expression is
nonzero.

The *while* structure executes a group of statements as long as a control expression is true. The control expression is tested before executing the statements (figure 6.1). The general form is

```
while control expression
      statements;
```

93

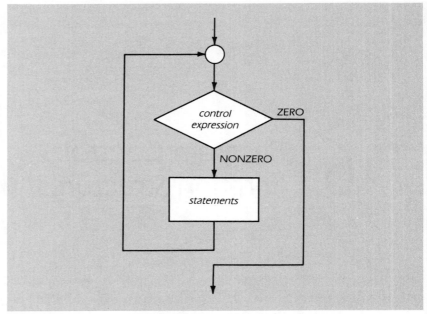

Figure 6.1 The while structure

The program begins by checking *control expression*. If *control expression* is nonzero, *statements* is executed. Otherwise, the program continues with the next statement after the semicolon. As with other control expressions, you can use brackets to indicate that a statement block is to be executed if the condition is nonzero.

Notice that *control expression* is tested before any statements are executed. If *control expression* is zero, no statements are executed. Generally the statements alter the value of the control expression. Notice that the *while* structure is very similar to the *if* structure, except that the *if* structure permits only a single iteration, whereas the *while* structure permits any number of iterations. As an example, try the following program:

```
/* WHILE loop example */

#include <stdio.h>
main()
{
        static char msg[17] = "This is a cycle.";
        int ctr;

        ctr = 1;
        while (ctr++ <= 6)
                printf("%s %d\n",msg,ctr);
}
```

The program will produce this output:

```
This is cycle  1
This is cycle  2
This is cycle  3
This is cycle  4
This is cycle  5
This is cycle  6
```

Notice that the value of a variable is part of the control expression and is changed for each iteration. Eventually the variable value reaches 6 and the loop execution is terminated. The control expression is tested before executing the statements in the loop.

Note | In creating an iterative structure, always be sure that you have a terminating condition. Otherwise, the loop will continue to execute indefinitely. There must be some way for the control expression to eventually reach a value of 0.

Now let's try a more practical example. This program calculates the greatest common denominator of two input numbers:

```c
/* Program to find the greatest common denominator */

#include <stdio.h>
main()
{
      int first,second,x;
      char firsta[10],seconda[10];

      printf("Please enter two positive integers\n");
      fgets(firsta, 10, stdin);
      fgets(seconda);
      first = atoi(firsta, 10, stdin);
      second = atoi(seconda);
      while (second != 0)
           {
           x = first % second;
           first = second;
           second = x;
           }
      printf("The greatest common denominator is %d\n",
           first);
}
```

The program uses an algorithm developed by Euclid. If **second** is zero, we've finished our work and the greatest common denominator is equal to first. If second is not zero, calculate:

```
x = first modulo second
second = x
```

and try again. A sample output could look like this:

```
Please enter two positive integers
26
39
The greatest common denominator is 13
```

Now try another example. This program will permit you to enter a series of numbers and will then display the average of the numbers:

```
/* Program to calculate the average of input numbers */

#include <math.h>
#include <stdio.h>
main()
{
        int ctr = 0;
        double number, average, sum;
        char numbera[10];

        sum = 0.0;
        number = -1.0;
        printf("Please enter the input numbers, \n");
        printf("terminating with a zero.\n");
        while (number != 0.0)
                {
                fgets(numbera, 10, stdin);
                number = atof(numbera);
                sum = sum + number;
                ctr++;
                }
        average = sum/(ctr-1);
        printf("The average is %f\n",average);
}
```

In this example the input numbers are read and summed in a *while* loop. As soon as a zero is entered, the *while* loop is terminated on the next iteration without executing the statements in the loop. The average is then calculated and displayed.

The readability of the example, however, is poor. In this type of problem it would be better to test for the condition after the input number has been read. That would eliminate the need for the somewhat crude initialization (`number = -1`) and the extra iteration. We can put the test at the end of the loop using a *do . . . while* structure.

The *do . . . while* Structure

The *do . . . while* structure executes a group of control expressions while a control expression is nonzero, testing the expression after the statements are executed.

The *do . . . while* structure executes a group of statements and checks a control expression. If the control expression is nonzero, the group of statements is executed again; if zero, the program exits the loop. Figure 6.2 shows the general structure. Notice the similarity to the *while* structure, except for the test being at the end of the loop. For this reason the group of statements will always be executed at least once.

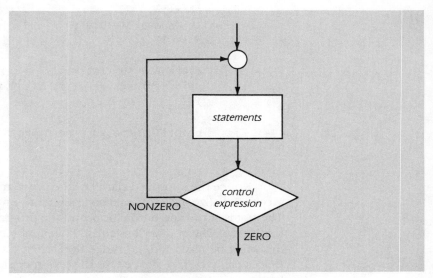

Figure 6.2 The do . . . while structure

The general form of the *do . . . while* structure is

```
do
        statements
while (control expression);
```

As with the *while* statement, you can use a statement block if the group is enclosed in braces.

Now you can rewrite the example of the previous section as:

```
/* Program to calculate the average of input numbers */

#include <math.h>
#include <stdio.h>
main()
{
     int ctr=0;
     double number,average,sum;
     char numbera[10];

     sum = 0.0;
     printf("Please enter the input numbers, \n");
     printf("terminating with a zero.\n");
     do   {
          fgets(numbera, 10, stdin);
          number = atof(numbera);
     sum = sum + number;
          ctr++;
     }    while (number != 0.0);
       if (ctr != 1)
            {
            average = sum/(ctr-1);
            printf("The average is %f\n",average);
            }
       else
            printf("There were no numbers entered\n");
}
```

Notice the improved clarity of the program. It is no longer necessary to initialize number, since no test is made until an input is received.
The test is at the end of the loop, and the program exits the loop if the
test is true. The counter has already been incremented at that time, so
this must be taken into consideration when the average is calculated.
Braces are used to indicate that the group of statements is part of the
loop.

The *for* Structure

In a *for* structure, a
group of statements is
executed a specified
number of times.

The *for* structure is used to execute a group of statements a specified
number of times. The general form of the *for* structure is

```
for (initializing_expression; control_expression;
       step_expression)
            statements;
```

Notice that there are three expressions inside the parentheses, and they are separated by semicolons. The first expression is an initializing statement. The second is the control expression. The loop continues as long as the control expression is nonzero. The third expression controls the step.

Using the *for* Structure

You can rewrite the first example of this chapter as:

```
/* FOR loop example */

#include <stdio.h>
main()
{
      static char msg[] = "This is a cycle";
      int ctr;

      for (ctr=1; ctr < = 6 ; ctr++ )
            printf("%s %d\n",msg,ctr);
}
```

Notice how much more compact the code is now than with the *while* structure. Inside the parentheses are the three expressions: the initializing statement, the control expression for testing, and the step statement that was formerly part of the loop. The expressions are separated by semicolons. If any one of these expressions is not used, the space for that expression should be blank:

```
/* FOR loop example */

#include <stdio.h>
main()
{
      static char msg[] = "This is a cycle";
      int ctr;

      ctr = 1;
      for ( ; ctr <= 6 ; ctr++ )
            printf("%s %d\n",msg,ctr);
}
```

As before, you can use a statement block in the loop if the statements are put in braces:

```
/* FOR loop example */

#include <stdio.h>
main()
{
      static char msg[] = "This is a cycle";
      int ctr;

      for (ctr=1 ; ctr <= 6 ; ctr++ )
          {
          printf("%s %d\n",msg,ctr);
          printf("End of this cycle);
          }
}
```

Other Variations

As you can imagine, the *for* structure is much more versatile than a similar statement in most other languages. Here are some features of the *for* structure:

- As with most languages, you can increment or decrement the counter and use a step function:

  ```
  for (ctr=10; ctr>0 ; ctr-=2 )
      printf("%d\n",ctr);
  ```

- You can also use geometrically increasing steps or any legal expression as the third component:

  ```
  for (ctr=1; ctr<10; ctr *= 2)
      printf("%d\n",ctr);
  ```

- You can use a variable in the condition test other than the loop variable:

  ```
  oldprice = 3.00;
  for (ctr=1; price<10.00; ctr++)
      {
      price = oldprice + ((ctr*oldprice)/10.00);
      printf("%6.2f",price);
      }
  ```

- You can omit an expression in the statement as long as the loop has some way to terminate. For what ctr value, for example, will the following terminate?

  ```
  result = 0;
  ```

```
for (ctr=1,result<10;)
     result = result*ctr;
```

- You can change the step expression dynamically while the loop is executing. For example, assume:

```
temp = 1;
for (ctr=1; ctr<10; ctr= temp*ctr)
     {
     if (ctr>5)
             temp = 2;
     printf("%d\n",ctr);
     }
```

In this case, after the first five iterations, the step is changed to a larger value.

Review

This chapter described three types of loop control: the *while*, the *do . . . while*, and the *for*.

1 | The *while* and *for* structures are used to execute one or more statements as long as a condition is true.

2 | The *do . . . while* structure is used to execute one or more statements until a condition is false.

Which structure to use in a given situation depends on the application. For example, deciding between *while* and *do . . . while* depends on when you wish to do the test. In about 90% of all applications, the *while* is preferred. One reason for this is that, with the *while*, the program statements can be skipped if the test fails. With the *do . . . while*, the statements will always be executed at least once.

Quiz for Chapter 6

1 | In what basic way does the *do . . . while* structure differ from the *while* structure?

    a | The loop execution terminates when the control expression is zero.

    b | The loop execution terminates when the control expression is nonzero.

    c | The condition is tested at the beginning of the loop.

    d | The statements in the loop are always executed at least once.

2 | In what basic way does the *while* structure differ from the *do . . . while* structure?

    a | The loop execution terminates when the control expression is zero.

    b | The loop execution terminates when the control expression is nonzero.

    c | The condition is tested at the beginning of the loop.

    d | The statements in the loop are always executed at least once.

3 | What is the most common type of loop structure?

    a | *do . . . while*

    b | *while*

    c | *switch . . . case*

    d | *if . . . else*

4 | Which of the following is not a loop control structure?

    a | *switch . . . case*

    b | *for*

    c | *do . . . while*

    d | *while*

5 | What is the value of $5 > 1$?

    a | 1

    b | zero

    c | -1

    d | None of the above

6 | What is the value of $2+4 > 2$ && $4 < 2$?

    a | 1

    b | zero

    c | -1

    d | None of the above

7 | What is the value of $x >= y$ || $y > x$?

    a | 1

    b | zero

    c | -1

    d | None of the above

8 | Which of the following expresses the condition that *ch* is not *a* or *b*?
    a | ch != 'a' && ch != 'b'
    b | ch != 'a' || ch != 'b'
    c | ch != 'a' || 'b'
    d | ch != 'a' && 'b'

9 | Which of the following conditions expresses the condition that *num* is between 1 and 9 but not 4?
    a | num > 1 && num < 9 && num != 4
    b | num > 1 || num < 9 && num != 4
    c | num >= 1 && num <= 9 && num != 4
    d | None of the above

10 | What is the output of the following program?

```
main()
{
for ( num = 18; num>0 ; num /=2)
        printf("%3d", num);
}
```

    a | 18 17 16 15 14 13 12 11 10 9 8 7 6 5 4 3 2 1
    b | 18 9 4 2 1
    c | 18 9 4 2 1 0
    d | None of the above

11 | What is the output of the following program?

```
main()
{
        int i = 0;

        while (++i < 4)
                printf("Hello! ");
}
```

    a | Hello! Hello! Hello!
    b | Hello! Hello! Hello! Hello!
    c | Hello! Hello! Hello! Hello! Hello!
    d | None of the above; the program has an error.

12 | What is the output of the following program:

```
main()
{
        int i = 0;

        do
                printf("Hello! ");
                while (i++ < 4);
}
```

a | Hello! Hello! Hello!
b | Hello! Hello! Hello! Hello!
c | Hello! Hello! Hello! Hello! Hello!
d | None of the above; the program has an error.

13 | What is the output of the following program:

```
main()
{
      int i;

      for (i = 0, i < 4, i++)
            printf("Hello! ");
}
```

a | Hello! Hello! Hello!
b | Hello! Hello! Hello! Hello!
c | Hello! Hello! Hello! Hello! Hello!
d | None of the above; the program has an error.

14 | What is the output of the following program:

```
/* FOR loop test */

#include <stdio.h>
main()
{
      int i, ch;

      for (i=0 , ch = 'A'; i < 4 ; i++, ch +=2 * 1)
            putchar(ch);
}
```

a | ABCDE
b | ABC
c | ACEG
d | None of the above; the program has an error.

15 | What is the output of the following program when *123* is entered?

```
#include <stdio.h>
main()
{
      int num,right;
      char numa[10];

      printf("Please enter an integer: ");
      fgets(numa, 10, stdin);
      num = atoi(numa);
      do    {
            right = num % 10;
```

```
            printf("%d",right);
            num = num / 10;
            } while (num != 0);
        printf("\n");
}
```

a | 123
b | 321
c | 3
d | None of the above

7 | Introduction to Pointers

About This Chapter

The C language permits you to use a variable to store the address of another variable. The variable is said to be a *pointer* because it points to the address of the variable. This chapter will show you the basic principles of using pointers.

What Is a Pointer?

A *pointer* is a symbolic representation of an address.

A *pointer* is a symbolic representation of an address. In chapter 4 you used an ampersand to point to the data stored at an address, for example:

```
int counter;

ptr = &counter
```

In this case `ptr` is a variable that points to the address of `counter` (figure 7.1).

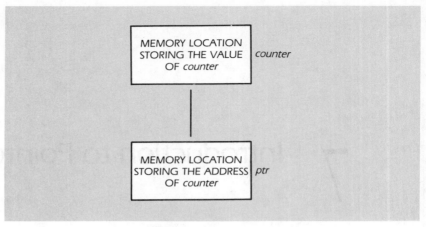

Figure 7.1 The pointer

Declaring Pointers

A pointer variable is declared as an address by beginning the variable name with an asterisk.

To declare a pointer variable as an address, begin the variable name with an asterisk:

```
char *message;
```

In this case, **message** is a pointer to the address of the beginning of a text string (figure 7.2).

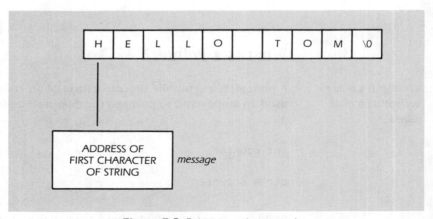

Figure 7.2 Pointers and a text string

You do not declare a pointer, but rather the

Notice that you do not declare the pointer, but rather the data to which the pointer points. That's because the computer needs to know

data to which a pointer points.

how much memory space to allocate for the data. There is no special pointer data type.

One of the major reasons why C is such a powerful language is its support of pointers. As you explore arrays (chapter 10) and create your own data structures (chapter 11), you will gain a greater appreciation of C's power to use pointers.

Pointer Operators

The two pointer-related operators are the address operator (&) and the indirection operator (*).

The pointer-related operators are special prefix codes that are used for performing operations with pointers. There are two pointer-related operators: the address operator (&) and the indirection operator (*).

The asterisk is used in declaring a variable that points to the address of the first character of the string. Note that `message` points to the address of the first character, not to the character itself; that is, in the following example `*message` is the same as `message[0]`, and `*message` is a pointer to `message[0]`.

```
/* Test for indirection */

#include <stdio.h>
main()
{
        int x;
        char *message;
        char xa[10];

        message = "HELLO THERE. \n";
        printf("Please enter an integer: ");
        fgets(xa,10,stdin);
        x = atoi(xa);
        printf("%s The number is %d\n",message,x);
}
```

The ampersand, or address operator, was used in the first example of this chapter and was also used earlier in chapter 4 to illustrate how to enter a numeric value with the *scanf( )* function.

In C, `*foo` refers to the data stored at address `foo`, and `&foobar` refers to the address of `foobar`. An array name represents a pointer to the first element of an array; that is, the address of the first pointer. You can then say that:

```
foo == &foo[0]
```

Using Pointers to Access Strings

As the previous example illustrated, another alternative in declaring strings is to declare a pointer:

```
main()
{
    char *message;

    message = "This is a test.";
    printf("%s\n",message);
}
```

In this case the declaration allocates space for a pointer called **message**. The first statement in the body of the program allocates space for a string and initializes the pointer to the value of the address of the first character of the string.

Notes on Pointers and Strings

Pointers are probably the most confusing feature of the C language. Here are two examples that show the right and the wrong way of using pointers and strings.

Example 1

Enter, compile, and execute this program:

```
/* Program #1 with a problem */

#include <stdio.h>
main()
{
    char *msg;

    printf("What is your favorite flower? ");
    fgets(msg,9,stdin);
    printf("Your favorite flower is the %s\n",msg);
}
```

With C, this program will compile and it may sometimes execute properly, but the program has a very serious problem. Here is how it probably executes—just as you would suspect:

What is your favorite flower: *rose*   ←Enter

Your favorite flower is the rose.

Avoid using the pointer method to declare an array for an input array unless the array is initialized when it is declared.

What is wrong with the program? The variable **msg** is a pointer to a character array. The problem is that no memory was allocated for the character string. The variable **msg** is a memory location that stores the starting address of the array. The input text will be stored beginning in whatever random address is stored in **msg**. This could be very dangerous if the address is used by some other part of the program or even DOS. In some compilers you may get a warning message, but you may also get nothing. This program will compile and may seem to execute correctly, but it contains this serious problem.

Note | With any input function, do not use the pointer form to declare a character string that is used for input. In the preceding example, the length of the string is determined at compile time and the compiler allocates the correct amount of space. When pointers are used to declare input strings, the string is stored in a local stack space dynamically, and the stack will be corrupted.

Here is the correct version of the same program:

```
#include <stdio.h>
main()
{
     char msg[20];

     printf("What is your favorite flower? ");
     fgets(msg,20,stdin);
     printf("Your favorite flower is the %s",msg);
}
```

Now you have assigned space for the text string (20 characters) by declaring the array variable.

Example 2

For another challenge, try this program:

```
/* Program #2 with a problem */

#include <stdio.h>
main()
{
```

```
        char msg[20];

        msg = "Hello out there!";
        printf("The computer's message is %s",msg);
}
```

This one won't even compile correctly. What's wrong? You have declared an array for the text, and then it appears that you tried to assign a text string to this array. When you try to compile it, however, you will get an error message.

An array name is a pointer to the first character of an array and thus cannot be assigned a value by the program.

Remember that `msg` is used to store the address of the first character of the text string. The problem is that the compiler thinks you are trying to assign the value of a character string to `msg`. An array name is a storage location for an address that contains a pointer to the array starting character. The array name is a pointer, a constant that cannot be modified or assigned a value. The correct form is

```
#include <stdio.h>
main()
{
        char msg[20];

        strcpy(msg,"Hello out there!");
        printf("The computer's message is %s\n",msg);
}
```

or here is another solution:

```
#include <stdio.h>
main()
{
        char *msg;

        msg = "Hello out there!";
        printf("The computer's message is %s\n",msg);
}
```

Now let's look at how those character string pointers really work.

Character Strings and Pointers

A character string is a *char* array with a terminating null character.

A character string, as already mentioned, is a *char* array terminated with a null character (\0). You have already seen one way of declaring a character string array. Let's look now at a second way and see how the two differ.

The Array Form

The array form declares a *char* array of a fixed size to store the string. You have already used this method:

```
static char msg[] = "rose";
```

An array of 5 bytes is declared for the storage of the text. There will be 4 bytes for the text string and another character reserved for the null character (\0). After the declaration, C will recognize `msg` as storing the address of the first array element:

```
msg == &msg[0]
```

It is important to realize that `msg` is a constant. It is fixed, and cannot be modified by the program. That is why, in Example 2, with QuickC you got the message:

```
2100 left operand must be lvalue
```

In the program of Example 2, you were trying to assign the address of a text string to `msg`, a constant:

```
msg = "Hello out there!";
```

With an array, you cannot use any operation like this, `++msg` or `msg = msg+1`, to find the next element of an array. The name of the array is a constant and is a pointer to the first element of the array. To put it another way, the array size is fixed and stored at a memory location determined at compile time. The constant `msg` is a storage location for a pointer to the first element of the array.

The Pointer Form

As a second alternative, you could use a pointer form and declare the array as

```
static char *msg= "rose"
```

Again, C will store this as an array of five elements, just as before. In addition, however, C sets aside a sixth storage location for a variable `msg`. The pointer to the text string is now a variable, and can be modified by the program as desired. You can now use the increment or decrement operators on the variable to output the string:

```
while ( *(msg) != '\0')
      putchar( *(msg++);
```

Which to Use?

Both methods work in many applications. For example, the following program

```
#include <stdio.h>
main()
{
      static char array_msg[]="Hello out there!";
      char *ptr_msg = "Hello out there!";
      int index=0;

      for (index = 0; index < 17; index++)
          putchar( *(array_msg + index) );
      putchar('\n');
      for (index = 0; index < 17; index++)
          putchar( *(ptr_msg + index) );
      putchar('\n');
}
```

would display

```
Hello out there!
Hello out there!
```

This little program uses both methods to store the same text string. The array pointer is a constant, but it is never incremented or altered, so the program works as indicated.

Now look at this form:

```
while ( *(ptr_msg) != '\0')
      putchar( *(ptr_msg++) );
```

It will work. The following form, however, will not work:

```
while ( *(array_msg) != '\0')
      putchar( *(array_msg++) );
```

In this case you are trying to increment a constant, which is not permitted.

In assigning one array to another, the same limitation holds. The following is valid:

```
ptr_msg = array_msg
```

The following is not valid because you cannot assign a value to a constant:

```
array_msg = ptr_msg
```

The ability to use pointers to process arrays gives C a strong advantage over other languages that do not provide much pointer support. For example, look at this program:

```
#include <stdio.h>
main()
{
        static char *msg = "Pointer copy test";
        static char *out_string;

        out_string = msg;
        printf("%s",out_string);
}
```

Your first impression of this program might be that a copy of the string is made and then displayed. In reality, however, only the pointer is copied. The text string is never copied. If you have a program with a very large array, copying the one pointer to an entire array is far faster and more efficient than trying to copy all the elements of an array.

Initializing a Character String Array

In order to initialize a character string array, you must declare it as *static* or *external*.

Remember that if you wish to initialize a character string array, it must be declared static or external. Using the previous example of chapter 2, we can include yet another method of declaring a string array:

```
static char msg1[] = "Hello";
static char msg2[] = {'H','E','L'.'L','O','\0'};
static char msg3[40] = "Hello";
static char *msgptr = "Hello";
```

In the first case, the array is declared and allocated 6 bytes (5 plus 1 for the null character), and is initialized. The second case is identical to the first. In the third case, the array is declared and allocated 40 bytes. The text string is stored in the first 5 bytes. All 35 of the remaining bytes are initialized to null (\0) characters.

In the fourth case, an array is declared and the initialization assigns 6 spaces for it (5 plus 1 for the null character). A seventh location is also reserved to store msgptr, which is a variable used as a pointer. The string length determines how much space will be reserved for the array.

Remember, when you declare an array using the third method, make sure that you allocate space for the largest string you expect to use, plus the null character. For example, to use the variable zip to store 5-character zip codes, you would need 6 bytes:

```
char zip[5+1];
```

Using Character String Arrays

In the last chapter you saw an example of an array of character strings:

```
#include <stdio.h>
main()
{
        static char *choices[]=
                {
                "A)dd an address",
                "E)dit an address",
                "D)isplay an address"
                };
        static char title[40] = "Main Menu\n\n";
        menu(title,choices,3);
}
menu(title,selections,size)
char *title;
char *selections[];
int size;
{
        int i;

        printf(title);
        for (i=0; i<size; i++)
                printf("%s\n",*(selections+i));
        return;
}
```

In this example selections is an array of three pointers to character strings. Each character string is an array of characters, so selections is really an array of three pointers to arrays. The first pointer, selections[0], is a pointer to the beginning of the first string; that is, selections[0] contains the address for the start of the first string. The second pointer, selections[1], points to the beginning of the second string.

```
*selections[0] == 'A'  *selections[1]=='E'
*selections[3] == 'D'
```

This form gives an array with rows of varying length, and the length of each row is determined by the string to which it was initialized.

You could also initialize the same array as

```
static char selections[3][40];
```

This would declare an array of three rows, each of 40 characters. The rows are all of equal length. This kind of array takes more space than the former, but in some cases it may be just what you need (as, for example, in the creation of fixed-length records for a file).

Using String Functions

The C language provides several functions for string operations.

The C library included with your compiler provides several functions for processing strings. You have already met the string input and output functions (chapter 4). Now let's look at a few more: *strlen( )*, *strcat( )*, and *strcpy( )*. In addition, we'll look at some variations of *strcmp( )*.

Finding a String's Length

The *strlen( )* function finds the length of a string.

The *strlen( )* function can be used to find the length of a string. One common use for *strlen( )* is to ensure that the length of an input string does not exceed the array space allocated for it. As we remarked earlier, C does not check this. If you wish it checked, you must include *strlen( )* in the program:

```
#include <stdio.h>
#define MAXLEN 10
main()
{
    static char name[80];
    :
    :

    if (strlen(name) > MAXLEN)
        puts("The name is too long")
    :
    :

}
```

In the example an input string is read, and then the length is compared with the maximum size of the array. If the string is too long, the last character in the space allocated for the array string is changed to a null character. The array here has 11 elements because the first element will be zero. The maximum input string is 10 characters plus the null character. The null character is not counted in the string length total.

Comparing Strings

The *strcmp( )* function compares two strings for equality.

In comparing strings, you must use caution or you may experience some interesting results. For example, try the following program:

```c
#include <stdio.h>
#define MAXNAMES   4
#define MAXNAMECHARS   10
#define NULL 0
#define END ""
main()
{
        char *name_ptr[MAXNAMES];
        static char name_array [MAXNAMES][MAXNAMECHARS+2];
        int i, index=0;
        void sort();

        printf("Enter Name: ");
        while ( index < MAXNAMES &&
                fgets(name_array[index],10,stdin) != NULL &&
                name_array[index] != END) )
                {
                name_ptr[index] = name_array[index];
                index++;
                printf("Enter Name: ");
                }
}
```

This routine reads a series of input names. The basic idea is that if the array size is exceeded, there is no input error and no null input string (carriage return entered); the name is accepted and a request is made for another name. This will work fine except for the last condition. If you enter only a carriage return, the program continues to ask for another name. You can't terminate the program.

The error is in the test condition:

```c
name_array[index] != END
```

END is a pointer. The pointer will never be equal to the value of name_array[index], so the condition always succeeds.

Now try this with a *strcmp( )* function:

```
#include <stdio.h>
#define MAXNAMES  4
#define MAXNAMECHARS  10
#define NULL 0
#define END ""
main()
{
    char *name_ptr[MAXNAMES];
    static char name_array [MAXNAMES][MAXNAMECHARS];
    int i, index=0;
    void sort();

    printf("Enter Name: ");
    while ( index < MAXNAMES &&
            fgets(name_array[index],10,stdin) != NULL &&
            strcmp(name_array[index],END) != 0)
            {
            name_ptr[index] = name_array[index];
            index++;
            printf("Enter Name: ");
            }
}
```

This routine will work. Notice that part of the test for ending the input is now

```
strcmp(name_array[index],END) != 0)
```

This compares the strings referenced by the two pointers. The *strcmp( )* function always takes two string pointers as arguments and returns a value of 0 if they are the same.

What if they are not the same? Here is an example of a string sorting function that uses the return value of *strcmp( )*:

```
/* BUBBLE sort routine */

/* sorts an array of character string arrays */
void sort(array,size)
char *array[];
int size;
{
    int i, j;
    char *temp;
```

```
for (i = 0; i<size-1; i++)
    for (j=i+1; j<size; j++)
        if (strcmp(array[i],array[j]) > 0)
        {
        temp = array[j];
        array[j]=array[i];
        array[i] = temp;
        }
}
```

This routine brings up an interesting point about *strcmp( )*: it compares strings, not arrays. Only the character string up to the null character is used in the test.

Now let's look at our original question. The return value for Turbo C or QuickC is the difference between the two ASCII values; that is, the following statement writes a −2:

```
printf("%d\n",strcmp("A","C"));
```

The value of the returned number is not the same for all C compilers, but with all compilers the *strcmp( )* function returns a negative value with this statement. If the first string precedes the second alphabetically, you will get a negative number. If the second precedes the first, you will get a positive number. The actual ASCII values (see appendix B) are used for comparison. An "A" is not equal to "a".

Tip | If you are comparing an input string with something and the input string might be in upper- or lowercase, use the *strupr( )* function to capitalize the input string before comparing.

Now what do you think is the output of the following statement:

```
printf("%d\n",strcmp("AA","AC"));
```

With Turbo C or QuickC, the output is the same as before, a −2. The *strcmp( )* checks the strings until the first mismatch; then it returns the difference of the ASCII values at that pointer.

There are several variations of the compare function in the C library:

Compare Function	Meaning
strcmp(string1, string2)	Compares two strings and returns 0 if the strings are equal, >0 if *string1* > *string2* and <1 if *string1* < *string2*.
strcmpi(string1, string2)	Case-insensitive version of

	strcmp( ) function. Uppercase and lowercase of the same character are considered equal.
stricmp(string1,string2)	Same as the preceding version. Case-insensitive version of *strcmp( )* function.
strncmp(string1,string2,n)	Compares first *n* characters of *string1* and *string2*, returning 0 if *n* characters are equal, >0 if *string1* $>$ *string2*, and <0 if *string1* $<$ *string2*.
strnicmp(string1,string2,n)	Case-insensitive version of *strncmp( )*. Uppercase and lowercase of the same character are considered equal.

As an example, the following program compares `last_name` with `name`, displaying the message if both are equal:

```
char last_name[40], name[40];
if (0 == strcmp(last_name,name))
    printf("The names are equal.\n");
```

The following program looks at the first 3 characters of `zip` to see if they are equal to or greater than 972:

```
char zip[5]
if (strncmp(zip,"902",3) >= 0)
    printf("The first three digits are greater than
    972.\n");
```

Now suppose you wanted this same program to test the last 2 characters for equality to 12. You would have

```
char zip[5]
if (strncmp(&zip[3],"12",2) == 0)
    printf("The last two digits are equal to 12.\n");
```

In the previous examples the name of the array was used. When the name of an array is used in a function or another expression, it actually represents the zero*th* element of the array. In this case we wish to reference the fourth element of the array. We use as an argument, then, a pointer to the fourth element. The **&** operator is used to indicate the address. The expressions **&zip[0]** and **zip** are equivalent, but you should avoid the former.

Concatenating Strings

The strcat( ) *function concatenates one string to another.*

You can also concatenate strings using the *strcat( )* function. Here is an example:

```
#include <stdio.h>
main()
{
        static char msg[10];
        static char add[80]="Your favorite flower is the ";

        printf("What is your favorite flower? ");
        fgets(msg,10,stdin);
        strcat(add,msg);
        puts(add);
}
```

The function has two arguments:

```
strcat(add,msg);
```

The function concatenates the second string to the first string, returning the concatenated string as a modified first string. The strings, not the arrays, are concatenated. As a result, the output is

What is your favorite flower? *rose*   ←Enter

Your favorite flower is the rose.

Even though the input array is 80 characters, the input string is suffixed only to the character string, not the array.

> **Tip** | C does not check to see if the concatenated string fits in the array. If you don't allocate enough array space for the first argument, you may experience serious problems.

Copying Strings

In an earlier section, you saw how you could copy the address of an array and save the time involved in moving an entire array:

```
#include <stdio.h>
main()
{
        static char *msg = "Pointer copy test";
```

```
      static char *out_string;

      out_string = msg;
      printf("%s",out_string);
}
```

Sometimes, however, you may wish to copy the entire array. In this case you would use the *strcpy( )* function:

```
#include <stdio.h>
main()
{
      static char *msg = "Pointer copy test";
      static char out_string[40];

      strcpy(out_string,msg);
      printf("%s",out_string);
}
```

This program uses two character arrays, and the function copies the first string to the second. The first argument is the destination array.

> **Tip** | C does not check to see if the destination array is large enough for the source. If you don't allocate enough array space for the first argument, you may experience serious problems.

An Example with String Functions

Here is an example of a program using string functions to read an input series of names, sort them, and then display the list:

```
#include <stdio.h>
#define MAXNAMES  4
#define MAXNAMECHARS  10
#define NULL 0
#define END ""
main()
{
      char *name_ptr[MAXNAMES];
      static char name_array [MAXNAMES][MAXNAMECHARS+2];
      int i, index=0;
      void sort();

      printf("Enter Name: ");
      while ( index < MAXNAMES &&
             fgets(name_array[index],12,stdin) != NULL &&
```

```
                        strcmp(name_array[index],END) != 0)
                        {
                        name_ptr[index] = name_array[index];
                        index++;
                        printf("Enter Name: ");
                        }
                sort(name_ptr,index);
                printf("\n\n");
                for (i=0; i<index; i++)
                        printf("%s\n",name_ptr[i]);
}


/* BUBBLE sort routine */
/* sorts an array of character string arrays */
void sort(array,size)
char *array[];
int size;
{
        int i, j;
        char *temp;
        for (i = 0; i<size-1; i++)
                for (j=i+1; j<size; j++)
                        if (strcmp(array[i],array[j])>0)
                        {
                        temp = array[j];
                        array[j]=array[i];
                        array[i] = temp;
                        }

}
```

Review

This chapter has discussed the concept of pointers and their use. It covered the following important points:

1 | The definition of a pointer.

2 | The indirection (*) and address pointer operators (&), and how to use them.

3 | How to declare a character string using a pointer, and some of the advantages and disadvantages of this method as compared with other methods of declaring a string.

4 | How to copy, compare, and concatenate strings.

Quiz for Chapter 7

1 | How many bytes are allocated with the following declaration?

```
char ch[]="A";
```

   a | 0
   b | 1
   c | 2
   d | None of the above

2 | How many bytes are allocated with the following declaration?

```
char ch='A';
```

   a | 0
   b | 1
   c | 2
   d | None of the above

3 | What is the second line of the output of the following program?

```
#include <stdio.h>
main()
{
        static char msg[] = "Hello out there!";
        char *msgptr;

        msgptr = msg;
        puts(++msg);
        puts(msg);
        msg[3] = '\0;
        puts(msg);
}
```

   a | Hello out there!
   b | ello out there!
   c | He
   d | None of the above; program has an error.

4 | What will be the first line of the output of this program?

```
#include <stdio.h>
main()
{
        static char msg[] = "Hello";
        char *msgptr;

        msgptr = msg + strlen(msg);
        while (--msgptr >= msg)
                puts(msgptr);
}
```

   a | o

   b | lo

   c | H

   d | None of the above; program has an error.

5 | In the following example, how many bytes are reserved in memory as a result of the declaration?

```
char *ptr = "C";
```

   a | 1

   b | 2

   c | 3 (1 for pointer, 2 for data)

   d | 4 (2 for pointer, 2 for data)

6 | What is the value of *ptr in this example:

```
char *ptr;
static char msg[] = "Test";

ptr = msg[0];
```

   a | Unknown (cannot be determined)

   b | T

   c | The address where the first character is stored

   d | None of the above

7 | What is the value of *(ptr+2) in the previous example?

   a | Unknown (cannot be determined)

   b | T

   c | The address where the first character is stored

   d | s

8 | Declare ptr as a pointer to an array of 20 characters.

   a | char ptr[20];

   b | char (*ptr)[20];

   c | *(ptr[20]);

   d | None of the above

9 | Declare ptr as an array of 20 pointers to an array.

   a | char ptr[20];

   b | char (*ptr)[20];

   c | *(ptr[20]);

   d | None of the above

10 | What is the array notation for the third element in an msg array of 4 characters?

   a | msg[3];

   b | msg[2];

   c | *msg[3];

   d | msg[4];

11 | What is the pointer notation for the third element of an `msg` array of 4 characters?

    a | *(msg+3)

    b | *(msg+2);

    c | *msg+3;

    d | *(msg+4);

12 | If the following is declared, which is valid?

```
char msg[10];
char value
```

    a | msg[2] = value;

    b | msg = value;

    c | Both are valid.

    d | Neither is valid.

13 | Which of the following is valid with this declaration?

```
char *ptr
char msg[10];
char value
```

    a | ptr = value

    b | ptr = msg

    c | Both are valid.

    d | Neither is valid.

14 | What is the pointer notation for an array of 3 charcters?

    a | (*ptr)[4];

    b | (*ptr)[3];

    c | *(ptr[4])

    d | *(ptr[3])

15 | What value does this return?

```
static char msg[]="Test";

printf("%d",strlen(msg));
```

    a | 0

    b | 6

    c | 5

    d | 4

8 | Using Functions and Macros

About This Chapter

When a company builds a complex machine, like a computer, it doesn't start from scratch with raw materials such as silicon, steel, and plastic. It assembles the computer from previously constructed parts, such as a power supply, function boards, and main circuit board. Each of these parts is, in turn, complex. The parts aren't assembled from raw materials but from still simpler parts such as integrated circuits, resistors, and capacitors.

Programs are built from functions and macros.

You can apply the same principle to building computer programs. Instead of trying to build your program from the raw materials offered by a particular programming language, you can build a program out of separately constructed parts. Each of these, in turn, can be built of still simpler parts, until you reach the level of the basic language statements of that particular program. The parts from which you build programs are called *functions* and *macros*.

What is more, these functions and macros have two very desirable properties that are not shared with the example of building a computer. First, using a function or macro does not "use it up." You can call the same function as many times as you desire in a program. Second, whereas the computer parts must be manufactured before the computer can be assembled, the functions and macros can be written either before or after the main program is written.

The creation and use of functions with the C language is one of the most important features of the language. This chapter introduces techniques for modularizing your program and reducing your development time with functions and macros. You will learn the basics of functions and macros and how to use them.

Functions

Functions relate a dependent variable to one or more independent variables. They are used to perform a single, specified action.

Functions are used to relate a dependent variable to one or more independent variables, or they are used to perform a single, specified action. The variables are said to be the *arguments* of the function. You have already used several functions in your programs. For example, the *printf( )* function has the form:

```
printf(format_string,argument_1,argument_2,
        argument_i...argument_n)
```

The independent variables are passed to the function as arguments.

The arguments (independent variables) are `format_string,argument_1,` `argument_2` to `argument_n`. Although a return value from this function has not been mentioned, both Turbo C and QuickC return a value (the dependent variable): the number of characters written.

You could also use this function as:

```
h = printf(format_string, argument_1, argument_2,
        argument_i...argument_n)
```

After execution, the variable h would be set to the number of characters sent to the display. If the function is used to initiate a specific action (such as writing to the screen or opening a disk file), the return value is often used to indicate if an error has occurred in performing the action.

In any program that you write, *main( )* is also a function. When the program is started, a hidden routine is initiated. This is the C support start-up module. The hidden routine, in turn, calls the function *main( )*. Like any other function, *main( )* returns a value. As we shall see later, there is also a way for the user to pass values to *main( )*.

The *main( )* function, in turn, can call other functions. Any application program is really a hierarchy of functions, with the hidden routine being topmost. This routine calls *main( )*, which eventually calls other functions (see figure 8.1).

Why Functions Are Important

The basic C language is really a medium-level language; that is, each statement compiles to at least one line of code. Thus, writing almost any program requires many, many lines of code.

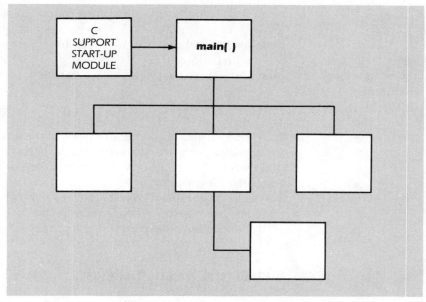

Figure 8.1 The structure of a C program

Now if you had to write all of your programs in the very basic C language, it would take a long time to write even a simple program. There are many things that you do over and over again in most programs. For example, in almost every program you will do writing and reading. Why write the code for this each time that you write a program? That is why almost every C compiler has a *printf( )* function in its library that is ready to do the output work for you. Turbo C and QuickC, like most languages, contain a library of C functions that can be used to do many of the repetitive actions and procedures found in most C programs. This reduces the number of program lines that you, as a programmer, have to write.

Types of Functions

C has three types of functions that you can use: functions in the C library provided with the compiler, functions purchased commercially, and functions you write.

There are three basic types of functions that you can use: functions in the QuickC or Turbo C library that come with your compiler, commercial functions, and functions that you yourself write.

C Compiler Functions

The Turbo C and QuickC products offer an extensive library of over 450 functions that you can use for many purposes. These functions include the basic C functions (such as *printf( )*) found in almost any C compiler, as well as some exciting graphics functions that enable you to add graphics to your application. The documentation with your C compiler includes an extensive listing of each function and how to use it.

Many C library functions require you to specify an *#include* file.

With many of these functions, you need to add a line at the beginning of the program to include one or more files, for example:

```
#include <stdio.h>
```

This line instructs the compiler to look in the *#include* file called *stdio.h* for the definitions needed by the function (such as buffer size, structure definitions). The number and names of the *#include* files needed for a particular function depend on the function, and are listed for each function in your compiler's library manual. The *#include* files are simple text files, and you can examine them with any text editor. The compiler reads the *#include* files as part of the process of compiling source code.

Commercial Function Libraries

Libraries of functions can be purchased from various suppliers (such as Vitamin C, FairCom, and Lifeboat). These add database management support, windowing, communications support, and other features.

Writing Your Own Functions

In writing a program, you will often find that you are entering lines of code identical to those you entered earlier in another program or, even worse, that you are entering lines of code already in your program. In this case you would want to write your own functions, keep them in a library, and then use them for frequent routines in your application programs.

Using Functions

By using functions as building blocks in programs, you avoid having to write the same code over and over.

Functions save you work. Each function represents several lines of code. Using the same functions in many programs eliminates the necessity of having to add the code to every program that you write. In fact, the function does not even have to be written in C. It could be written in any compiler language that is compatible with the language's linker. For QuickC, this includes Microsoft's QuickBASIC, assembly language, or even a C compiler from another manufacturer. To some extent, you can mix functions written in several languages, taking advantage of the best of each language.

Note | This concept is more ideal than practical. You probably won't have much trouble mixing object modules from various Microsoft compilers, but use caution when dealing with compilers from other manufacturers. For example, if you mix object modules from Turbo Prolog and QuickC, the object module conventions may or may not be compatible.

Functions can be written in any language compatible with your compiler's object code (including assembly) and can be compiled for use with your C programs.

Functions, then, give you the capability of converting low-level or medium-level C languages to powerful high-level languages of your own making. Once this language is created, you can build many applications from your creation. As an example, if you like to create object-oriented adventure games, you can create powerful functions to support the objects and actors you use in your games. A good example of this is David Betz's adventure authoring system in *Byte* (May 1987), which was written in C. If you like animation, you can build functions to support this. You can also write database managers, spreadsheets (Lotus 1-2-3 was initially written in C), word processors, or whatever. In each case you are creating functions that are application-specific.

The use of functions is an integral part of using structured programming techniques.

Finally, functions are an extension of structured programming techniques. Functions should have a single entry and exit.

Let's review, then, the advantages of functions:

- Development time and cost are reduced, since functions already written and debugged are portable to other programs and C compilers.

- You can create your own high-level language that is application-oriented and can be used for many applications.

- Functions improve the readability of the program because each function has a single purpose.

Don't be hesitant to use functions wherever you can in your programs. Build up your own libraries. Purchase those that are relevant to programs you are developing.

This chapter will introduce you to the basics of writing functions. With C, you can also create libraries of functions that you use frequently.

Tip | Use as many functions as you can in your program. Check public domain libraries for ones that you can use free of charge, and purchase any others that you need for your applications. The cost of purchasing almost any function is far, far less than trying to write it yourself. Write those that you can't obtain and build your own proprietary library.

A Simple Function

This simple *delay( )* function requires no input arguments.

Now try your hand at a simple program that uses a function. This program displays a message, initiates a delay, and then displays another message:

```
/* Program to test a delay function */

#include <stdio.h>
main()
{
        void delay();

        printf("Starting\n");
        delay();
        printf("Ending\n");
}

/* DELAY function */
void delay()
{
        unsigned int i, j, n;

        n = 1000;
        for (i=0; i<n; i++)
                for (j=0; j<n; j++);
        return;
}
```

The preceding example was a simple one, but it does illustrate some important features of writing a function:

1 | In the example the calling program uses the function name followed by two parentheses. There are no arguments here, but even when no arguments are used the two parentheses must be there. This enables the compiler to distinguish between variables and function names.

2 | The function return value is declared in the main program by the process of *prototyping* or *forward referencing* the function. If you don't declare the function, the return value is assumed to be *int*. Even if you don't plan to use any return value, it is still a good idea to prototype the function as *void*. This gives some protection and returns an error message if you use the function improperly. In this case there is no return value, and the function is prototyped as *void*.

3 | In the function itself, there is no semicolon after the function name. This tells the compiler that you are defining the function, not using it. (In the main program, where you are using it, a semicolon follows the function name if the function terminates the statement.)

4 | When writing the function, the return value (*void* here) is declared and must match the declared return value of the calling function.

5 | The body of the function, like the main program, uses an opening and a closing brace.

6 | Variables used in the function are defined inside the braces. These variables are local to the function. If a variable by the same name exists outside of the function in the main program or in another function, it is not the same variable.

7 | Function names follow the same rules as variable names: they must start with a letter or underscore, you can use digits after the first letter, and you cannot use spaces in the name. The rules for function names are the same as those for any other type of identifier (see chapter 2).

The *delay( )* function now requires a single input argument. It returns no value and performs a single operation: delays the program for a specified time.

Now let's take the example one step further by enabling the calling program to define the length of the delay:

```
/* Program to test a delay function */

#include <stdio.h>
main()
{
        void delay();

        printf("Starting\n");
        delay(1000);
        printf("Ending\n");
}


/* DELAY function */
void delay(n)
unsigned int n;
{
        unsigned int i,j;

        for (i=0; i<n; i++)
                for (j=0; j <n; j++);
        return;
}
```

In the example the function creates a delay with a length defined by the variable n in the function. This controls two loops, one inside the other. The total number of loop iterations is n^2.

In this case we have added a single argument, and this argument enables a value to be passed to the function to control the length of the delay. The actual value is passed to the variable n in the function. This variable, as before, controls the number of loop iterations.

Note | The function argument types are declared before the first brace. Other variables in the function are defined after the first brace.

You could also write this program as:

```
#include <stdio.h>
main()
{
        unsigned int c;
        void delay();

        printf("Starting\n");
        c = 1000;
        delay(c);
        printf("Ending\n");
}
```

Here, the argument variable in the main program enables a value to be passed to the function. The arguments, as you can see from this example, can have different names. Even if they are the same name, they are not the same variable. If the function has more than one argument, the values are passed, matching argument for argument (see figure 8.2). Both the program and the function must have the same number of arguments for the function.

Here is a third way to write the same program:

```
#include <stdio.h>
main()
{
        void delay();

        printf("Starting\n");
        delay(500*2);
        printf("Ending\n");
}
```

In this case the result of the calculation is passed to the function, not to the formula.

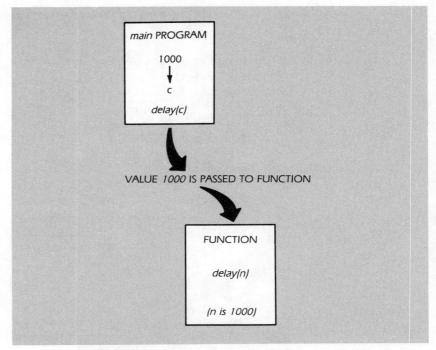

Figure 8.2 Passing argument values to a function

Returning Single Values Using *return( )*

Sometimes a function is used to calculate one or more dependent variables from one or more independent variables. For example, suppose that you want to use a function to calculate the area of a circle when the radius is known (figure 8.3).

To do this, a *return( )* statement is used to return the area value as:

The *return( )* statement can be used to return a single value: the result of the expression specified by the *return( )*.

```
/* CIRCLE function */

#include <math.h>
#include <stdio.h>
main()
{
        double radius, area, circle();
        char radiusa[10];

        printf("Please enter radius: ");
        fgets(radiusa,10,stdin);
        radius = atof(radiusa);
        area = circle(radius);
```

```
        printf("The area is %12.4f\n",area);
}


/* function to return area of circle from radius */
#define PI 3.141593
double circle(r)
double r;
{
        double a;
        a = PI * r * r;
        return(a);
}
```

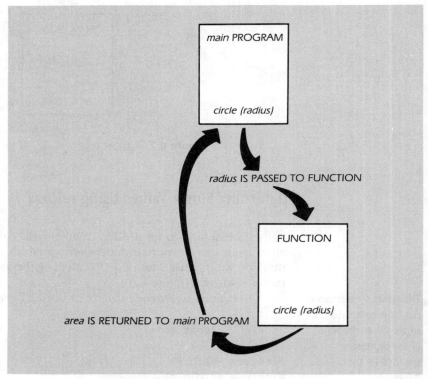

Figure 8.3 Calculating the area of a circle

The radius of the circle is passed to the function as an argument. The area is then calculated. The *return( )* statement does two things: it terminates the function, and it returns a value to the calling program. Any statements after the *return( )* will not be executed. The *return( )* statement has the form:

```
return (expression);
```

where *expression* is a value which is then passed back to the main program. With *return( )*, you can send only one value back to the calling program. If there are no values to be passed back, you can use *return* (without parentheses and with no return value) to cause a simple termination.

Notice that `circle(r)` must be declared in the main program. This declaration actually defines the type of the value that will be returned from the function.

In this example the variable **a** is assigned to the returned value. If you fail to declare the return value of the function in the program in which it is used (prototype the function), the value will be returned as an *int* type.

The *atof( )* function converts an ASCII string to an equivalent floating point number.

The *atof( )* function is used in this example to convert the string entered by the user to a floating point number of the *double* type. When using this function, always be sure to include the *math.h* file. The *atof( )* and *atoi( )* functions, which are provided with the compiler, convert an ASCII string to a floating point or integer value, for example:

```
address_no=atoi(address_noa)
```

This expression assigns the integer value of the ASCII string **address_noa** to the variable **address_no**. In the same way:

```
kwh = atof(kwha);
```

assigns the float value of the ASCII string **kwha** to **kwh**.

> **Note** | If at all possible, use integer values in your program instead of *floats* or *doubles*. Functions to support *float* operations are generally large (a considerable amount of executable code is added) and slow. If possible, you are better off managing the decimal point yourself and using integer functions.

You could write the previous program in a shorter form as:

```
/* Using the CIRCLE function */

#include <math.h>
#include <stdio.h>
main()
{
        double radius, circle();
        char radiusa[10];

        printf("Please enter radius: ");
        fgets(radiusa,10,stdin);
        radius = atof(radiusa);
```

```
        printf("The area is %12.4f\n",circle(radius));
}

/* function to return area of circle from radius */
#define PI 3.141593
double circle(r)
double r;
{
        return( PI * r * r;);
}
```

Returning Multiple Values

Now assume that the objective is to create a function that will swap two integer values. This is useful with sort programs, which generally do swaps in sorting and must return two values. For this purpose the function must be able to accept two input values and return two output values. You might think that you could pass two integers to the function and that two would be returned. That won't work, but let's see why:

```
/* We've got a problem here */

#include <stdio.h>
main()
{
        void swap();

        int a,b;
        a = 3;
        b = 5;
        swap(a,b);
        printf("%d %d",a,b);
}
void swap(a,b)
int a,b;
{
        int c;

        c = a;
        a = b;
        b = c;
    return;
}
```

This looks like a typical subroutine in any language, but if you try it, you will find that it doesn't work. This mistake is an easy one to make, and the problem is simple: *a function doesn't change any variable in the main program if a variable value is passed to the function from the main program*. The variable in the main program remains unaltered. If you want to change a variable in the main program, you must pass the *address* of the variable as an argument to the function, not the variable. The function then uses this address to access the value and change it.

In this example remember that the *a* and *b* in the function are not the same as the *a* and *b* in the main program. The function doesn't do anything to the values of *a* and *b* in the main program.

You can get this program to work by changing it so that it will pass the addresses of the variables instead of the variable values. Then you will be able to modify the variables in the main program:

```
/* SWAP to swap two integers */

#include <stdio.h>
main()
{
        int x,y;
        void swap();

        x = 3;
        y = 5;
        swap(&x,&y);
        printf("x now equals %d, y now equals %d\n",x,y);
}

/* the swap function */
void swap(x1,x2)
int *x1,*x2;
{
        int temp;
        temp = *x1;
        *x1 = *x2;
        *x2 = temp;
        return;
}
```

You can return multiple values from a function by returning the addresses of the values.

Now the addresses (integer pointers) of the variables to swap are passed to the function as &x and &y. This means that x1 and x2 in the function are integer pointers, or the pointers to the addresses of the variables to swap. A variable `temp` is used to hold one of the values. The asterisk operator is used to recover the actual values, which are then swapped.

Here is a brief review of the use of the & and * operators for this purpose:

&foo is the address of variable foo.

pointer_foo is &foo.

*pointer_foo is the value stored at &foo, or foo.

This next example illustrates how you can return two or more values from a function. For example, you could write a program that returns the square, cube, and fourth power of a number as:

```
/* Returns the first four powers of a number */

#include <stdio.h>
main()
{
        int number,square,cube,quad;
        char numbera[10];
        void power();

        printf("Please enter an input number: ");
        fgets(numbera,10,stdin);
        number = atoi(numbera);
        power(&number,&square,&cube,&quad);
        printf("%d squared is %d\n",number,square);
        printf("%d cubed is %d\n",number,cube);
        printf("%d to the fourth power is %d\n",number,quad);
}


/* the power function */
void power(no,sq,cu,qu)
        int *no, *sq, *cu, *qu;

{
        *sq = *no * *no;
        *cu = *no * *sq;
        *qu = *no * *cu;
        return;
}
```

In this example the function is called with a pointer to the square, cube, and quad of the number. The function calculates the powers and returns the pointers to the second, third, and fourth powers as the arguments.

Note | Be cautious when using this method to change the value of a variable. See the discussion in the next chapter.

Recursion

The C language permits you to define a function in terms of itself, or *recursively*.

C permits you, if you wish, to define a function partially in terms of itself. A function is said to be *recursive* if it is defined in terms of itself or if it calls itself.

The most common example is the use of recursion to create a factorial function. In particular, the function *factorial(n)* should return the product of all integers 1 through *n*:

factorial(1) = 1

factorial(2) = 2

factorial(3) = 6

factorial(4) = 24

.
.
.

factorial(n) = n!

This formula can be written in a C program as:

```
/* FACTOR - Program to compute the factorial of a number */

#include <stdio.h>
main()
{
      unsigned factorial();
      unsigned  x,y;
      char numbera[10];

      printf("Please enter input number: ");
      fgets(numbera,10,stdin);
      x = atoi(numbera);
      y = factorial(x);
      printf("The factorial of %u is %u\n",x,y);
      exit(0);
}


unsigned factorial(n)
unsigned n;
{
      if (n <= 1)
            return(1);
      else
            return(n * factorial(n-1));
}
```

The example shows the *factorial(n)* function with a *main( )* program to test the function. The *factorial(n)* function calls a copy of itself, which in turn calls a copy of itself until it is called with the value 1 (figure 8.4).

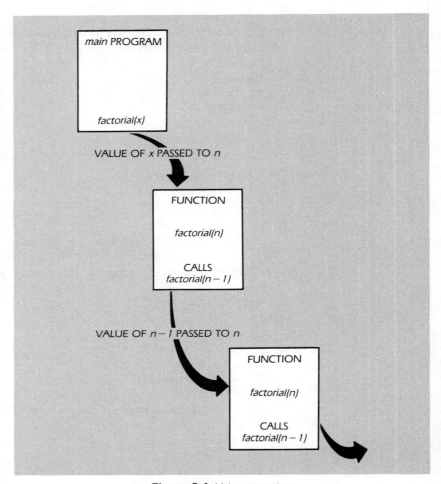

Figure 8.4 Using recursion

In recursive calls, the program does not call itself but calls a copy of itself. The program "winds down" until a specified condition is met (n=1 in this example), and then it unwinds through each invocation again. There must be a terminating condition, or the program will *recurse* (wind down) indefinitely.

Here are some general program design rules for recursion:

• Recursion improves the efficiency of some types of programs (as in the last example) but does make the program difficult to read and understand. Use recursion sparingly.

- Make the recursive function do its work on the way down, not on the way up; that is, avoid the use of statements in the function after the recursive call. In the factorial function, the call to another copy of the function is at the end of the function.

- Minimize variables and complex structures in the function.

Command Line Arguments

Since the main C program —*main( )*— is a function, you can pass arguments to it in the form of command line parameters to be read in when the program starts.

In some cases you might wish to pass a value to your program at start-up. For example, for a word processor you might wish to pass the name of a document file to open. For a compiler program, you might wish to pass the compiler options.

Suppose you begin an adventure game and wish to use an r parameter to indicate where to start from a previously saved game:

```
C>ADV -r
```

Since the primary program module *main( )* is also a function, you might expect to be able to pass argument values to this main function when you start the program. C provides a method of doing this by using two arguments with the call *argc* and *argv*. For example, the following program will work to pass one command line argument to the program:

```
#include <stdio.h>
main(argc, argv)
int argc;
char *argv[];
{
        int rflag = 0;
        int debugflg=0;

        while (--argc > 0)
            {
            ++argv;
            if (**argv != '-')
                break;
            switch(argv[0][1])
                {
                case 'r' :
                        ++rflag;
                        continue;
                case 'd' :
```

```
                              ++debugflg;
                              continue;
                    default :
                    printf("unknown flag: %c\n",
                              argv[0][1]);
                    continue;
              }
         }
    }
```

The `argc` argument defines the argument count, and `argv` is an array of pointers to the argument values. If this were part of the main program for an adventure game in C, it would initiate a *restore* function from the program with the r parameter, as previously indicated. This would set `rflag`, which could be used in a test to read a *restore* file later in the program.

Guidelines for Using Functions

Here are a few guidelines that can help you make better use of functions:

- Always prototype the function in the calling program, declaring the arguments and return value, for example:

  ```
  float circle(float);
  ```

  Put the prototypes in the *include* file.

- Minimize the use of recursion.

- Use functions as much as possible to modularize your program and to make your procedures portable to other programs that you develop.

- Build functions around the application concepts. If you are writing an object-oriented application program, the functions should support these type of concepts.

Using Macros

You can define a procedure as a macro by using a *#define* statement.

In C, procedures can be written as either functions or macros. If the procedure is simple, it can be defined by a *#define* statement and used in this way instead of writing it as a function. For example, here is a macro that returns the cube of a number:

```
/* MACRO definition */

#include <stdio.h>
#define CUBE(a)  ((a) * (a) * (a))
main()
{
     int no,y;
     char noa[10];

     printf("Please enter an input number: ");
     fgets(noa,10,stdin);
     no = atoi(noa);
     y = CUBE(no);
     printf("The cube of %d is %d.\n",no,y);
}
```

When this program is compiled, the formula defined in the *#define* statement is substituted in the program for CUBE(no). This calculates the cube, which is then displayed.

> **Note** | In defining a macro, be sure that the case of the function name in the program matches the case in the *#define* statement.

Macros versus Functions

When should you use macros, and when should you create a function instead? Here are two primary considerations:

1 | Macros are faster than functions to execute. Whenever a function is used, it must be called each time that it is executed. Values or addresses must be passed to the function and then values must be returned. Macros, in contrast, are program code substitutions.

Macros are substitutions, and will expand the program each time they are used in the program. Functions expand the program only once (regardless of how many times they are used) but are generally slower than macros.

2 | Functions can reduce the length of the program. When the program is compiled, whatever is in the *#define* statement is substituted at compile time for each instance. The program can execute, then, without taking any time to call a function and then return. Macros, however, are at a disadvantage if the same macro is used several times in the program. In that case the *#define* statement will cause the program to be expanded for the substitution each time the macro is used, resulting in a larger program. In contrast, functions are added only once to the program.

In addition to these primary considerations, here are some further points to consider about macros:

1 | Macros are better for short routines that can be put on a single line. You can put a long routine in a macro, but it will be difficult to read and understand.

2 | You cannot use pointers as arguments with macros, and you can use them to return only a single value.

3 | Macros do have some good points, however. The same macros can be used with any type of argument. They only define a substitution, and do not have type-specific arguments. You can use the same macro with *char*, *int*, *short*, or *long* data types. This enables macros to be particularly useful if you need to use the same macro with different types of arguments.

Keeping this in mind, let's return to the *getchar( )* and *putchar( )* routines used in chapter 4. As we mentioned in that chapter, these routines are defined as macros in the *stdio.h* file that comes with your C. If you examine this file, you will find:

```
#define getchar() getc(stdin)
#define putchar(c) putc((c),stdout)
```

This means that you use them as macros. If you wish to use them as functions, C provides the *fgetchar( )* and *fputchar(c)* functions, which are identical to *getchar( )* and *putchar(c)*, respectively, but which operate as functions. (The *f* prefix indicates that it is a function.) You may use either in your program. In using either the macro or the function versions, you must include the *stdio.h* file in the program. Definitions needed for macros that you write can be part of an *include* file at the beginning of your program.

Types of Macros

There are three basic types of macros: *function* macros, *definitional* macros, and *expression* macros. The following program shows an example of each:

```
#include <stdio.h>
#define TWELVE 12
#define PRINTX(x)  printf("The answer is %d\n",x)
#define CUBE(y) ((y)*(y)*(y))
main()
{
     int x, y, z;
     x = TWELVE;
     z = CUBE(x);
```

```
    PRINTX(z);
}
```

The second *#define* in this program defines a *function* macro. This routine emulates a user-created function. The function macro returns a single output value for given input values. Remember, however, that it does not behave like a true function (see table 8.1). Unlike a function, there are no calculations, only substitutions. A function call passes the value of the argument to the function during program execution. A macro call does only substitution during the compile process.

There are two other types of macros that also prove useful. The first *#define* shown, the *definitional* macro, equates an identifier name with a value. Wherever the variable name occurs in the program, the compiler substitutes the value. The third *#define* creates an *expression* macro. In this case a frequently used expression is reduced to a single variable name. None of the macro definitions ends with a semicolon.

Table 8.1 Macros versus Functions

Macros	Functions
Faster than functions.	Slower than macros.
Generic. Can accept multiple data types.	Can accept only a single data type.
Expands a program each time that it is used.	Expands a program only once, even when used many times.
Can have side effects.	No side effects.
Does not support recursion.	Supports recursion.
Difficult to debug.	Easy to debug.
Not modular or hierarchical.	Modular and hierarchical.
Returns a single value.	Can return multiple values.
Flexibility for expression or statement substitution.	No expression or statement substitution.

Guidelines for Using Macros

Here are a few guidelines for using macros:

- You can use substitutions within substitutions; that is, you can expand a term in a definition with another term:

```
#define TWELVE 12
#define ACE(x) (TWELVE * (x))
```

```
main()
{
        int x,y;
        x = 4;
        y = ACE(x);
        printf("%d",y);
}
```

This is dangerous, however, and should be avoided unless necessary. The results are unpredictable and can vary with the compiler.

- Keep the macros in *include* files and use an *#include* directive to add them to the program.

- You can create a macro that is longer than one line by using the backslash operator at the end of the line to indicate a continuation. You can also use curly braces, putting each statement of the macro on a separate line and ending each with a semicolon. As a general rule, however, keep your macros to a single line.

- Avoid recursion in macros.

- Capitalize the name of the macro in the body and in the definition to indicate that it is a macro and not a variable or function name.

Review

This chapter introduced functions and macros and illustrated the basic concepts of how to use them. It covered the following important points:

1 | What a function is and how to declare a function.

2 | How to use functions in the C library.

3 | How to write simple functions.

4 | How to send data to a function using arguments.

5 | How to return single values from a function with the *return( )* statement.

6 | How to return multiple values from a function by passing the variable addresses to the function as arguments.

7 | How to declare the function as *void* when there is no returned value.

8 | What macros are and how to use them.

9 | The advantages and disadvantages of macros as compared with functions.

Quiz for Chapter 8

1 | The input values for a function are passed as
   a | Dependent variables
   b | Prototypes
   c | Arguments
   d | Macros

2 | The output value of a function is
   a | An independent variable
   b | A dependent variable
   c | An argument
   d | None of the above

3 | Which of the following is not true of a macro:
   a | It is generic and the same macro can accept many data types.
   b | It is faster than a function.
   c | Macros improve the readability of the program.
   d | If a macro is used many times in a program, it generally results in a smaller executable file than if a function were used.

4 | Which of the following is not true of a function:
   a | A function is generally easier to debug than a macro.
   b | Functions support recursion.
   c | A function generally executes faster than a macro.
   d | Functions are portable to many source programs.

5 | What is the maximum input value that can be used in the factorial recursion example shown earlier in the section titled "Recursion"?
   a | 8
   b | 12
   c | 6
   d | None of the above

6 | How could you modify the factorial example to accept a larger input value?
   a | Change the function to a macro.
   b | Change the data type to *long*.
   c | Change the input statement.
   d | Change the declaration of xa to a larger array size.

7 | What is wrong with this example?

```
void test(no)
{
        int no, ctr;

        for (ctr = 0; ctr<no; ctr++)
            printf("I like ice cream\n");
```

a | There should be a colon after `test(no)`.

b | The variable no should be declared before the first brace, not after.

c | The *void* keyword should not be used.

d | There is nothing wrong with it.

8 | What is wrong with this function that should return the largest of three integers:

```
void max(x, y, z)
int x, y, z;
{
        if (x > y)
                if (x > z)
                        return x;
                else return z;
        else if (y > z)
                return y;
        else return x;
}
```

a | The x, y, and z variables should be declared after the opening brace.

b | The colon should not be used after the declaration statement.

c | The *void* keyword should be *int*.

d | The entire functional concept is wrong because you can't use a function to return multiple values.

9 | Which of the following is not true?

a | Functions generally reduce development time and cost.

b | Functions produce a faster executable program than macros.

c | Functions make the program easier to debug because procedures are modularized and placed in hierarchies.

d | Functions can be used to convert C to a type of high-level language.

10 | Which of the following is not true?

a | Functions support recursion.

b | Functions cannot alter a variable in the calling program.

c | Functions support only a single data type for each argument.

d | Functions can use a *return( )* statement to return only a single value.

11 | Why should the function return value and arguments always be declared in the calling program?

a | It reduces the chance of misusing the returned value or the arguments.

b | It improves the execution speed of the function.

    c | The C language requires it.

    d | It makes the program more portable to other C compilers.

12 | Which of the following is not a proper way of using a function name?

    a | To declare or define a function

    b | To invoke or call a function

    c | As an argument when invoking a function

    d | All are proper.

13 | What is the maximum number of exits that a function can have?

    a | None

    b | 1

    c | One for each argument

    d | As many as desired

14 | Which of the following is not true?

    a | A function can return information only to the procedure that called it.

    b | More than one function can be executing at a time.

    c | A function remembers the name of the calling procedure and from where it was called in the procedure. After terminating, it returns to the procedure and the next statement in the calling procedure.

    d | A function can be executed only if it is called from another procedure.

15 | Which of the following is a valid use of a function name?

    a | Using the function name as a value of a pointer to a function

    b | Using the function name with the *sizeof* operator

    c | Performing arithmetic operations using a function pointer

    d | Assigning a function pointer to a value other than zero

9 | Variable Storage and Memory Models

About This Chapter

C provides the programmer with great flexibility in controlling how variables are used. It is the programmer who manages how variables are used, not the language. This puts more power in the hands of the programmer, but it also requires knowledge on the programmer's part to be able to use this power. This chapter will introduce you to the basic concepts of managing the storage of variables. You will also learn more about special variable types and other variable management techniques.

Storage Classes

A variable has three attributes: type, value, and storage class.

You have already learned two attributes of a variable: *type* and *value*. To identify the type of variable, you use a declaration statement. Variables are given values by the process of assignment, either in the declaration statement or in the body of the program. Now let's look at a third attribute of a variable: its storage class.

Local variables are known only to the statement block of which they are a part.

The variables that you used in the first eight chapters were *local*; that is, they were known only to the functions containing them. In chapter 8, for example, you used a function to return multiple values. In doing this, you had to use pointers, since the value could not be passed back as an argument. You could return only an address. If the main program had a variable named **cube** and the function had a variable named **cube**, the program treated them as two separate variables.

Global variables are those known to several functions or statement blocks.

There is a way, however, to make a variable common to both the main program and the functions. You can do this by using a different storage class for the variable, that is, by making the variable global. A *global* variable is a variable known to several functions. You can create global variables by declaring the variable before the main program and then using the *extern* keyword as part of the variable declaration in each function in which it is used. The program then becomes:

```
/* Returns the first four powers of a number */

#include <stdio.h>
int number, square, cube, quad;
main()
{
        extern int number, square, cube, quad;

        void power();
        char numbera[10];

        printf("Please enter an input number: ");
        fgets(numbera,10,stdin);
        number = atoi(numbera);
        power();
        printf("%d squared is %d\n",number,square);
        printf("%d cubed is %d\n",number,cube);
        printf("%d to the fourth power is %d\n",number,quad);
}

/* The power function */
void power()
{
        extern int number, square, cube, quad;
        square =  number * number;
        cube = number * square;
        quad = cube * number;
        return;
}
```

The *extern* keyword is used in a statement block to refer to a global variable declared external to the block.

Notice that the function no longer has any arguments, nor are they needed. There is no returned value or address. Four global variables are defined before the main program. These are used by both the main program and the function. The *extern* keyword in the main program and in the function references the global variables.

Declaring the variable external to the functions of which it is a part

The storage class of a variable defines its scope and how long the variable remains in memory.

and using the *extern* keyword to reference the function, changes the *storage class* of the variable, a third attribute of every variable you use. The storage class of a variable defines its *scope* (the availability of the variable to other functions) and how long the variable remains in memory. As this example shows, declaring a variable as global opens up a real opportunity. There are, however, hidden dangers in declaring a variable global. This chapter will help you see both the benefits and the dangers of sharing variables between functions and will show you how sharing is done.

The C language supports four storage classes: automatic, external, static, and register.

Every variable has a storage class, whether or not it is declared explicitly. C provides four storage classes for variables: automatic, external, static, and register. The class for a variable is defined when you declare it. If you do not declare it explicitly, the class defaults to automatic. All of the programs in the first eight chapters used automatic variables. Now let's look at each of the four storage classes.

Automatic Variables

Automatic is the default storage class for a variable. If you omit any keyword for the storage class, the storage class is assumed to be automatic. You can also specifically define the storage class by using the *auto* keyword.

```
#include <stdio.h>
main()
{
        auto int x, y, z;

        x = 3;
        y = 4;
        z = x + y;
        printf("The sum is %d",z);
}
```

The default storage class is automatic, and an automatic variable is available only to the statement block of which it is a part.

Any variable declared as automatic is available only to the statements in the function of which it is a part. The variable is not available to any functions called by the block or to any statements outside of the defining block. If the same name is used in another function, it is assumed to be a different variable and has a different memory location.

The scope of an automatic variable is local to the block of which it is a part. The variable is declared immediately after the opening brace of the function (or block). The variable comes into existence when the function or block is called. When the function returns control to the calling program, the variable ceases to exist and no longer takes memory space. An automatic variable in the *main( )* procedure, for example, becomes active when the procedure is started. It is not available in any called function but is still active when the function returns control to the *main( )* procedure. Since an automatic variable uses memory space only when its function is active, using automatic variables saves memory space.

External Variables

External variables are declared outside of the first routine that uses them. You then use the *extern* keyword to refer to the global declaration.

Global variables are variables available to all functions and modules of a program. You can create global variables by defining them outside of the first routine that uses them and then by using the *extern* keyword in any subsequent modules and functions in which the variables refer to the global definitions.

```
#include <stdio.h>
int x=3, y=4;
main()
{
        extern int x,y;

        int z

        z = x + y;
        printf("The sum is %d",z);
}
```

It is not necessary to use the *extern* keyword if the variables are used in the same file as the declaration and in the function immediately following the declaration. For example, in the preceding case the *extern* keyword is not needed. It is still a good idea, however, to include the keyword to improve the readability of the program.

In this example the variables x and y are declared before the *main( )* procedure. You can also initialize them at this time if you wish. The *extern* reference in the main program or in any subsequent functions does not declare the variable again. It simply tells the compiler to use the variable that was previously declared with its present value. A statement with an *extern* keyword always refers to a previous declaration.

Use external variables for global values that you use in your programs. For example, if your company name is displayed on several screens, it could be put in a global variable and used for the entire program. In the same way, the default drive to use could be stored as a global variable.

Note | Use global values with caution (see the discussion later in this chapter). They do not make functions portable, and programs with a lot of global values are difficult to debug because so many of the modules can affect the variable.

Using external variables raises some real dangers that can trap the unwary programmer. For example, suppose you wrote the previous example as:

```
/* Don't do it this way */

#include <stdio.h>
short number, square, cube, quad;
main()
{
        extern int number, square, cube, quad;
        .
        .
```

The variables are declared globally as *short* and then are accessed within the function by using the *extern* keyword as *int*. The results are unpredictable and will vary with the compiler. As a first step to preventing this type of problem, declare all globals in one place—the *include* file. A comment statement in the *include* file should label them as globals. An even better idea is described later in this chapter in the discussion "Global Variable Management."

Static Variables

A *static* variable is a variable that doesn't disappear when the function returns control to the calling program.

Static variables are variables that do not disappear when the function returns control to the calling program. The scope is the same as for automatic variables; that is, the variables are local only to the block of which they are a part. The difference is that when the function returns, the variable value is not lost and is available if the function is called again. Let's look at an example to clarify this:

```
/* AUTO variable test */

#include <stdio.h>
main()
{
        int ctr;

        void counter();

        for (ctr=0;ctr<5;ctr++)
            counter();
```

```
}
void counter()
{
     static int y = 1;
     int x=1;
     printf("x = %d   y = %d\n",x,y);
     x = x + 1;
     y = y + 1;
     return;
}
```

If you try this little example, you will get the output:

```
x = 1   y = 1
x = 1   y = 2
x = 1   y = 3
x = 1   y = 4
x = 1   y = 5
```

In the example the function `counter` is called five times from the main program. The variable x is an automatic variable; its value (and the storage area for the variable) is lost each time that the function returns to the main program. The variable y is a static variable. When the function returns, the value of y remains set to the previous value and is not reset by the declaration statement. The function does not release the memory space for the y variable on exiting the program. Both x and y are local only to the function in which they are used. All static variables have memory allocated to them as long as the program is running.

You can make a static variable global in a module by putting it outside of the function in which it is used and by using the *extern* keyword in the functions to refer to it:

```
/* AUTO variable test */

#include <stdio.h>
main()
{
     int ctr;

     void counter();

     for (ctr=0; ctr<5; ctr++)
          counter();
}
static int y = 1;
void counter()
```

```
{
      extern static int y;
      int x=1;
      printf("x = %d   y = %d\n",x,y);
      x = x + 1;
      y = y + 1;
      return;
}
```

Register Variables

A *register* variable is a variable that doesn't disappear when the function returns control to the calling program.

The computer processor chip has several internal registers that can be used for temporary storage. These are useful in some cases because accessing a register to get a variable value is much faster than trying to access a memory location for a variable value. Use register variables when the variable will be accessed frequently. Register variables are particularly useful for loop counters:

```
#include <stdio.h>
main()
{
      register int ctr;
      void counter();

      for (ctr=0; ctr<5; ctr++)
            counter();
}
```

In using register variables, you are making a request that may or may not be fulfilled. A register will be used only if one is available. If no register is available at the time, the variable reverts to an automatic variable.

Register variables can be used only for *char*, *short*, and *int* data. They cannot be used with *long*, *float*, or *double*, since a register is only 16 bits (2 bytes) in size.

Special Data Types

C provides several special data types that are useful for many applications. We will look at the *enum* and *void* types.

The *enum* Type

The *enum* keyword defines a list of valid values for an identifier.

The *enum* keyword can be used to define a list of valid values for an identifier, for example:

```
enum flag {true,false};
enum flag delete_flag, update_flag;
```

Two statements are used. The first declares enum flag as a variable type that can have one of two values: true or false. Note that enum flag is not a variable, but a variable type. The second statement assigns the two variables delete_flag and update_flag as enum flag type.

Here is another variation:

```
enum days {sun,mon,tue,wed,thu,fri,sat};
enum days today;
```

Here enum days is a variable type that can have any one of seven values—the days of the week. The second statement declares today to be of that type.

Look at this program using the *enum* keyword:

```
#include <stdio.h>
main()
{
        enum month {jan,feb,mar,apr,may,jun,jul,aug,sept,oct,
        nov,dec} ;
        enum month now_month;

        now_month = jun;
        printf("The present month number is %d.\n",now_month);
}
```

This declares the variable now_month to be of the enum month type, which can have any of 12 values. Internally, C tracks the list with an integer value assigned to each item, which means that the enum month variable must be printed with %d. If you try this example, you will get

```
The present month number is 5.
```

which is not correct (it should be 6). The reason is that C starts the list numbering from zero, so jan is assigned the value of 0. To get this program to work, simply reassign the first month:

```
#include <stdio.h>
main()
{
```

```
enum month {jan=1, feb, mar, apr, may, jun, jul,
        aug, sept, oct, nov, dec} ;
enum month now_month;

now_month = jun;
printf("The present month number is %d.\n",now_month);
}
```

You can use integer values only for assignments, but the use of both negative and positive integers is permitted. You can put assignments on multiple list values, and unassigned list items are numbered sequentially from the last assigned list item. (These assignment rules vary with compilers and are not too portable.)

The use of the *enum* keyword is somewhat limited, since C still assumes the variable to be an integer value. The *enum* keyword also has limited portability. Some C compilers will not permit arithmetic expressions with *enum*-declared variables. The primary advantage is that the program is more readable. For example, you might have a menu structure and switch on any of several *enum* variable values. You can also use *enum* variable values in logic decisions to improve readability:

```
enum available_colors {blue,green,red};
enum available_colors color;

color = red;
if (color == red)
    printf("You picked red, one of the available
            colors.\n");
```

The *void* Type

The *void* keyword is useful for prototyping functions when no return value is expected.

Good programming style requires that the programmer always define the type of variable returned from a function, even when nothing is being returned. For example, in chapter 8 the short program that returns the powers could better be written as:

```
#include <stdio.h>
main()
{
    void power();
    int number,square,cube,quad;
    char numbera[10];

    printf("Please enter an input number: ");
    fgets(numbera,10,stdin);
    number = atoi(numbera);
```

```
        power(number,&square,&cube,&quad);
        printf("%d squared is %d\n",number,square);
        printf("%d cubed is %d\n",number,cube);
        printf("%d to the fourth power is %d\n",number,quad);
}


/* the power function */
        void power(no,sq,cu,qu)
        int no, *sq, *cu, *qu;
{
        *sq = no * no;
        *cu = no * *sq;
        *qu = no * *cu;
        return;
}
```

This style immediately tells the user that no return value is expected.

Modifiers

C provides certain modifiers that can also be used in a declaration. These are not really types; rather, they modify other types.

The *volatile* modifier declares a variable that can be modified from outside the program.

If a variable can be modified from outside the program, it should be declared with the *volatile* modifier. This will prevent the compiler from performing certain optimizing that could do strange things with the data. Variables used for modem and clock data are typical candidates for this modifier.

> **Note** | With QuickC, the *volatile* modifier does not do anything. It is accepted, but does nothing more, since QuickC is not an optimizing compiler. The variable is available to be used external to the program.

The *const* modifier declares a variable that cannot be changed during program execution.

Variables that cannot change during program execution can be locked to a value with the *const* modifier. The attempt to hold a variable constant may seem a contradiction, but it is really a protection for the programmer against unintentional program execution that might modify something that shouldn't be modified. The best candidates here are arrays. As you will see in the next chapter, you cannot pass array values to a function, only the address of an array. Array functions, then, modify the original array data.

For example, suppose you were creating a function that writes an error message using a pointer to a message string. The pointer is passed to the function. You could then begin your function as

```
int errmsg(string)
const char *string
{
        .
        .
        .
}
```

Here `string` is a pointer to an array of characters. Now the `errmsg()` function can use `string` but cannot alter it.

Symbolic Data Types

You can create your own data type names by using the *typedef* keyword.

When you have a complex data declaration that is used several times for several variables, it is often better to define the declaration with a symbolic name and then use the name to declare each variable. You can assign a symbolic name to a declaration by using the *typedef* keyword:

```
typedef int CTR;
CTR i, j, k;
```

In this example `CTR` is defined as *int*. This symbolic declaration can then be used in subsequent variable declarations. As an example, suppose that you planned to declare your integers *int,* but later you wished to change them to *short*. This would be easy if you created a `CTR` type as shown above and used it to declare your integers. Then, by changing the one *typedef* statement, you could switch all your integers from *int* to *short*.

We could also have done this with a *#define* statement:

```
#define CTR int
```

The *typedef* keyword, however, is more powerful than a *#define* statement with respect to variables. For example, you could define a string type as:

```
typedef char    STRING[81];
STRING          last, first, address, city, state;
```

This has the same effect as:

```
char last[81], first[81], address[81], city[81], state[81];
```

In this case you could not have used the *#define* statement to create an equivalent. You are not defining a new variable type, only a new name for a variable type that already exists. Unlike a *#define* statement (which is processed before compiling by a preprocessor), the *typedef* statement is processed during the compiling.

Here is a similar application:

```
typedef char *STRING;
STRING last, first, address, city, state, buffer;
```

Again, this could not be done with a *#define* statement. Another application is for the assigning of a name to a complex data structure that will be used for several variables (see chapter 11). The structure is defined once, given a name, and then used to declare several variables.

In using symbolic names, remember these rules:

1 | Put the symbolic name in capital letters to distinguish it from other variables.

```
typedef int CTR;
```

2 | Use the *typedef* statement as you would a declaration: put it inside the function for local variables, outside for global variables.

```
test()
{
        typedef int CTR;
        CTR         counter;
        .
        .
        .
}
```

3 | Do not define the storage class of a variable with a *typedef* statement.

4 | Use the *typedef* keyword to improve readability and to reduce the need for multiple entry of complex declarations.

Stack Management

Automatic variables are kept on a local stack. Global and static variables are kept in data segments that are separate from the program segments.

Automatic variables are kept on a stack. A *stack* is a continuous series of memory locations that function much like a stack of cafeteria trays. The last piece of data pushed on the stack is always the first off when the stack is popped. Global variables, in contrast, are stored in a separate data segment area. Knowing how the stack works is important for efficient C programming. When a function is called, the stack is used to save the return point in the calling program as well as the arguments for the function. As local variables are declared, they are pushed to the stack. Once the function has finished its work, the local variables are lost (freeing up stack space) and the return address is used to return to the place in the calling program from which the function was called. Using automatic variables keeps the variables local and conserves memory, as they need storage only while the function is active. Global and static variables, in contrast, are using memory space during the entire time that the program is in memory.

Techniques for Managing Variables

Keep the scope of your variables as small as possible.

The golden rule of managing variables is to keep the scope as small as possible. The temptation is to use global variables and external references to pass values to and from a function. This gives the appearance of simplifying the program, as in the first example of this chapter. This appearance, however, is deceiving. The function then becomes locked to special variable names and to a single program, and is no longer portable to other C programs that you may develop.

In using a global variable, you may sometimes need to use it for only two or three functions. In this case you can define the variable before the first function in which it is used, keeping it semiglobal. (This works only if the function group using the variable is compiled as a group.) A good example of this is a set of two or three modules that work together as a single function. In this case you could create semiglobal values that are shared by the functions, yet the unit acts as a single function with complete portability. Values and addresses are passed to and from the unit by using arguments.

Avoid overloading and superseding of variables. *Overloading* refers to the practice of using one variable for several purposes, such as a single variable *x* over and over again for various purposes. Its meaning at any one time depends on the context of the program.

Superseding refers to the redeclaring of a variable. The new declaration supersedes the original. For example, a variable defined as global might be temporarily redefined as automatic. The results are unpredictable and vary with the compiler. The result is a loss of portability if the program works at all.

Table 9.1 shows a summary of the four storage classes. Here are some good general rules:

1 | Keep the scope of your variables as small as possible. Pass values and addresses with arguments and return values, not by using global variables. This keeps your functions portable, and you can use them in other programs. It also simplifies debugging.

Table 9.1 Storage Class Summary

Storage Class	Keyword	Duration	Scope
automatic	*auto*	temporary	local
external	*extern*	permanent	global
static	*static*	permanent	global
register	*register*	temporary	local

2 | Don't use the same variable name for two different variables. If `square` is used as an auto variable in the main program, don't use the same name for an auto variable in a function. If you need to use a similar variable locally, use a consistent naming convention such as:

```
counter  global variable
1_counter   local variable
```

3 | Don't initialize a variable unless necessary. For example, it is not necessary to initialize a *for . . . else* loop counter, since the *for . . . else* construct initializes the counter:

```
/* Don't do this */

int ctr = 0;

for (ctr = 0; ctr <10; ctr++)
   :
   :
```

4 | Put global variables in the *include* file and label them as such.

5 | In declaring a *static* array, you can omit the value for the array size if you initialize it. For example, instead of:

```
static char msg[16] = "Hello out there";
```
use
```
static char msg[] = "Hello out there";
```
This eliminates the need to count the characters.

6 | Use register variables for loop counters.

7 | Avoid superseding a declaration. Do not redeclare a variable that you have already declared. (Note that the *extern* keyword does not redeclare a variable but only references a variable already declared.)

8 | Avoid overloading, or trying to minimize, variables by using a variable name for multiple purposes.

9 | Insert declarations at the beginning of the block in which they are used.

10 | Place references to external variables in a function before local declarations.

C Memory Models

The processor families used in the current IBM-compatible architectures allocate memory in 64K segments.

The processor family used by the IBM PC, XT, AT, and PS/2 compatibles (8088, 8086, 80286, and 80386 microprocessors) employ a segmented memory architecture in which the memory is allocated to the program in 64K segments. Most C implementations, including Turbo C and QuickC, allow you to control the memory allocation to be sure that adequate memory is allocated for execution.

The minimum memory size required for the execution of a C program compiled to an EXE file is 128K, or two segments.

The minimum memory required for execution of a C program compiled to an EXE file is two segments, or 128K. Turbo C does support a tiny model, which permits execution in a single segment (compiling to a COM file). In the two-segment model, one segment is used for the program code, the second for the data. This specification for memory allocation is referred to as the *C small model*.

You will need to use an alternative memory model if either of the following is true:

- You are compiling a program with the internal QuickC or Turbo C environment that has more than 64K of static data.

- A program compiled external to the QuickC or Turbo C environment has more than 64K of code or 64K of data.

If either is true, you must use one of the alternative memory models. The alternative models use a *far* addressing technique in which the segment and offset values are passed in addressing.

The C language supports six memory models: tiny, small, medium, compact, large, and huge. All compilers do not support all models.

The C language supports six memory models (table 9.2). The models are named *tiny, small, medium, compact, large,* and *huge.* The Turbo C environment supports all of them. The QuickC environment supports only the medium model unless the external compiler is used. From this you can see that the memory model required for a particular application is determined by the number of code and data segments required.

In the QuickC environment, compiling is limited to the medium model. The Turbo C environment supports compiling to all seven models.

With either environment, however, the *near* and *far* keywords allow you to override the default addressing convention and use more than two segments for your program. These keywords are not a

The *near* and *far* keywords allow you to override the default addressing conventions and use additional segments.

standard part of the C language, and are useful only for systems with a segmented architecture similar to the 8086 processors. Here are some examples:

```
int far item; /* integer declaration */
char far parts[1000]; /* array declaration */
int far prompt(); /* function forward declaration */
```

Table 9.2 C Memory Models

Model	Code Segments	Data Segments	Segments/Data Item
tiny	————(1 segment total)————		
small	1	1	1
medium	many	1	1
compact	1	many	1
large	many	many	1
huge	many	many	many

(*Note*: The QuickC environment supports only medium.)

Global Variable Management

Preprocessor directives are commands to the C preprocessor (which is an automatic part of a C compiling). You have already met two of these directives: the *#include*, which permits you to include external files at compile time, and the *#define*, which permits you to define substitutions for compiling.

Another important directive is the *#if . . . #endif*, which permits you to include code at compile time based on a specified condition. Let's see how this directive can be used to improve global variable management.

The use of global variables in a program introduces the need for control on the part of the programmer. A variable can be declared one way and then externally referenced as another type:

```
/* Error example */

short counter;
main()
{
    extern int counter;
    .
    .
```

Declare all globals in an *include* file and label them as such.

To minimize this problem, you should declare all globals in the *include* file and label them as such. Even this, however, is often not quite sufficient.

Now suppose we create an *include* file for the globals:

```
GLOBAL int counter;
GLOBAL char buffer[100]; /* array - no initialization */
GLOBAL char string[] /* this is a char string */
#ifdef INIT /* blocks initialization except in globals.c */
= "This is a dummy message" /* initialization string */
#endif
; /* note that the semicolon is here */
GLOBAL int filecount /* an int to be initialized*/
#ifdef INIT
= 200 /* here is the initialization */
#endif
;


/* ====================C o m m e n t ==================== */

/* GLOBAL is always defined in THE BODY OF THE PROGRAM.
   In only one place is it defined as blank. Everywhere
   else it is defined as "extern". That piece of code
   contains the actual declarations, and only in that
   piece of code should "INIT" be defined. That way the
   initializations occur only in one place. */
```

Now, in the program, we use

```
/* GLOBALS.C Copyright 1987 Michael Maurice */
/* All rights reserved */
#include <stdio.h>
#include "config.h" /* configuration declarations */
#include "std.h"  /* a file of standard typedefs */

#undef GLOBAL /* be sure no define for GLOBAL */
#define GLOBAL /* create a define that is blank */
#define INIT /* turns on initialization of globals */
#include "globals.h" /* where the globals are */

/* ==================================================== */

/* This is what the declarations in globals.h look like */
     int      counter;
     char     buffer[100]
     char     string[]
```

```
= "This is a dummy message"

;

        int         filecount

= 200

;

/* ========================================================= */
/* This is what globals.h looks like in other code. */
extern int      counter;
extern char     buffer[100]
extern char     string[]




;




extern int filecount /* the semicolon is 4 lines down */



;
```

Notice the carriage returns (blank lines) before the semicolon. This white space is not seen by the compiler.

Using this type of *include* file gives us the protection needed for the global variables.

Review

C provides the user with a large amount of flexibility in declaring variables, but it is up to the user to take advantage of it properly. This chapter has covered the following important points:

1 | Every variable has a type, value, and storage class.

2 | The storage class of a variable defines its scope (the availability of the variable to other functions) and how long the variable remains in memory.

3 | The four basic storage classes are: automatic, external, static, and register.

4 | The default storage class is automatic. If the variable is declared as automatic, its value is kept in a local stack and is active only while the block is active. The value is lost when the function returns control to the calling program.

5 | If the variable is declared as *extern* or global, its value is kept in a separate data segment, but the memory space is allocated as long as the program is active.

6 | If a variable is declared as *static*, the value is stored in a separate data segment. The memory space for the variable is continuously used (as with a global), but the variable is known only to the block locally and cannot be referenced outside of the block.

7 | Register variables are variables in which the value is stored in a processor register. This provides the fastest type of access, but it can be used only for *char*, *short*, and *int* data.

8 | The golden rule of managing variables is to keep the scope as small as possible.

9 | The C language provides an *enum* keyword to define a set of values for a variable.

10 | The *void* keyword should be used to declare a function that does not return a value.

11 | C provides two modifier keywords. The *const* modifier can be used to prevent a variable from being modified. The *volatile* keyword should be used with variables that can be modified external to the program from real-time events. Using the *volatile* keyword prevents the compiler from using certain optimizing techniques with the variable.

12 | The *typedef* keyword permits you to define your own data types.

13 | Turbo C and QuickC permit you to select from a variety of memory models to control the total amount of memory allocated for the program.

Quiz for Chapter 9

1 | Which of the following is not a C storage class?
    a | Automatic
    b | Register
    c | Static
    d | Void

2 | What is the default storage class?
    a | Automatic
    b | Register
    c | Static
    d | Void

3 | Which of the following cannot be used with a *float* variable?
    a | Extern
    b | Automatic
    c | Register
    d | Static

4 | Which of the following is not true of an *extern* variable?
    a | The variable value is stored in a separate data segment.
    b | It uses memory during the entire time that the program is in memory.
    c | It can be used by any function in the program.
    d | The variable is declared with the *extern* keyword.

5 | What are the C modifiers?
    a | Volatile
    b | Const
    c | Both of the above
    d | Neither of the above

6 | In declaring a counter as an *int* type, which of the following would give the fastest execution time?
    a | Extern
    b | Automatic
    c | Register
    d | Static

7 | In declaring a counter as an *int* type, which of the following would use less memory?
    a | Extern
    b | Automatic
    c | Register
    d | Static

8 | Which of the following keywords causes a variable to use local stack space?

    a | Extern
    b | Automatic
    c | Register
    d | Static

9 | Examine the following program:

```
#include <stdio.h>
main()
{
        enum av_colors {blue,green,red};
        enum av_colors color;
        char colora[10];

        printf("Please enter a color: ");
        fgets(colora,10,stdin);
        color = atoi(colora);
        if (color == red)
                printf("You picked the red color");
}
```

What data must you enter to get the text message?
    a | 1
    b | 2
    c | red
    d | 3

10 | Which do you use to declare a function with no return value?
    a | Extern
    b | Automatic
    c | Register
    d | Void

11 | Which of the following is not placed in the stack?
    a | The return address in the calling program
    b | The argument values
    c | The values for the automatic variables used by the function
    d | The values for the static variables used by the function

12 | What is the advantage of the *typedef* keyword?
    a | It permits you to create your own data types.
    b | It improves the readability of a program.
    c | It provides more flexibility than the *#define* statement.
    d | All of the above

13 | What is the advantage of the *enum* keyword?
    a | It permits you to create your own data types.
    b | It improves the readability of a program.
    c | None of the above
    d | All of the above

14 | Which of the following is not a variable attribute?
   a | Storage class
   b | Value
   c | Type
   d | All of the above are variable attributes.

15 | What is wrong with the following program?

```
int ctr;
char inchar;
float price;
main()
{
        extern price;
        extern short ctr;

        price = 10.00;
        for (i=0; i < ctr; i++)
                print("%f\n",price);
}
```

   a | extern price should be extern float price.
   b | extern short ctr should be extern int ctr.
   c | char inchar is not defined as extern.
   d | a and b

10 | Arrays

About This Chapter

An *array* is a data structure in which all the elements are of the same type.

An *array* is a data structure in which all the elements are of the same type. You have already met one type of array, since any character string in the C language is represented as an array of characters:

```
static char msg[] = "This is a test.";
```

This chapter will introduce you to the basic concepts of using arrays in C.

Arrays and C

An array is a special type of data structure, a method of organizing data. In particular, an array is a variable that holds multiple values in an ordered sequence. The values are called the *elements*, and must all be of the same data type. When iterative structures are used, arrays are often used with them.

Arrays offer the advantage of quick access to specific data. The reason for this is that the subscript in the array variable name is used to identify the element to which you are referring. The members of the array are identified by a subscript, or index. The index value is an integer value that, with C, always begins at zero. For example, `msg[2]` represents the third member of the `msg` array.

An array has three attributes: type, location, and length. The *type* of the array is the common type of all elements of the array. The *location* is the address of the first element of the array. The *length* of the array is the number of elements of the array and is defined either by the value in brackets when the array is declared or by the number initialization values.

Let's look at an example using an array:

```
#include <stdio.h>
main()
{
        static char msg[] = "This is a test.";

        printf("%s",msg);
}
```

In this example `msg` is declared as an array of 16 characters (the length of the string plus 1 null character). In declaring `msg`, you are defining the type of each element of the array (*char*) and the length of the array. All elements of the array must be of the same type. The array, like any variable, also has a storage class. In this case it is *static*. The brackets after `msg` identify it as an array. If there is a number within the brackets, it indicates the size of the array.

In the body of the program, use brackets with a subscript to refer to any element of an array.

In the body of the program you can use brackets with a subscript to refer to any element of an array. In the example the fourth element of the array is the character `s`. The subscript number always starts from zero in C, so the fourth element is `msg[3]`. This makes it easy to locate any element of the array quickly:

```
msg[0] = "T";
msg[1] = "h";
msg[2] = "i";
msg[3] = "s";
```

Arrays can be used with almost any type of data structure.

In the same way, you can create an array of integers, real numbers, or any other type of data structure:

```
int partno[24];
float price[24];
```

In this case an integer array of 24 part numbers is defined, as well as a floating point array of 24 prices. Notice that, although the first array subscript is 0, when declaring an array you always specify the total number of elements, not the number minus one. This is true of both numeric and character arrays.

You must use a constant to declare the array. You cannot declare the size of the array with an expression containing a variable. You can, however, use a constant expression. The following is valid:

```
int partno[3*8];
```

Arrays can be single dimensional (as shown here) or, as we shall see later in this chapter, multidimensional. Here are a few examples:

```
#define ANYSIZE 100
int illegalsize;
int myint[100]; /* OK */
int myint[ANYSIZE]; /* OK */
int yourint[illegalsize]; /* NOT OK */
```

Initializing Arrays

In declaring a variable, you discovered that you could initialize it at the same time:

```
int flag = 1;
```

Only external and static arrays can be initialized.

An array, however, can be declared and also initialized *only* if the array is static or declared externally. For example, here is a simple program using a static array to calculate the mean of a group of numbers:

```
#include <stdio.h>
main()
{
        static float values[]={12.0,6.0,7.0,3.0,15.0,10.0,
        18.0,5.0};
        int index, size;
        float sum, temp;
        float mean;

        sum = 0.0;
        size = sizeof(values /(sizeof (float)) ;
        for (index=0; index < size; index++)
                sum += values[index];
        printf("The mean is %f\n", sum/size);
}
```

The array is declared as *static float* and initialized. Notice that the initial values are placed between braces. The number of array elements is calculated by dividing the size of the array by the size of each element of the array. To obtain the mean, the elements are summed and then divided by the array size.

Here is the same program with the array declared externally:

```
#include <stdio.h>
float values[]={12.0,6.0,7.0,3.0,15.0,10.0,18.0,5.0};
main()
{
        extern float values[];
        int index, size;
        float sum, temp;
        float mean;

        sum = 0.0;
        size = 8;
        for (index=0; index < size; index++)
                sum += values[index];
        printf("The mean is %f\n", sum/size);
}
```

In functions that operate on arrays, the address of the array is passed to the function, not the value.

In either case, the array variables remain in memory occupying memory space during the entire execution of the program. Moreover, as we shall see later, if you call a function that operates on an array (such as a function to print a character string), you must pass the *address* of the array to the function rather than the value. With most functions you pass a copy of the data, which is used by the function. With arrays you are passing the address of the actual data, and the function operates on the data itself.

Arrays of class automatic (local) are created out of stack space and are not cleared to zero on starting. For this reason, you should always initialize any automatic class (local) arrays. Arrays that are declared *static* or *external* are cleared by the C run-time start-up code.

An easy way to initialize a local array is to use the *memset( )* function, for example:

```
char first[25+1];

memset(first,'\0',sizeof(first));
```

Inputting to an Array

Suppose that you want to enter data to an array that has been previously defined. You could do this for the preceding example as follows:

```
#include <math.h>
```

```
#include <stdio.h>
#define MAXSIZE 20
main()
{
       double values[MAXSIZE];
       int index = 0, size;
       double sum = 0.0;
       char inputa[10];

       do    {
             printf("Please enter a number: ");
             fgets(inputa,10,stdin);
             values[index] = atof(inputa);
             } while (values[index++] > 0.0);
       size = index - 1;
       for (index=0; index < size; index++)
             sum += values[index];
       printf("The mean is %f\n", sum/size);
}
```

The maximum size of the array here is defined with a *#define* statement. The array is declared automatic (it can be declared automatic since it is not initialized). The values are entered with a *do . . . while* loop. The array will permit the entry of any number of values up to the maximum (20 in this example), so some means must be provided to determine when all input values have been entered. In this case the entry of zero terminates the entry. C also does not check to see if the maximum size of the array has been exceeded (20 in this case). For most programs you should check the number of entries to be sure that the maximum array size is not exceeded.

As an exercise, use the previous example and enter more than **MAXSIZE** entries. What does your compiler do?

Pointers and Arrays

The use of arrays requires knowledge of how C uses pointers. For the moment, remember that the following is true in C:

*foo refers to the data stored at address **foo**.

&foobar refers to the address of **foobar**.

The array name is a pointer to the first element of an array.

The array name represents a pointer to the first element of an array, that is, the address of the first pointer. You can then say that:

```
foo == &foo[0]
```

Now let's look at an array example using pointers:

```
/* ARRAYPTR array pointer demonstration */

#include <stdio.h>
main()
{
    int partno[4], *pts, index;
    float price[4], *ptf;

    pts = partno;
    ptf = price;
    for (index = 0; index <4; index++)
        printf("base + %d: %10d %10d\n",
            index, pts+index, ptf+index);
}
```

If you run this program, the output will look like

```
base + 0:    5228    5208
base + 1:    5230    5212
base + 2:    5232    5216
base + 3:    5234    5220
```

There is an interesting aspect of C here that is very important to understand. When the pointer is incremented, it is incremented by the number of storage units, not by the actual value of the index. Adding 1 to a *float* pointer increments it by 4, and adding 1 to a *short* pointer increments it by 2 (figure 10.1).

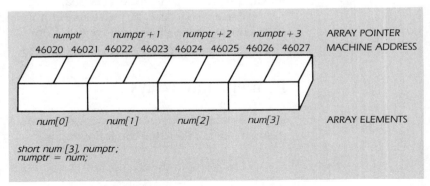

Figure 10.1 Pointers and array storage

Note | In C, whenever a pointer is incremented or decremented by an integer type, the value of the pointer is scaled by the size of the object pointed to. This ensures that the compiler uses the sizing functionality built into itself, and incrementing the pointer by

1 will always point to the next data item, regardless of the size of the item.

As a result, the following conditions are all true:

```
partno + 2 == &partno[2]
*(partno+2) == partno[2]
```

In the first condition the two addresses are the same; in the second the two values are the same.

Using Arrays in Functions

Arrays can be used either as local variables in a function or as arguments. The previous discussion applied to arrays used in the body of a function. Passing arrays as arguments, however, involves some special precautions that must be addressed by the programmer.

As an example, let's examine the problem of sorting. This is a very common use of arrays, so much so that most programmers create or purchase a collection of array sort functions for various types of applications. Here is an example of a sort function used to sort a series of input float numbers:

```c
#include <math.h>
#include <stdio.h>
#define MAXSIZE 20
main()
{
    static double values[MAXSIZE];
    int index = 0, size;
    double sum = 0.0;
    char inputa[10];

    printf("\033[2J"); /* clear screen */
    do  {
        printf("Please enter a number: ");
        fgets(inputa, 10, stdin);
        values[index] = atof(inputa);
        }
    while (values[index++] > 0.0);
    size = index - 1;
    sort(values,size);
    printf("The sorted list:\n");
    for (index=0; index < size; index++)
        {
```

```
                    sum += values[index];
                    printf("%f\n",values[index]);
                    }
            printf("The mean is %f\n", sum/size);
    }


/* BUBBLE sort routine */
/* sorts an array of floats */
sort(array,size)
double array[];
int size;
{
        int i, j, temp;
        for (i = 0; i<size-1; i++)
            for (j=i+1; j<size; j++)
                if (array[i] > array[j])
                    {
                    temp = array[j];
                    array[j]=array[i];
                    array[i] = temp;
                    }

}
```

This program is a modified version of our earlier one that calculated the mean. The difference is that the input numeric array is sorted in ascending order and then listed before the mean is displayed.

The sort technique used here in the function is known as a *bubble sort*. The function starts by trying to find the smallest item in the list and putting it as the first element of the array. The procedure is then repeated with the remainder of the list, putting the next smallest item as the second element of the array. This continues until the entire list is in ascending order. The bubble sort is one of the easiest sorts to understand and program, but it is one of the least efficient. For larger lists, you would probably want to use a better algorithm.

The outer loop, with the i index, determines which element of the array will be used for comparisons. It starts with the first array element. The inner loop, with the j index, steps through the remaining array items, comparing each with the first. If the comparison shows the elements are out of order, a swap is initiated. To initiate a swap, one item must first be stored in a temporary location.

Functions that operate on an array operate on the original values, not a copy of the values.

Remember that it is the original array that is swapped, not a copy of the array. This saves C the time involved in dragging all the array values into an array in the function and then returning all the sorted values. It also reduces the requirements for memory space, since a duplicate of the array does not have to be stored in the function stack space. There is a danger, however, in sorting the original array. If the function is improperly designed, it can destroy the original array values.

Tip | In passing an array to a function for sorting, always include an argument for the size of the array.

Character String Arrays

Character strings are defined as arrays in C.

String arrays should be handled carefully in C. Remember that you can declare a character string by using either an array or a pointer:

```
char msg1[40];
char *msg2;
```

The first method actually reserves space for the character string array. The second only declares a pointer to a character. You can use the *scanf( )* function to read input characters to an array declared in the first way. You would get an error message trying to use *scanf( )* to input values for a variable declared in the second way, since the declaration reserved no storage for the array.

The following two examples are identical:

```
static char msg[5] = "Test";
static char msg[5] = {'T', 'e', 's', 't','\0'};
```

The first example will, like the second, store a null character at the end of the array. Notice that the array size specification must include space for this null character. If you use a larger array size, the extra elements are initialized to zero in each of the above cases. If you omit the array size, it is assumed to be the number of initializing characters. If you use your C library's *strlen( )* function to return the length of the string, it will not include the null character in the count. The following example returns the value 4:

```
#include <stdio.h>
main()
{
        static char msg[5] = "Test";

        printf("%d\n",strlen(msg));
}
```

In using string arrays, then, you should observe the following precautions:

1 | Make sure that any function or operation that creates a string also creates the null character at the end, for example:

```
char msg[3+1];
char[0] = '1';
char[1] = '2';
char[2] = '3';
char[3] = 0;
```

2 | Before copying a string array, make sure that the source string (with null character) is less than or equal to the size of the destination array, for example:

```
char oldname[21+1];
char msg[19+1];

strncpy(msg, oldname, sizeof(msg)-1);
msg[19] = 0;
```

3 | Make sure that the null character is copied when a string is copied (see the last example).

Multidimensional Arrays

Arrays of multiple dimensions are indicated by using a set of square brackets for each dimension.

You can create arrays of multiple dimensions by using a set of square brackets for each dimension:

```
int values[2][3];
```

You can also initialize a multidimensional array if it is external or static:

```
#include <stdio.h>
main()
{
        static int values[2][3] = {{0,1,2},{3,4,5}};

        printf("%d",values[0][2]);
}
```

In this example the program would display the output value of 2.

Now let's try an interesting experiment. We will attempt to modify the sort function used earlier so that it will work with a multidimensional array. In this case the array is used to store the codes for each salesperson and for his or her corresponding sales total. The program will permit us to enter each sales code and sales total. It will then use a sort function to sort the codes in order of decreasing sales volume. The program then displays the output list.

```
#include <math.h>
#include <stdio.h>
#define ROWS 20
#define COLUMNS 2
main()
{
      static double sales [ROWS] [COLUMNS];
      int index = 0, size;
      char agent_number[10], agent_sales[10];

      printf("\033[2J"); /* clear screen */
      printf("Please enter salesperson number and\n");
      printf("sales. Enter two zeros to terminate:\n\n");
      do {
            printf("Enter agent number: ");
            fgets(agent_number,10,stdin);
            printf("Enter agent's sales: ");
            fgets(agent_sales,10,stdin);
            sales[index][0] = atof(agent_number);
            sales[index][1] = atof(agent_sales);
         }
      while (sales[index++][0] > 0);
      size = index - 1;
      sort(sales,size);
      printf("The sorted list:\n");
      for (index=0; index < size; index++)
            printf("%3.0f %6.2f\n",sales[index][0],
                   sales[index][1]);
}


/* BUBBLE sort routine */
/* sorts an array of floats */
sort(array,size)
double array[][COLUMNS];
int size;
{
      int i, j, k;
      double temp [COLUMNS];

      for (i = 0; i<size-1; i++)
            for (j=i+1; j<size; j++)
                  if (array[i][1] < array[j][1])
                        {
                        for (k=0; k<COLUMNS; k++)
                              temp[k] = array[j][k];
                        for (k=0; k<COLUMNS; k++)
                              array[j][k] = array[i][k];
```

```
                        for (k=0; k<COLUMNS; k++)
                             array[i][k] = temp[k];
                    }
}
```

Here is a sample execution of the program:

```
Please enter each salesperson number and
sales. Enter two zeros to terminate:
```

```
    Enter agent number: 007                    ←Enter
    Enter sales for this agent: 12.0            ←Enter
    Enter agent number: 100                     ←Enter
    Enter sales for this agent: 48.00           ←Enter
    Enter agent number: 125                     ←Enter
    Enter sales for this agent: 6               ←Enter
    Enter agent number: 167                     ←Enter
    Enter sales for this agent: 23.0            ←Enter
    Enter agent number: 0                       ←Enter
    Enter sales for this agent: 0               ←Enter
    The sorted list:
    100   48.00
    167   23.00
    007   12.00
    125    6.00
```

The two-dimensional array is declared in the main program by defining two constants, **ROWS** and **COLUMNS**. The corresponding codes and sales volumes are entered in the array, after which the function is called and the array sorted.

Notice that the function has now lost some of its independence, since some information used by the function **COLUMNS** must be passed as constants without using arguments. You can pass the size of a one-dimensional array to a function in C, but with two or more dimensions you can pass only the first subscript.

The temporary storage in the function for swapping (**temp**) must now be an array, since each element of a row must be swapped if a row is swapped. Notice how this temporary array is defined (compare it with the last sort example).

Now let's look at a multidimensional example in which an array of character strings is used as an argument for a *menu( )* function. This is also a multidimensional array:

```
#include <stdio.h>
main()
```

```
{
        static char *choices[] =
            {"A)dd an address",
             "E)dit an address",
             "D)isplay an address",
             0
            };
        static char title[40] = "Main Menu\n\n";
        void menu();

        menu(title,choices,3);
}

void menu(title,selections,size)
char *title;
char *selections[];
int size;
{
        int i;
        printf(title);
        for (i=0; i<size; i++)
                printf("%s\n",*(selections+i));
        return;
}
```

The main program uses character arrays within another array or, more accurately, an array of pointers. This array is declared as *static* and is initialized to the menu choices. Another character array is used for the menu title.

The function is called as `menu(title,choices,3)`. The first two arguments are arrays. From the previous section, you should realize that in both cases you are passing the address of the first element of the array to the function. You are not passing the values of the array to the function. The function uses the address (pointer) to recover the actual data:

```
printf("%s\n",*(selections+i));
```

Guidelines for Using Arrays

Here are some helpful guidelines and rules to remember when you are using arrays:

1 | The first element of the array is always subscript 0. The last element will have a subscript of one less than the number of elements in the array.

2 | Variables cannot be used in any expression to declare the size of the array.

3 | Only *static* and externally declared arrays can be initialized. If you do not initialize an array, the program will execute, but it will assume garbage values in the array unless the program dynamically initializes the array.

4 | C does not check to see if the index exceeds the array bounds. The programmer must do this.

5 | Remember that functions access the original array data (using pointers), not a copy of the data. A function can change the original array data.

6 | In using functions with array arguments, remember that the function has no way of knowing the size of the array. As a safety precaution, always pass the size of an array to a function with the array. The exception is when passing character string arrays. In this case you can use the *strlen( )* function to get the size of the array.

7 | In loops involving arrays, set the initial condition to 0, set the terminating condition as one less than the highest subscript, and increment it after using the index variable as:

```
for (index=0; index < MAXSIZE; index++)
    ...;
```

Review

This chapter has introduced the basic concepts of using arrays. You should have learned the following important points:

1 | Arrays permit you to store an ordered set of data of the same type.

2 | The size of an array is defined by using brackets with the variable name:

```
float price[25];
```

3 | Arrays can be initialized just like any other variable, but any initialized array must be *static* or declared *extern*.

4 | Local arrays declared as automatic (the default class) are not automatically initialized in execution. The programmer must initialize local arrays.

5 | Arrays can be multidimensional.

Quiz for Chapter 10

1 | Which of the following is not true?
   a | The first array element has a subscript value of 0.
   b | Array elements in the same array can be of different types.
   c | Arrays permit fast access to ordered data.
   d | Arrays can be used with *int*, *short*, *long*, *char*, *float*, and *double* data types, as well as with data types defined with the *typedef* keyword.

2 | Why was C designed to require the address of the array rather than the array values passed to a function?
   a | Passing the array values would require too much computer memory for large arrays.
   b | Passing array values would require too much execution time for large arrays.
   c | Both of the above
   d | Neither of the above

3 | How would you express the starting address of an array element declared as

   ```
   static int location[0][0];
   ```

   a | *location[0][0];
   b | &location[0][0];
   c | location[0]; *or* location;
   d | b and c are correct

4 | Which of the following are valid:
   a | ptr = &i
   b | ptr = &++i
   c | ptr = &(i+1)
   d | a and b

5 | What is the value of *ptr in the following:

   ```
   int *ptr;
   static int foo[4] = {1,2,3,4};

   ptr = foo;
   ```

   a | 1
   b | Indeterminate
   c | 2
   d | 0

6 | What is the value of *(ptr+1) in the previous example?
   a | 1
   b | Indeterminate
   c | 2
   d | 0

7 | What is the value of `*(ptr+2)` in the following?

```
float *ptr;
static float foo[2][2] = { {1.1,2.2}, {3.3,4.4}};

ptr = foo[0];
```

   a | 1.1
   b | Indeterminate
   c | 3.3
   d | None of the above

8 | If `price` is an array of 10 *floats*, how would it be declared?
   a | float price[11];
   b | float price[10];
   c | float price[9];
   d | float price[ ];

9 | If `ptr` is a pointer to an array of 20 characters (and the null), how should it be declared?
   a | char (*ptr)[20];
   b | char pstr[20];
   c | Neither of the above
   d | Both of the above are correct.

10 | How would you declare an array `rate` of four *ints* and initialize it to the values 1, 2, 3, and 4?
   a | int rate[5] = {1,2,3,4,'\0'};
   b | int rate[4] = {1,2,3,4};
   c | int rate[4] = {1,2,3,4,'\0'};
   d | None of the above

11 | For a 12-element array, the index range is:
   a | 1 to 12
   b | 0 to 12
   c | 0 to 11
   d | 1 to 13

12 | How would you express the address of location `[20][30]`?
   a | *location[20][30];
   b | *(location[20][30]);
   c | &location[20][30];
   d | a and b

13 | How would you express the address of location `[5][0];`
   a | *location[5][0];
   b | &location[5][0];
   c | location[5];
   d | b and c are correct

14 | Which of the following is not true?

a | Arrays can have three, four, or more dimensions.

b | The name of the array is a pointer to the first element.

c | The size of an array cannot be changed dynamically while the program is executing.

d | Arrays are always stored in a program's data segment.

15 | Which of the following is not true?

a | You can store a variable declared as *int* and another declared as *float* in the same array.

b | Strings are stored as character arrays.

c | An array has three attributes: type, location, and length.

d | The *char* data type is used to store character strings.

11 | Using Data Structures

About This Chapter

Arrays permit you to store a list of data in memory and access it quickly—even multidimensional lists. Arrays do, however, have a serious limitation. Each element of the array for all dimensions must be of the same type and must use the same amount of storage space. This often poses a problem. Remember the sales program of the last chapter in which the salesperson number and sales were both stored in the array? It worked because the salesperson number and the sales amount were both *float* data; but, suppose we wish to store the salesperson's name instead of the number? The array approach would not work because you would be trying to store strings (character arrays) and *float* data in the same array. You cannot mix element types in an array. Moreover, each element must be the same size. If you create an array of addresses, each field of the address (name, address, city, state, etc.) must be the same size.

Data structures permit you to build your own data types, combining data of different types in the same structure.

Data structures allow you to build your own data types, mixing data of different types and sizes in the same structure. This chapter will show you how this is done.

A Simple Data Structure

Let's begin with a simple example of a program using a data structure. The following program allows you to enter and then display an address:

```c
#include <stdio.h>
#define PAD 2;
main()
{
      struct address_rec
            {
            char address_no[3+PAD];
            char name[40+PAD];
            char street[40+PAD];
            char city[20+PAD];
            char state[2+PAD];
            char zip[5+PAD];
            };
      struct address_rec address;

      printf("Name: ");
      fgets(address.name,sizeof(address.name),stdin);
      printf("Address: ");
      fgets(address.street,sizeof(address.street),stdin);
      printf("City: ");
      fgets(address.city,sizeof(address.city),stdin);
      printf("State: ");
      fgets(address.state,sizeof(address.state),stdin);
      printf("Zip: ");
      fgets(address.zip,sizeof(address.zip),stdin);
      printf("Number: ");
      fgets(address.address_no,sizeof(address.address.no),
      stdin);
      printf("\n\n%s\n",address.address_no);
      printf("%s\n",address.name);
      printf("%s\n",address.street);
      printf("%s %s %s\n", address.city,
            address.state, address.zip);
}
```

If you execute this program, you will get something like this:

Name: *George Washington*   ←Enter
Address: *1600 Pennsylvania Ave*   ←Enter
City: *Washington*   ←Enter
State: *DC*   ←Enter
Zip: *30070*   ←Enter
Number: *1*   ←Enter

1
George Washington

```
1600 Pennsylvania Ave
Washington DC  30070
```

Now let's see how the program works.

Defining the Structure Template

The *struct* keyword defines a template for the data structure and assigns it to an identifier.

We need a data structure to store the address that will consist of six parts: name, street, city, state, zip, and an address number. This structure is defined using the *struct* keyword:

```
struct address_rec
       {
       char address_no[3+PAD];
       char name[40+PAD];
       char street[40+PAD];
       char city[20+PAD];
       char state[2+PAD];
       char zip[5+PAD];
       };
```

This structure does not define or reserve any space for a variable. All you have done is define a template or format and assign this template a tag called **address_rec**. The members of the template can be integers, floats, characters, arrays, or even other data structures. The definition ends with a semicolon.

In using character string arrays in the structure, be sure to insert space for the padding, which in this example includes a carriage return and newline character. The zip code may be only 5 characters, but you will need 2 additional bytes, making it an array of 7 characters. The state name is 2 characters but needs an array of 4 characters.

Declaring a Structure Variable

Once you have defined this template, you can use it as a data type in your program, just as you would any other data type:

```
struct address_rec address;
```

In this example the variable name is **address**. This variable is declared to be of the **struct address_rec** type. Variable space is reserved for the variable **address**. The variable will take 122 bytes. The template name is called a *tag*, and is not a variable.

You can use the same structure for several variables if you wish. It is a data type, just like any other data type:

```
struct address_rec input_address;
struct address_rec output_address;
```

Here, both `input_address` and `output_address` are declared to be of the `struct address_rec` type. Both variables will take 122 bytes of storage.

You can find the size of the structure with a simple program:

```
main()
{
    struct address_rec
        {
        char address_no[3+PAD];
        char name[40+PAD];
        char street[40+PAD];
        char city[20+PAD];
        char state[2+PAD];
        char zip[5+PAD];
        };
    struct address_rec address;

    printf("%d",sizeof(address));
}
```

You may wish to experiment with this program, changing or eliminating various structure elements or changing types to see how it affects the structure size. For example, change `zip` to an *unsigned long* type.

In the next example both the template and the variable are defined inside the function. You can also put the template outside the function:

Variables can be declared with the structure by using the struct keyword and the identifier.

```
#include <stdio.h>
struct address_rec
    {
    char address_no[3+PAD];
    char name[40+PAD];
    char street[40+PAD];
    char city[20+PAD];
    char state[2+PAD];
    char zip[5+PAD];
    };
main()
{
    struct address_rec address;
```

When the template is defined within the function, it can be used only to declare variables within that function. When the template is defined outside of the functions or main program, it can be used by the main program or any function.

It is possible to define the structure and declare the variable at the same time:

```
#include <stdio.h>
#define PAD 2
main()
{
    struct
        {
        char address_no[3+PAD];
        char name[40+PAD];
        char street[40+PAD];
        char city[20+PAD];
        char state[2+PAD];
        char zip[5+PAD];
        } address;
```

In this case there is no structure name (**address_rec**). The variable name, **address**, is added at the end after the closing brace of the definition. This is acceptable if the structure will be used only for one variable, but it is not advisable if the structure is used for multiple variables.

If you wanted to use this method with multiple variables, you could add them with commas after the closing bracket:

```
#include <stdio.h>
#define PAD 2
main()
{
    struct
        {
        char address_no[3+PAD];
        char name[40+PAD];
        char street[40+PAD];
        char city[20+PAD];
        char state[2+PAD];
        char zip[5+PAD];
        } input_address, output_address;
```

Tip | Although structures can be used without tags (names), using tags improves the readability of the program and is considered better form.

Initializing a Structure Variable

Structure variables can be initialized in the same way as other variables.

The rules for whether or not a structure variable can be initialized are the same as for an array variable. Structure variables can be initialized if the variable is *external* or *static*. Whether a variable is external depends on where the variable is declared, not where the template is defined.

```
#define PAD 2
main()
{
        struct parameters
                {
                char company_name[40+PAD]; /* company name */
                char default_drive; /* default drive */
                int access_level; /* access level */
                };
        static struct parameters address =
                {
                "ACME Manufacturing Company"
                'D'
                3
                };
}
```

In initializing a structure, it is not necessary that all components be of the same type. In the preceding example, a character array, a character, and an *int* integer are all components of a single structure.

Accessing Structure Components

C permits only four operations with a structure variable: you can access one of the members, you can assign one structure equal to another, you can use *sizeof(structure)* to get the size of the structure, or you can use the & operator to access the address of a structure. The first two operators are discussed in this section. The third and fourth are discussed later in the chapter under "Pointers and Structures."

Variables that are part of a structure are accessed by using the structure name, the period operator, and the component name.

Once you have declared a structure variable, you can access the variable by using the structure name, the *period* operator, and the component name. The period operator is also called a *dot* or *member* operator:

```
fgets(address.name,sizeof(address.name),stdin);
printf(address.name);
```

In this example the input text is stored as the **name** component of the

address array. You can use **address.name** just as you would any other character string variable. If you have multiple variables of the same type, each is a separate variable:

```
#define ASS_STRUCT(a,b) movemem(&(a), &(b),sizeof(b));

struct address_rec input_address;
struct address_rec output_address;

fgets(input_address,sizeof(input_address),stdin);
ASS_STRUCT(output_address,input_address)
printf(output_address);
```

The preceding example illustrates another important aspect of data structures: you can assign a value of one structure to another. Here, the entire structure contents (and not just a pointer) is copied to the other structure.

Arrays of Structures

You can build arrays of structures.

Our little address program is not very useful now, since we will usually wish to enter multiple addresses. To do this, the program must be modified to permit storing an array of structures:

```
#include <stdio.h>
#define MAXADDR 5
#define PAD 2
#define END ""
main()
{
     struct address_rec
          {
          char address_no[3+PAD];
          char name[40+PAD];
          char street[40+PAD];
          char city[20+PAD];
          char state[2+PAD];
          char zip[5+PAD];
          };
     struct address_rec address[MAXADDR];
     int count = 0;
     int index;

     printf("Name: ");
     while (count<MAXADDR &&
```

```
        strlen(fgets(address[count].name,
            sizeof (address[count].name),stdin) !=
                NULL )
        {
        printf("Address: ");
        fgets(address[count].street,
            sizeof(address[count],street),stdin);
        printf("City: ");
        fgets(address[count].city,
            sizeof(address[count].city),stdin);
        printf("State: ");
        fgets(address[count].state,
            sizeof(address[count].state),stdin);
        printf("Zip: ");
        fgets(address.zip[count],
            sizeof(address.zip[count]),stdin);
        printf("Number: ");
        fgets(address.address_no[count++],5,stdin);
        if (count<MAXADDR)
                printf("Name: ");
        }
    for (index=0; index<count; index++)
        {
        printf("\n\n%s\n",address[index].address_no);
        printf("%s\n",address[index].name);
        printf("%s\n",address[index].street);
        printf("%s %s %s\n",address[index].city,
                address[index].state, address[index].zip);
        }
}
```

This program is a little more complex but is really not difficult to understand. The template is defined exactly as before. The first clue to the difference is when the variable is defined:

```
struct address_rec address[MAXADDR];
```

At this point you are reserving variable space for an array of type struct address_rec. The array has a maximum dimension of 5, which means that the declaration will reserve 5 × 122 bytes for the address[5] variable, or 610 bytes. As you can imagine, complex array structures can use a lot of memory if you are not careful.

Accessing members of the array means that you will have to use a subscript to identify the member. The subscript in this case is used as part of the structure name, not as part of the name of the structure member:

```
gets(address[1].name);
```

If the component is an array, you can also use subscripts with the component name to identify the member of that array:

```
printf(address[1].name[3]);
```

This statement would print the fourth letter in the name of the second address.

The program mechanics of the example are quite simple. A *while* loop is used to enter the addresses until either the maximum number of addresses has been entered (5) or a null name has been entered (carriage return with no name entered). After all the addresses are entered, a *for* loop displays the list.

Nested Structures

You can use data structures as components of other data structures.

You can use structures as part of other structures, creating nested structures. For example, assume that you are working on a job-costing program in which you are tracking various jobs and the time and cost of each:

```
struct time
       {
       int days;
       int hours;
       int minutes;
       };
struct job_rec
       {
       int job_code
       char  desc[30]
       struct time billing_time
       };
struct job_rec job;
```

Now if you've worked with database management programs (such as dBASE III), you've probably recognized something very interesting here. The address program of the earlier example used a data structure (figure 11.1) to define a record and the fields of the record. Now, however, the field itself becomes like a record within a record with its own subfields—something that can't be accomplished with dBASE III or other high-level languages (figure 11.2).

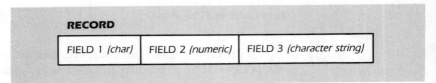

Figure 11.1 Traditional database management structure

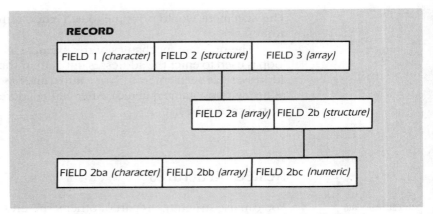

Figure 11.2 Database structures permitted with C

Members are accessed by using two period operators on the structures with substructures. For example, the following statement will assign the number of job hours as 8:

```
job.time.hours = 8;
```

Pointers and Structures

Pointers can be used with data structures, just as with other data types.

C permits the use of pointers with structures, just as with other data types. This provides three useful advantages:

- As with arrays, pointers to structures are easier to manipulate than the structures themselves. You don't need to copy one structure to another; just use the assignment operator.

- Pointers enable the creation and use of many interesting data structures, such as hierarchical record fields.

- You can use structures with functions and pass the structure pointer to the function. This eliminates the time needed to copy the structure values to the function variables.

The indirect membership operator (->) is used to represent the data of a member.

As with arrays and other variables, the ampersand operator (&) is used to refer to the address of the pointer to the structure. As with arrays, this operator is used with the structure name as an argument when a function is used with a structure. The asterisk (*) is used to indicate the data in an address. One new operator, the indirect membership operator (->) is also used to indicate the data of a member.

Let's see how these operators work. Try this program:

```
#include <stdio.h>
#define PAD 2
main()
{
        struct address_rec
               {
               char name[40+PAD];
               char street[40+PAD];
               char city[20+PAD];
               char state[2+PAD];
               char zip[5+PAD];
               };
        static struct address_rec address[2]=
               {       {"James Smith",
                       "Box 34",
                       "Portland",
                       "OR",
                       "97211" },
                       {"Bill Roberts",
                       "34 Fairlane Dr.",
                       "Seattle",
                       "WA",
                       "98732"}
               };

        struct address_rec *one_address;
        one_address = &address[0];
        printf("The first address is %u\n",one_address);
        printf("Here is the address again: %u\n",&address[0]);
        printf("The first name is %s\n",one_address->name);
        one_address=&address[1];
        printf("The second address is %u\n",one_address);
        printf("Here is the address again: %u\n",&address[1]);
        printf("The second name is %s\n",one_address->name);

}
```

Here we have declared an address array as before and initialized it. After the initialization a pointer is defined:

```
struct address_rec *one_address
```

The expression **one_address** is now defined as a pointer to the structure. The next statement assigns it the value of the address of the first address:

```
one_address = &address[0]
```

The next statement prints the value of the address that holds the pointer to the first address:

```
printf("The first pointer is %u\n",one_address)
```

Since **one_address** is also **&address[0]**, the next statement prints the same number.

The following statement introduces a new operator, the indirect membership operator:

```
printf("The first name is %s\n",one_address->name);
```

This prints the actual data value in the variable name that is part of the address pointed to by **one_address**.

The address pointer is then set to the next address and the cycle repeated. The actual output with QuickC would be similar to

```
The first address is 3280
Here is the address again: 3280
The first name is James Smith
The second address is 3397
Here is the address again: 3397
The second name is Bill Roberts
```

In Turbo C the output is

```
The first address is 158
Here is the address again: 158
The first name is James Smith
The second address is 275
Here is the address again: 275
The second name is Bill Roberts
```

Notice that the following are all equal:

```
address[0].name   (*one_address).name
one_address->name
```

if

```
one_address == &address[0]
```

Functions and Structures

When using data structures with functions, the address of the data structure is passed to the function.

Data structures can be used with functions in the same way as arrays are used. The address of the structure is passed to the function, and the function operates on the data using the address. As a general rule, you should not pass the structure itself to the function because that would be too time-consuming and require too much memory. This means that, as with arrays, you must use caution, since a function can unintentionally modify the original data if the address is passed to the function.

As an example of using structures with functions, let's take a function that creates screen forms. The desired form is defined as a structure and is passed to the function and used to draw the screen:

```
#include <stdio.h>
struct data_frame
       {
       int row,col;
       char *msg;
       };
main()
{
       static struct data_frame main_menu[] =
              {
              10, 25, "MAIN MENU",
              13, 20, "A)dd an address",
              14, 20, "E)dit and address",
              15, 20, "D)isplay an address",
              0,  0,  NULL
              };
       int index;
       void display_form(struct data_frame *);

       display_form(main_menu);
}
void display_form(form)
struct data_frame form[];
{
       int index;
       void displayline(struct data_frame *);

       printf("\033[2J");
       for (index=0; form[index].msg != NULL; ++index)
              displayline(&form[index]);
}
void displayline(ptr_form)
struct data_frame *ptr_form;
```

```
{
        printf("\033[%d;%dH",ptr_form->row,ptr_form->col);
        fputs(ptr_form->msg,stdout);
}
```

The preceding program is used to write **msg** at coordinates **row, col**. The graphic aspects are described in chapter 13, but for now let's look at the indirect operator. First, let's use this structure to initialize an array of these structures:

```
static struct data_frame main_menu[] =
        {
                10, 25, "MAIN MENU",
                13, 20, "A)dd an address",
                14, 20, "E)dit and address",
                15, 20, "D)isplay an address",
                0,  0,   NULL
                };
```

In this example the NULL is an empty string used to indicate the end of the list of display lines.

The next statement declares the return value of the **display_form()** function as *void*. It also defines the argument to be used with the function as a **structure data_form** pointer:

```
void display_form(struct data_form *);
```

Here the main program does nothing but call the **display_form** function, passing a pointer to the form to be used.

The **display_form()** function clears the screen and then accesses each line of the array for display. The pointer to the structure that contains the display message, row, and column is passed as:

```
displayline(&form[index])
```

The **NULL** is used to sense the end of the array and is defined in the *stdio.h* file.

The **displayline()** function is used to display each line of the array. The first line in the function is

```
printf("\033[%d;%dH",ptr_form->row,ptr_form->col);
```

This statement moves the cursor to **row, col**. For example, the following statement moves the cursor on an IBM screen to row 10, column 8:

```
printf("\033[%d;%dH",10,8);
```

The only difference between the two is that the membership indirection operator (->) is used to obtain the row and column from the structure passed to the function. The following are equivalent:

```
ptr_form->row(*ptr_form).row
```

In both cases the expression represents the actual value of row in the structure. The final function statement outputs the message at the cursor location.

Be very careful in using pointers. You can make some simple changes in the program and the program may still compile and execute properly. Even more strange, you may find that you can compile the program and execute it external to the C compiler environment; but, if you compile it under the Turbo C or QuickC environment, the computer locks up or does other unusual things. The problem is usually the improper use of pointers.

> **Tip** | C does not check completely for proper use of pointers. If you experience compiling problems, check for proper use of pointers.

Applications for Data Structures

There are three basic reasons for using structures in a program: to permit the use of complex data forms, to permit the use of multiple data types in an array-like structure, and to improve readability.

Structures permit you to create complex data forms, and are particularly useful when data members need to be grouped as part of a larger unit of data. You have already seen that, for database management, the data fields become the structure members and the record becomes the unit structure. Data structures can also be used to create binary trees for indexing in database management. Queues, heaps, hash tables, stacks, and graphs can all be represented with data structures. You can also create linked structures, building a network of data with items linked in complex interrelationships.

Structures also permit you to combine data of different types in a single structure. In this chapter you saw how you could store a numeric value with character strings in an address structure, yet you could access each member as easily as if it were part of an array.

Structures also improve the readability of a program. In the array example of the last chapter sales[2][1] was the sales of the third salesperson. Using a data structure, this could become

```
salesperson[2].sales
```

Structures permit you to create complex data forms and to group related data.

which is much more readable.

Structures are the building blocks of complex data types, which form the foundation of object-oriented programming. In such applications a structure is used to store all the attributes of the object, which can then be used in the program as a single entity.

Here are some guidelines for using structures:

- Group data that is related by content or usage in a single structure.

- Build larger and more general data groupings from smaller, more specific ones.

- Link data of different types that are related.

Unions

Unions permit the storage of different data types in the same memory space.

A *union* is a method in C for storing different data types in the same memory space. It is used in much the same way as a structure; that is, you create a tag or structure and then use this tag to declare variables.

As an example, you could create a union tag called `table`:

```
union table {
      int number;
      long  address;
      char  code;
      };
```

You could then declare three variables:

```
union table co_address;
union table code_string[10];
union table address_no;
```

C allocates enough space to hold the largest value that will be stored. (See chapter 14 for a union application in which the computer's register values are set up to be accessed as 8-bit or 16-bit by means of a union.)

Review

This chapter has covered the following important points:

1 | Data structures permit you to store and process data of different types as a unit.

2 | A data structure can be defined with a template, and the template can be used with any number of variable names in a program. The template should be given a name, or tag.

3 | C permits you to perform four operations with a structure: access one of its members, assign one structure equal to another, use the *sizeof* operator to get the size of a structure, or use the **&** operator to obtain the address of a structure.

4 | You can build arrays of structures, or a structure can contain an array. You can also nest structures.

5 | As a general rule, you should pass the address of a structure to a function rather than a copy of the values.

6 | Structures can be used in a wide variety of applications, such as queues, heaps, hash tables, stacks, and graphs.

7 | A union is a method in the C language for storing different data types in the same memory space.

Quiz for Chapter 11

1 | What is wrong with this structure?

```
structure parts
    {
    int part_no;
    char descrip[20];
    float price;
    char *ptr;
    }
```

a | The keyword should be `struct`, not `structure`.
b | Pointers cannot be used in a structure.
c | A semicolon must be placed at the end.
d | a and c

2 | How would you represent the `partno` member of `parts`?

```
struct inven
    {
    int partno;
    };
```

```
struct inven parts;
struct inven *ptr = &parts;
```

a | parts.partno
b | ptr—>partno
c | partno
d | a and b

3 | Which of the following would read input to `zip`, a member of address?

```
struct ad
    {
    char name[60];
    char address[60];
    char city[20];
    char state[4];
    char zip[7];
```

```
struct ad address;
struct ad *ptr = &address;
```

a | fgets(address.zip, sizeof(address.zip), stdin)
b | fgets(ptr—>zip, 6, stdin)
c | a and b
d | None of the above

4 | Which of the following is not an advantage of using structures?
 a | You can process mixed data types as a single unit.
 b | You can store character strings of different lengths in a single structure.
 c | Data can be stored in a modular and hierarchical form.
 d | Less memory storage space is needed for the same data.

5 | Which statement is not true?
 a | Using a data structure instead of an array permits you to store strings and numbers in a single structure.
 b | Data structures make the program more readable.
 c | Both a and b are not true.
 d | Both a and b are true.

6 | Which of the following is not true?
 a | When a structure tag is defined within a function, it is recognized only within the function.
 b | A structure can be reused for several variables in a program.
 c | A structure tag is a programmer-defined symbol, but it has a scope that resembles that of a variable.
 d | All of the above are true.

7 | Which of the following is not true?
 a | You can create an array of structures.
 b | You can create a structure that contains one or more array elements.
 c | You can create a structure that contains one or more data structures, which in themselves can contain structures.
 d | All of the above are true.

8 | Which of the following is not true for Turbo C and QuickC?
 a | Several variables can share the same structure.
 b | You can name structures as function arguments, and functions can return structure values.
 c | You can transfer data from one structure to another using the form:

```
struct
    {
    char name[40];
    char address[60];
    char city[20];
    char state[4];
    char zip[7];
    } address_in address_out;


address_out = address_in;
```

 d | All of the above are true.

9 | Construct an identifier for the third letter of the **name** variable of address:

```
struct fullname
        {
        firstname[20];
        char lastname[20];
        };

struct ad
        {
        struct fullname name;
        char address[60];
        char city[20];
        char state[4];

struct fullname
        {
        firstname[20];
        char lastname[20];
        };

struct ad address;
struct ad *ptr = &address;
```

   a | address.name.firstname[2];
   b | ptr—>name.firstname[2]
   c | Both of the above
   d | Neither of the above

10 | Write an expression that returns the total number of characters in the first and last name (excluding any null characters that pad the character array) in the previous example.
   a | strlen(address.name.firstname) + strlen
     (address.name.lastname)
   b | strlen(ptr—>name.firstname + strlen
     (ptr—>name.lastname)
   c | Both of the above
   d | Neither of the above

11 | In the following example, what would the program print?

```
main()
{
        struct name
                {
                char name_long[60];
                char name_short[15];
                };
```

```
struct inven
    {
    int partno;
    struct name descrip;
    float price;
    char material[10];
    };

struct invent part =
    {
    1020,
    {"Terzel bicycle widget-fastening bolt",
    "Terzel bolt"},
    "steel"
    };

ptr = &part

printf("%d",part.partno);
}
```

  a | 1020
  b | Nothing, the program will not compile.
  c | 0
  d | The program compiles but displays an error on executing.

12 | In the previous example, what is the output if the print statement is changed to:

```
printf("%s",ptr->material+2)
```

  a | teel
  b | Nothing, the program will not compile.
  c | eel
  d | steel

13 | In the example for question 11, how would you represent the name_long description in structure notation?
  a | part.descrip.name_long
  b | part.name.name_long
  c | ptr->name.name_long
  d | ptr->&descrip.name_long

14 | The following structure is for creating a 10-element array of addresses. What is wrong with it?

```
typedef struct
    {
    name[40];
```

```
          address[60];
          city[20];
          state[4];
          zip[7];
          } ADDRESS;

ADDRESS names[10];
names[2].name = "John Doe";
names[2].address = "Box 2";
names[2].city = "Portland";
names[2].state = "OR";
names[2].zip = "97211";
```

    a | The *typedef* keyword should be omitted.

    b | You cannot initialize an array in this way.

    c | The array was not declared to be of the proper storage class.

    d | There is nothing wrong.

15 | Which of the following is not true?

    a | Structures can be compared for equality.

    b | In any situation (except for bit fields) in which the & address operator can be applied to a structure to obtain a pointer to the structure, it is also permitted to apply the operator to a structure component to obtain a pointer to the component; that is, a pointer can point to the middle of a structure.

    c | A component of a structure cannot be of the type *void*.

    d | A structure cannot contain an instance of itself, but it can contain a pointer to an instance of itself.

12 | Using Files and Other Input and Output

About This Chapter

Up to now, you have been using a variety of input and output (I/O) functions without regard to the technical aspects of the internal workings of these functions. This chapter will take you into another level of creating input and output. You will learn how to direct output to the printer, control keyboard echo on the display, use buffer control, and read and write files.

Let's begin by looking at general aspects of input and output. Then we will apply these to some applications.

Using Buffers

Most input and output functions use a buffer to temporarily store the data that is to be transferred.

In most input and output functions data is stored temporarily in a memory location until it is ready to be used (figure 12.1). This temporary location is called a *buffer*. Buffering is done automatically. The CON-FIG.SYS file that is used by DOS defines the maximum number of buffers that the operating system is permitted to open, such as

```
BUFFERS = 20
```

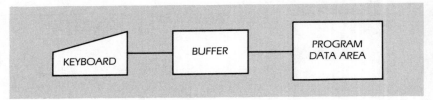

Figure 12.1 Using a buffer

You can edit or change this number as necessary to customize the operating system for your applications.

As an example, for most applications you will want incoming keyboard characters saved in a buffer until an entire line has been entered. This permits you to backspace, correct any errors, and then continue to enter more characters. Once you press the carriage return, the buffer contents are sent to the program and the buffer is cleared for the next line. The *getchar( )*, *scanf( )*, and *gets( )* functions are all buffered input functions. This means that for each of these functions no action is taken by the program until the carriage return is pressed. The *stdin* (keyboard) identifier used by the *fgets( )* function usually refers to buffered input, and the Enter and Ctrl-Z keys are handled in a special way in this type of buffered input.

The C language also supports input and output using unbuffered functions.

Sometimes you will want unbuffered input. For example, after a menu is displayed, you will want the program to wait for the user to enter an option. The user should press one key (but not carriage return), after which the option is initiated. The action should be immediate, without requiring the pressing of the Enter key. In this case you want direct input without buffering. To do this, use the *getche( )* function:

```
printf("Option: ");
option = getche();
```

Another use for unbuffered input is to wait for a user response after an error has been detected:

```
printf("Answer must be 'Y' or 'N'\n");
printf("Press any key to continue\n");
getche();
```

Any command to the program generally should be entered as unbuffered input, since you want immediate action.

Echoing

During most input you will want the keyboard entry to echo on the screen immediately after a key is pressed. All of the I/O functions that you have used up to this time have provided this immediate echo, whether they were buffered (such as *fgets( )*) or unbuffered (such as *getche( )*). Sometimes, however, you may not wish the keyboard input echoed.

Suppose that you are entering a password; you will not want the password echoed to the screen as it is typed. For single character input when you do not wish an echo, use the *getch( )* function. For example, to enter a password you could use:

```
printf("Please enter password: ");
for (i=0; i<strlen(password)+1; i++)
        {
        reply[i]=getch();
        putchar('*');
        }
strcat(reply,"\0");
if (strcmp(reply,password) != 0)
        {
        printf("Illegal password.\n");
        printf("Press any key to continue.\n");
        getche();
        exit(0);
        }
```

The *getch( )* function permits the entry of keyboard data without echoing the data to the display device.

The *getch( )* function is very similar to the *getche( )*, except that the input character is not echoed. The program loads the keyboard entry to a reply buffer and then compares it to the password previously stored in the password variable.

Files

Files are named sections of storage on a disk or other storage device.

Data stored in computer memory is *volatile*; that is, it is lost as soon as you turn off the computer. To save something for later sessions, files are used. *Files* are named sections of storage on a floppy disk, hard disk, tape, or other storage device. C uses many files, for example, source program files, library files, and *include* files. Of course, you will use files to store data. For example, suppose you write a program to process addresses. You will want to store the addresses in a file so that you can use them in later sessions.

Data is physically stored on the disk in bytes, sectors, and tracks (figure 12.2). Each of these divisions has a fixed length on a given machine. Programs, however, view data in logical records. Records may be of varying length or of fixed length. The records, in turn, are composed of one or more fields (figure 12.3). For example, assume that you wish to store a collection of addresses in a file. Each address in the file is a record. The last name, first name, street address, city, state, and zip code are all separate fields in the record.

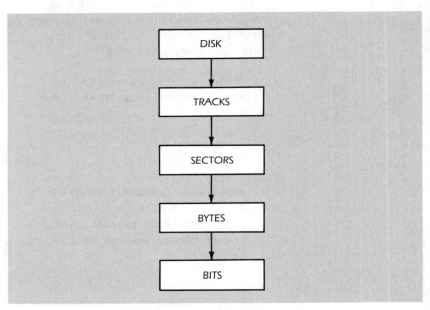

Figure 12.2 Physical file storage

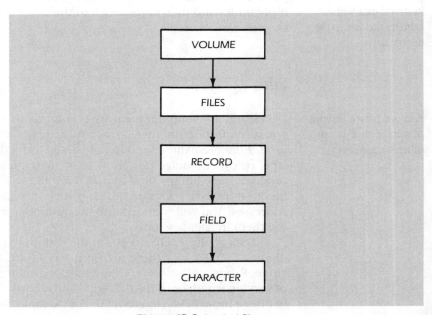

Figure 12.3 Logical file storage

It is the file buffer that permits the transfer between physical and logical storage. For example, in both Turbo C and QuickC the buffer size for file transfers is defined in the *stdio.h* file as 512 bytes. When addresses (records) are written to this buffer, the transfers from the program to the buffer continue until the buffer becomes full. At that time the I/O system automatically transfers all 512 bytes to the disk, clears the buffer, and then begins reading to the buffer again wherever it left off in the current record.

Types of File Transfer

File transfer functions can be grouped as character, string, or record I/O.

File transfer functions can generally be divided into three groups, depending on how they transfer data. For the moment, we'll use as examples the I/O functions with which you are familiar:

1 | *Character I/O*—data is transferred one character at a time. Examples are *putchar( )* and *getchar( )*.

2 | *String I/O*—data is transferred as a character array. With some functions the string may be formatted; with others it is not formatted. Examples of unformatted string I/O functions include *gets( )* and *puts( )*. Examples of formatted string I/O functions are *scanf( )* and *printf( )*.

3 | *Record I/O*—data is transferred as a fixed-length character string. We will not give any examples just yet, since record I/O will be introduced in this chapter.

High-Level versus Low-Level Access

File I/O functions can also be grouped as high- or low-level.

The file read and write functions can be divided into two mutually exclusive groups: high-level and low-level. The high-level functions support buffered transfer, are generally portable with different C compilers, are easier to use, and provide more internal error checking. The low-level functions provide more direct access of the data and require less memory, but they support less error checking and contain no buffering. (Table 12.1 at the end of this chapter compares the two groups of functions.) For most file operations, you will want to use high-level data transfers.

Later in the chapter you will be introduced to low-level functions such as *open( )*, *close( )*, *write( )*, and *read( )*. These are low-level functions for nonbuffered transfers. They are less portable with various implementations of C (they perform differently with different C compilers), but they are useful in some applications.

Buffered File Transfers

This section will introduce the most common file transfer functions: those used for buffered file transfers. They are high-level functions and are portable to all C languages; that is, if a program is written using any of them, it is not likely that the call will need to be changed to compile under another C implementation.

Opening a File

Before a file can be used, it must be opened.

Before you can use a file, you must open it. Opening the file creates a buffer for any file input or output and sets up other necessary control variables (figure 12.4).

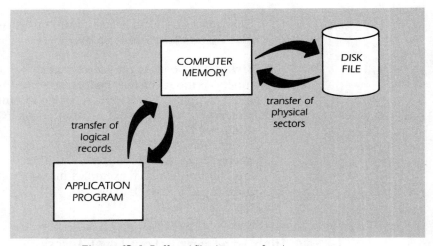

Figure 12.4 *Buffered file data transfers in a computer*

To open a file, you need to use a data structure that is already defined in *stdio.h*:

```
#define FILE     struct _iobuf
extern FILE
     {
     char *_ptr; /* current buffer pointer */
     int  _cnt; /* current byte count */
     char *_base; /* base addr. of I/O buffer */
     char  _flag; /* control flags */
     char  _file; /* file number */
     } _NEAR _CDECL _iob[];
```

You can then open a file by defining a pointer to this structure and using the *fopen( )* function to open the file. In its simplest form, the program for opening a file becomes

```c
#include <stdio.h>
main()
{
      FILE *param_file;

      param_file=fopen("ADDRESS.DAT","r");
      .
      .
      .
```

This program defines *param_file as a pointer to a structure for the file ADDRESS.DAT. The *fopen( )* function has the general form:

```
fopen(file_name,access_type)
```

where the access type is defined as:

r   = Read only. The file must exist.

r+   = Read and write. The file must exist.

w   = Write only. Any current file is deleted.

a   = Append to current file. Create if it does not exist.

The actual list for available access types is much longer than this, but this list will do for our present purposes. The function returns a pointer to the open file. If an error is detected, a null is returned.

Tip | Always check for an error return from *fopen( )*. This saves you from trying to read a file that does not exist, for example:

```c
#include <stdio.h>
main()
{
      FILE *param_file=NULL;
      static char file_name[] = "PARAM.DAT";

      if (NULL== (param_file=fopen(file_name,"r")))
            {
            printf("Error opening file!\n");
            printf("Press any key to continue.\n");
            getche();
            exit(0);
            }
```

Closing a File

Once you are through
with a file, it must be
closed.

Once you are through with a file, you should always close it. For an output file, closing the file writes any data still in the buffer to the file. For any file, it releases the buffer space for another file. The file close function takes the general form:

```
fclose(file_pointer)
```

Notice that the file pointer is the argument, not the filename. In its simplest form, the close statement becomes:

```
fclose(param_file);
```

> **Tip** | Check to be sure that the file is closed properly. Failure to close a file that is used for writing can cause a loss of data. The function returns a value of 0 if the file is closed properly, and a 1 if an error occurred:

```
if (fclose(param_file) != NULL)
      {
      printf("Error on closing.\n");
      printf("Press any key to continue.\n");
      getche();
      exit(0);
      }
```

Reading and Writing Data

The functions for reading and writing data are similar to those that you have already used for inputting and outputting data. Let's look at the file I/O functions by pairs.

The *fprintf( )* and *fscanf( )* Functions

For high-level I/O, the
fprint( ) function is used
for formatted writing
and the *fscanf( )*
function for reading.

The *fprintf( )* and *fscanf( )* functions work like the *printf( )* and *scanf( )* functions, permitting the input and output of formatted data with a file. The difference is the inclusion of an extra argument for the file pointer. The general form for each is

```
fprintf(file_pointer,format_string,string_pointer)
```

```
fscanf(file_pointer,format_string,string_pointer)
```

Since both functions are processing arrays, pointers must be used to the arrays. Here is an example of a program to create a **PARAM.DAT** file of three input character strings:

```c
#include <stdio.h>
#include <string.h>
#define PAD 2
main()
{
     FILE *param_file=NULL;
     static char file_name[] = "PARAM.DAT";
     char reply[80];
     static char ctitle[60+PAD];
     static char pass[2+PAD];
     static char password[40+PAD]="\n";
     int z, i

     puts("Enter Company Name: ");
     fgets(ctitle,sizeof(ctitle),stdin);
     puts("PASSWORD CONTROL ON? (Y/N): ");
     fgets(pass,sizeof(pass),stdin);
     if (stricmp(pass,"Y\n") == 0)
          {
          puts("PASSWORD: ");
          fgets(password,sizeof(password),stdin);
          }
     if (NULL== (param_file=fopen(file_name,"w")))
          {
          printf("Error opening file!\n");
          printf("Press any key to continue.\n");
          getche();
          exit(0);
          }
     fprintf(param_file,"%s",pass);
     fprintf(param_file,"%s",password);
     fprintf(param_file,"%s",ctitle);
     if (fclose(param_file) != NULL)
          {
          printf("Error on closing.\n");
          printf("Press any key to continue.\n");
          getche();
          exit(0);
          }
}
```

Numeric data is converted to ASCII on writing. For example, if you use *fprintf( )* to write the *short* integer number 254 to a file, it would read 254 from memory as 2 bytes. It would write 254 to the file as 3 characters, or 3 bytes. On reading data, the *scanf( )* function does just the reverse, converting the file ASCII data to numeric values if that is the format in *fscanf( )*.

In using *scanf( )* to read a file, the return value will be `EOF (-1)` if the end of the file is reached. The return value should always be checked for end-of-file:

```
z = fscanf(param_file,"%s",name);
if (z == EOF)
        {
        printf("The end of the file was reached.\n");
        exit(0);
        }
```

The *fputs( )* and *fgets( )* Functions

The *fputs( )* and *fgets( )* functions can be used for writing and reading character strings.

The *fputs( )* and *fgets( )* functions are similar to *puts( )* and *gets( )*, except that an extra file pointer argument is added. They have the general form:

```
fputs(string_pointer,file_pointer)
```

```
fgets(string_pointer,no_of_characters,file_pointer)
```

Notice an important difference between these two functions and the *fprintf( )* and *fscanf( )* functions: the file pointer is the last argument here, not the first. The function returns a string pointed to by `string_pointer`, and it reads characters until one of the following conditions is met:

- A newline character is read.

- The end of the file is encountered.

- `no_of_characters-1` is read.

You can use the *fgets( )* function, then, to read either sequential record fields in a file of variable length separated by newline characters or to read fixed-length record fields of `no_of_characters-1`.

We could read the file written in the previous section by using the following program:

```
#include <stdio.h>
#include <string.h>
main{
        FILE *param_file=NULL;
```

```
static char file_name[] = "PARAM.DAT";
static char ctitle[60+2];
static char pass[1+2];
static char password[40+2]="\n";

if (NULL != (param_file=fopen(file_name,"r")))
     {
     fgets(pass,80,param_file);
     printf("%s",pass);
     fgets(password,80,param_file);
     fgets(ctitle,sizeof(ctitle),param_file);
     printf("%s",password);
     printf("%s",ctitle);
     if (fclose(param_file) != NULL)
          {
          printf("Error on closing.\n");
          printf("Press any key to continue.\n");
          getche();
          exit(0);
          }
else {
     printf("Error on opening.\n");
     printf("Press any key to continue.\n");
     }
   }
}
```

The *fputs( )* function, like *fprintf( )*, does not copy the newline character or a null to the output device.

As with *fscanf( )*, you should always check the return value of *fgets( )*. If an error or end-of-file is reached, the return value will be null.

The *fgets( )* function is the preferred input function because it offers protection against the overflow of local stack space if the input string is too long.

In this book we have used *fgets( )* as the preferred input function. The reason is that *fgets( )*, unlike *gets( )*, monitors the length of the input line and ensures that there is no buffer overflow. The *gets( )* function, if reading an input character string that is too long, can overflow the allocated stack space and destroy local variables.

There is a trade-off, however. For the *fgets( )* function, the buffer must be padded by 2 bytes. For example, try the following:

```
#include <stdio.h>
main()
{
     char msg[10];

     printf("Enter a character string: ");
     fgets(msg,10,stdin);
```

```
        puts(msg);
        puts(msg);
}
```

If you are using QuickC, set up **msg** as a watch variable and single-step the program execution with F8. The output will look like:

```
Enter a character string: rose

rose

rose
```

After the *fgets( )* is executed, the **msg** buffer will look like:

```
"rose\n\0\0\0\0\0"
```

(The last 4 characters will be garbage.) In other words, you need 2 extra buffer characters: one for the newline, one for the null. The input stream is read up to and including the newline character (carriage return and line feed). For Turbo C or QuickC, the input string is padded by 2 bytes. Both a carriage return and a line feed are read. The last byte is converted to a null. Try this with a 5-byte buffer, and you will see that the \n is not in the **msg** buffer, since the last byte is converted to a null. Now try this using the *gets( )* function for input and notice the difference.

The *getc( )* and *putc( )* Functions

The *gets( )* and *putc( )* functions can be used for reading and writing characters.

The *getc( )* and *putc( )* functions are file versions of the single character I/O functions *getchar( )* and *putchar( )*. These functions work like their counterparts except that the file pointer is included. For example, to read one character from the **PARAM.DAT** file previously opened, you could use

```
ch = getc(param_file);
```

and to output you could use

```
putc(ch, param_file);
```

In fact, if you remember from earlier in this chapter, the *getchar( )* and *putchar( )* functions are defined in terms of *getc( )* and *putc( )*:

```
#define getchar() getc(stdin)
#define putchar(c) putc((c),stdout)
```

Always check the return value. If the end-of-file is reached, an EOF will be returned:

```
#include <stdio.h>
main()
{
        FILE *param_file=NULL;

        static char file_name[] = "PARAM.DAT";
        static char ctitle[60+2];
        static char pass[1+2];
        static char password[40+2]="\n";

        int ch; /* note ch is declared as int */

        if (NULL !=  (param_file=fopen(file_name,"r")))
            {
            fgets(pass,80,param_file);
            while (ch = getc(param_file) != EOF)
                  printf("%c",ch);
            fclose(param_file);
            }
        else
            puts("Error on opening");
}
```

In Turbo C and QuickC, the EOF value is −1.

Random Access

C supports random reads and writes in a file by using the *fseek( )* function to position the file pointer.

C permits you to randomly access a file, moving quickly to a specific record. Suppose, for example, that you have a file of addresses and that each address takes exactly 130 bytes. If Betty Adams is the 51st address in the file, you could use the *fseek( )* function to move directly to the first byte of the address. You would take the length of each address, multiply it by 51, and then move directly to that byte in the file by using *fseek( )*. This saves the time of having to read all of those first 50 addresses.

The *fseek( )* function takes the general form:

```
fseek(file_pointer, offset, mode)
```

Let's look at each of these arguments. The `file_pointer` argument is familiar, but what about the other two?

The `offset` argument tells the function how far to move in the file. It must be a *long* value and can be positive or negative. The `mode` argument tells from where the offset is measured and has the following values:

Mode	Measure from
0	Start of file
1	Current position in file
2	End of file

To find the 51st address in our file, we would use

```
fseek(param_file, (long) (51-1) * sizeof(address), 0);
```

The offset must be a *long* value. The file pointer points to the byte in the file where the next access will occur. The *fseek( )* function moves this pointer.

Tip | Whenever possible, use a mode value of 0. This ensures an absolute reference point for your positioning. The mode value of 1 should be avoided unless absolutely necessary, since the current file position may not be what you expect.

The *sprintf( )* Function

The *sprintf( )* function permits formatted writes to a character array.

There is one other buffered I/O function that is useful for creating records, the *sprintf( )* function. This function does not do any output or input, but it does permit the creation of a formatted text string. The output is sent to a buffer that you create, which can then be displayed, printed, or written to a file. Here is a simple program using the *sprintf( )* function:

```c
#include <stdio.h>
#define DELIM '~'
#define EOR '\n'
main()
{
        char name[40+1];
        char password[20+1];
        int len_record;
        char pass_rec[80+1];
        char access_level[9+1];

        printf("Please enter user's first name: ");
        gets(name);
        printf("Please enter password for this user: ");
        gets(password);
```

```
    printf("Please enter access level permitted: ");
    gets(access_level);
    len_record=sprintf(pass_rec,"%s%c%s%c%s%c",name,
        DELIM,password,DELIM,access_level,EOR);
    printf("%s %d",pass_rec,len_record);
}
```

Note | Input using the *gets( )* function can overflow the local stack space.

Here is a sample session with this program

```
Please enter the user's first name: bob        ←Enter
Please enter the password for this user: able  ←Enter
Please enter the access level permitted: 2      ←Enter
bob~able~2
11
```

The function creates a composite record from several fields. In this case **pass_rec** is created from **name**, **password**, and **access_level**. The fields can be a combination of various data types. Since the fields will be concatenated, it is up to the user to add any necessary delimiter (**DELIM**, or ~ in this case) to separate the fields. The string will be terminated with null characters, but you may choose to add some type of end-of-record character to mark the end. The function returns the number of characters in the record.

Standard C libraries do not provide any internal function to recover a specific field from records created with *sprintf( )*, but you can write your own function to do just that:

```
/* Routine to extract field from record */

#define DELIM ~
recfield(dest_string,sourc_string,field)
char dest_string[];
char sourc_string[];
int field;

{
    int dest,source;

    /* get to start of field */
    for (source = 0; --field && sourc_string[source] !=
        '\0';)
        {
        while (sourc_string[source] != '\0' &&
```

```
                          sourc_string[source] != DELIM) ++source;
                      if (sourc_string[source] == DELIM) ++source;
                      }

                /* copy from source to destination */
                for (dest = 0; sourc_string[source] !='\0' &&
                      scurc_string[source] != DELIM;
                      ++source, ++dest)
                      dest_string[dest] = sourc_string[source];
                dest_string[dest] = '\0';
                return;
         }
```

This function extracts the field number **field** from **sourc_string** and returns it with a null terminator as **dest_string**. The first field will be 1.

Binary Transfers

C supports binary writing and reading.

At times you may wish to save data in a file in binary form. In a nonbinary mode (the default), carriage-return–line-feed configurations are translated to a single line-feed input, and line-feed characters are translated to carriage-return–line-feed combinations on output. With nonbinary files a Ctrl-Z is used to mark the end of the file. When reading the file, reading terminates with Ctrl-Z. In a binary file the Ctrl-Z could be a part of the data, and reading would continue until the physical end of the file.

To use buffered binary transfers, append a "b" to the access type when opening the file. For example, to open a binary file for reading and writing, use:

```
fopen(file_name,"rb+")
```

Note | Avoid editing a binary file with a text editor. The results are unpredictable.

Low-Level I/O

Low-level I/O permits more control of the data transfer, but it leaves most of the buffering and error checking to

Sometimes you may wish to use low-level file transfers. Low-level, or unbuffered, data transfers permit more direct control of the data transfer and can be more efficient than high-level functions. In low-level transfers most of the buffering and error checking is done in the program itself, rather than in the library function.

routines written by the programmer.

As an example, assume that you have a mailing list file using random-file access. The file is opened in binary mode. Here is the program to create and list the file:

```c
#include <stdio.h>
#include <fcntl.h>
#define ERROR_MSG(x) printf("%s\7\n", x); exit(1)
#define QUERY(msg,reply) puts(msg); fgets(reply, 80, stdin)
#define TRUE 1
#define FALSE 0

main()
{
    int fh_address;
    int cmd;
    char *msg, *x, buffer[20];
    char reply[80];
    long address_no;
    struct address_rec
        {
        long num;
        int flag;
        char last[25+1];
        char first[25+1];
        char street[40+1];
        char city[20+1];
        char state[2+1];
        char zip[5+1];
        };
    struct  address_rec address;

    /* open the file in binary mode */
    if (-1==(fh_address=open("address.dat",O_RDWR |
        O_CREAT | O_BINARY )))
        ERROR_MSG("No file: address.dat");
    while (TRUE)
    {
    QUERY("Add or List? ",reply);
    cmd=reply[0];
    if (cmd !='a' && cmd !='l')
        {
        close(fh_address);
        return(0);
        }
    QUERY("Number: ",reply);
    address_no = atol(reply);
    printf("%dL",address_no * (long) sizeof (address));
```

```
            lseek(fh_address,(long) (address_no * (long) sizeof
                 (address)),0);
        if (cmd== 'a')
              {
              QUERY("Last name: ",address.last);
              QUERY("First name: ",address.first);
              QUERY("Address: ",address.street);
              QUERY("City: ", address.city);
              QUERY("State: ",address.state);
              QUERY("Zip: ",address.zip);
              write(fh_address,&address,sizeof address);
              }
        else if (cmd='l')
              {
              read(fh_address,&address, sizeof address);
                   {
                   puts(address.last);
                   puts(address.first);
                   puts(address.street);
                   puts(address.city);
                   puts(address.state);
                   puts(address.zip);
                   }
              }
        }
        return(0);
}
```

Notice that the file is opened with *open( )*. The record is located with *lseek( )*. Records are read with *read( )* and written with *write( )*. The file is closed with *close( )*. The argument definitions vary somewhat from the buffered access versions and can vary with the C implementation. Notice here that the *open( )* function uses the filename, not the pointer to the file. This program will work using Turbo C or QuickC.

To open a file in binary mode, the access code uses a masked template with bits that were set using previously defined codes. The bits are defined by **O_RDWR**, **O_CREATE**, and **O_BINARY**. The bits are ORed together. These definitions are defined in *fcntl.h*, so this file must be included. One of these bits sets the access for binary mode.

Here is an example of using unbuffered functions with a program buffer to create a password file:

```
/* Low-level I/O example */

#include <stdio.h>
#include <string.h>
#include <fcntl.h>
```

```
#define DELIM '~'
main()
{
      int param_file;
      static char file_name[] = "PARAM.DAT";
      char reply[80];
      char ctitle[60+1];
      char pass[1+1];
      static char password[40+1]="\n";
      char param_record[80];
      int cmd;
      int z, i, len_record;

      puts("Create or List Parameter File?");
      fgets(reply,80,stdin);
      cmd = reply[0];
      if (cmd != 'c' && cmd != 'l')
            return(0);
            if (cmd=='c')
                  {
                  printf("Create option\n");
                  puts("Enter Company Name: ");
                  gets(ctitle);
                  puts("PASSWORD CONTROL ON? (Y/N): ");
                  gets(pass);
                  if (stricmp(pass,"Y") == 0 )
                        {
                        puts("PASSWORD: ");
                        gets(password);
                        }
                  if(-1==(param_file=open("PARAM.DAT",O_RDWR
                        | O_CREAT | O_BINARY)))
                        {
                        puts("Error on opening file.\n");
                        puts("Press any key to continue\n");
                        getche();
                        exit(0);
                        }
                  len_record = sprintf(param_record,
                        "%s%c%s%c%s",
                        ctitle,DELIM,pass,DELIM,password);
                  if ((z = write(param_file,param_record,
                        80))==(-1))
                        {
                        puts("Error in writing to file.\n");
                        puts("Press any key to continue\n");
                        getche();
```

```
                                     exit(0);
                                     }
                        if (close(param_file) == (-1))
                                {
                                printf("Error on closing.\n");
                                puts("Press any key to continue\n");
                                getche();
                                exit(0);
                                }
                }
        }
        else if (cmd=='l')
                {
                if(-1==(param_file=open("PARAM.DAT",
                        O_RDONLY | O_BINARY)))
                                {
                                puts("Error on opening file.\n");
                                puts("Press any key to continue\n");
                                getche();
                                exit(0);
                                }
                if (z = read(param_file,param_record,80)
                        == (-1))
                                {
                                puts("Error in reading file\n");
                                puts("Press any key to continue\n");
                                getche();
                                exit(0);
                                }
                recfield(ctitle,param_record,1);
                puts(ctitle);
                recfield(pass,param_record,2);
                puts(pass);
                recfield(password,param_record,3);
                if (close(param_file) == (-1))
                                {
                                puts("Error on closing.\n");
                                puts("Press any key to continue\n");
                                getche();
                                exit(0);
                                }
                if (strcmp(pass,"Y") == 0 )
                                {
                                printf("Please enter password: ");
                                for (i=0; i<strlen(password); i++)
                                        {
                                        reply[i]=getch();
                                        putchar('*');
```

```
                    }
           if (strcmp(reply,password) != 0)
              {
              printf("\nIllegal
                     password\n");
              printf("Press any key to
                     continue\n");
              getche();
              }
           }
        }
    }
```

The listing for the *recfield( )* function was given earlier in this chapter. In this example, input data is concatenated with the *sprintf( )* function to a record and then written with a *write( )* function. The record is then read with the *read( )* function and the fields removed.

Note | Avoid mixing buffered and unbuffered I/O functions with the same open file.

Printing: Using Standard Devices

Printing is done by using the same C output functions to direct the output data stream to the standard printer device.

If you will examine the *stdio.h* file that came with C, you will find the *getchar( )* and *putchar(c)* functions defined as macros:

```
#define getchar() getc(stdin)
#define putchar(c) putc((c),stdout)
```

Notice from this that the *getchar( )* and *putchar(c)* functions are defined in terms of the *getc( )* and *putc( )* functions that reference *stdin* and *stdout* arguments. These arguments are defined in the same file to point to the keyboard and display, respectively. Notice in this same file that several other standard devices are defined:

Device Name	Description
stdin	Keyboard
stderr	Output device for error messages
stdaux	Auxiliary port
stdprn	Printer port

You might imagine, then, that you could define your own output printing function as

```
/* Printing routine */

#include <stdio.h>
#define prnchar(c) putc((c),stdprn)

main()
{
    int character;
    character = getchar();
    prnchar(character);
}
```

This new *prnchar( )* function works identically to *putchar( )*, except that the output goes to the printer. The program receives one input character from the keyboard and then prints the one character.

As you will see, this concept of standard devices gives the C language tremendous versatility. In BASIC, to change output from a display to a printer, you would need to change all the respective PRINT statements to LPRINT. In C, it is necessary only to change a single *#define* at the beginning of the program. You could test a program output on the display and then, when it is close to what you wish, switch it to the printer. You could also have the user queried for the desired output device and then select the proper function using an *if . . . else* structure.

Each of the standard devices has a buffer reserved by DOS. There are five standard devices. This means that the actual number of buffers available for file transfers is five less than the number specified in the CONFIG.SYS file. For example, if the CONFIG.SYS file specifies **BUFFERS=20**, a maximum of 15 files could be open at a time.

As you shall see later, there are also variations of the *puts( )* and *printf( )* functions that permit you to direct output to the printer. For example, you could output a string to the printer as

```
fputs("This is a test.\n\r",stdprn);
```

Before looking at these, however, let's see how the C language processes file input and output.

General Design Rules

This chapter has introduced you to the most common file I/O functions (table 12.1). However, you will find even more I/O functions in your library manual, such as *fwrite( )* and *fread( )*. All of these are useful, but try to be consistent with your program because mixing different types of buffered functions can add unnecessary length to your program.

Table 12.1 C Routines for File Operators

Operation	Nonbuffered Routine (low-level)	Buffered Routine (high-level)
Open a file	*open*	*fopen*
Close a file	*close*	*fclose*
		fcloseall
Read from a file	*read*	*fread*
		fgets
		fgetc
		fgetchar
		fscanf
Write to a file	*write*	*fwrite*
		fputs
		fputc
		fputchar
		fputf
Reposition file pointer	*lseek*	*fseek*
		rewind
Get file pointer position	*tell*	*ftell*

By writing your own functions for input, you will have more control than if you used the library C input functions.

As you gain experience, you will find that you want to write your own I/O functions. Most of the standard library functions have limited abilities. For example, here are some ideas for sample functions that you might wish to write:

- A function to accept as input a *Y*, *y*, *n*, or *N* (without a carriage return) and return an error code if any other value is entered.

- A function to accept input against a defined template that is passed to the function.

- A function to accept input between two specified values inclusively, with the range passed as arguments to the function. Any value outside of the range results in the function returning an error value.

The *getchar( )* and *putchar( )* functions permit a lot of flexibility in the design of such functions.

Here is a function to read an input string `text` of length `len` from `row, col` to a QuickC program. Although it uses a few graphics functions (which will be described in the next chapter), it does show how you can make good use of library functions to create your own input functions.

```
void get_reply(row,col,text,len)
COUNT row,col,len;
char *text;
{
      char buffer[80];
      COUNT ich, cont;

      /* copy to buffer & display current value */
      strcpy(buffer,text);
      for (ich = strlen(buffer); ich < len; ++ich)
            buffer[ich] = '_';
      buffer[ich] = '\0';
      _settextposition(row,col);
      _outtext(buffer);
      _settextposition(row,col);
      strcpy(buffer,text);
      /* read input value */
      for (ich=0, cont=TRUE; ich<len && cont;)
            {
            _displaycursor(_GCURSORON);
            buffer[ich] = getch();
            _displaycursor(_GCURSOROFF);
            buffer[ich+1] = '\0';
            switch(buffer[ich])
                  {
                  case '\x05': /* ^E, restart */
                        strcpy(buffer,text);
                        for (ich = 0; ich < len; ++ich)
                              buffer[ich] = '_';
                        _settextposition(row,col);
                        _outtext(buffer);
                        ich = 0;
                        buffer[ich] = text[ich] = '\0';
                        _settextposition(row,col);
                        break;
                  case '\r' : /* carriage return */
                  case '\n' : /* send default value back */
                        if (ich == 0 && text[0] != '\0')
                              {
                              strcpy(buffer,text);
                              cont = FALSE;
                              }
                        else
                              {
                              buffer[ich] = '\0';
                              cont = FALSE;
                              }
```

```
                                    break;
                          case '\b': /* backspace */
                                    buffer[ich] = '\0';
                                    if (ich > 0)
                                            {
                                            buffer[--ich] = '\0';
                                            _settextposition(row,col+ich);
                                            _outtext("_");
                                            _settextposition(row,col+ich);
                                            }
                                    break;
                          default : /* legal character */
                                    buffer[ich+1] ='\0';
                                    _outtext(&buffer[ich]);
                                    ich++;
                                    if (ich>len)
                                            cont = FALSE;
                                    break;
                                    }
                            }
                    strcpy(text,buffer);
                    ich = strlen(text);
                    _settextposition(row,ich+col);
                    for (; ich<len; ++ich)
                            _outtext("_");
                    return;
}
```

Review

This chapter has introduced the file I/O functions and described how to use them. It has covered the following important points:

1 | The three types of file transfer are character I/O, string I/O, and record I/O.

2 | The two basic I/O function groups are high-level and low-level. High-level functions are generally preferred, since they provide internal buffering and better error control.

3 | A file must be opened before it is used. After all reading or writing is completed, the file must be closed.

4 | High-level file reading and writing is done with the *fprintf( )*, *fscanf( )*, *fputs( )*, *fgets( )*, *getc( )*, and *putc( )* functions.

5 | The *fseek( )* function permits random access of a file.

6 | The *sprintf( )* function supports a formatted write to a buffer.

7 | Binary reading and writing is supported by using the "b" option when the file is opened.

8 | Low-level read and write functions permit unbuffered file access.

9 | Printing is done with any function that supports stream I/O (such as *fputs( )*) by naming the printer standard device.

Quiz for Chapter 12

1 | Which statement is not true?

    a | High-level I/O functions are more portable to other compilers than low-level I/O functions.

    b | In C programming, high-level functions are the preferred functions for file I/O in most applications.

    c | There are fewer high-level I/O functions than low-level I/O functions in most C libraries.

    d | High-level I/O functions provide more error checking than low-level I/O functions.

2 | Which *include* file is necessary for all high-level functions?

    a | *fcntl.h*

    b | *stdio.h*

    c | *string.h*

    d | None

3 | Which Turbo C *include* file(s) is necessary for most low-level functions?

    a | *stdio.h*

    b | *fcntl.h, io.h, sys\types.h, sys\stat.h, stdlib.h*

    c | *fcntl.h, io.h*

    d | None

4 | Rewrite the low-level I/O program example in this chapter to a high-level program example. How many extra bytes of memory does the executable file take in Turbo C or QuickC?

    a | Approximately 4.5K

    b | Approximately 1.2K

    c | None

    d | Approximately 9.4K

5 | What is wrong here?

```
#include <stdio.h>
main()
{
        FILE *fp;
        int x;
        fp = fopen("test","w");
        for (x = 0; x < 25; x++)
                fputs(fp,"This is a test");
        fclose("test");
}
```

    a | The *fputs( )* arguments should be reversed.

    b | The file should be closed with the file pointer, not the filename.

    c | Both a and b

    d | There is nothing wrong with the program.

6 | Which file defines the value of EOF and the structure for **FILE**?

    a | *fcntl.h*

    b | *stdio.h*

    c | *io.h*

    d | *sys/types.h*

7 | What is the value of EOF in Turbo C and QuickC?

    a | 1

    b | 0

    c | −1

    d | None of the above

8 | Which of the following is not a high-level I/O function?

    a | *fopen*

    b | *fwrite*

    c | *rewind*

    d | *read*

9 | Which of the following functions performs formatted input?

    a | *fscanf*

    b | *freadf*

    c | *fgetc*

    d | *fgetf*

10 | What value does the *fread( )* function return?

    a | The number of items read

    b | The value read

    c | There is no return value.

    d | An error value, or zero if there is no error

11 | What value does the *fopen( )* function return?

    a | A pointer to the open file

    b | A null value if an error is indicated

    c | There is no return value.

    d | a and b

12 | What value does the *fclose( )* function return?

    a | A zero to indicate a successful close, and an EOF if an error was encountered

    b | An EOF to indicate a successful close, and zero if an error was encountered

    c | An EOF to indicate a successful close, and −1 if an error was encountered

    d | There is no return value.

13 | In the following example, what argument is used in a subsequent *fclose( )* function?

```
FILE *in;

in = fopen("TEST.DAT","rb");
```
    a | "TEST.DAT"
    b | in
    c | Either of the above
    d | Neither of the above

14 | Which argument type is used to specify the place to seek in the *fseek( )* function?
    a | *int*
    b | *short*
    c | *long*
    d | *int, short,* or *long*
    e | *char*

15 | What is the preferred mode value for random access using *fseek( )*?
    a | −1
    b | 0
    c | 1
    d | 2

Chapter

13 | Using Graphics

About This Chapter

One of the outstanding features of modern C compilers is their ability to support color graphics and animation on computers having the proper monitor. This chapter will introduce the basic concepts of using graphics with C.

There are four methods of supporting graphics with Turbo C or QuickC (table 13.1):

You can use any of four methods to support graphics in C: ANSI driver, C graphics library, BIOS services, and direct input.

1 | **Using the ANSI driver** (often called text graphics). This method is very portable to other C compilers and hardware.

2 | **Using a special internal graphics library** provided with the compiler. Although not as portable, this method provides fast and extensive graphics support.

3 | **Using the BIOS services**. This method is portable to almost any compiler on the PC compatibles, but it is slow.

4 | **Writing the graphic image directly to the memory location** from which it is displayed. This is a fast method, but portability is very limited, even to other PC compatibles.

The first two methods, using text graphics and using an internal graphics library, are relatively simple and are described in this chapter. The

247

third and fourth methods are more complex and should be used only by advanced programmers; they are covered just briefly in this chapter.

Table 13.1 The Four Graphics Support Methods

Text Graphics	C Functions	BIOS Services	Direct
Very portable	Limited portability*	Very portable	Limited portability
Slow	Fast	Slow	Fast
Limited features	Extensive features	Extensive features	Extensive features
Easy to use	Easy to use	Complex	Complex
DOS compatible	DOS compatible	DOS compatible	Not DOS compatible**

*Portability implies the program can be compiled with a wide base of C compilers for execution on many operating systems.

**Not supported by Microsoft or IBM, and may fail in some DOS systems, multitasking modes, and future DOS versions.

Introduction to Graphics

MS-DOS supports any of 19 modes that are basically one of two types: text or graphics.

When you are writing to a video screen, you can choose from any of several modes. These modes are of two types: text and graphics. In a typical *text mode,* the screen displays text in 25 lines of cells in 80 rows, with each cell containing an ASCII character and an attribute (intensity, color, etc.). The display image is stored as 2 bytes per cell, with 1 byte containing the character to be displayed and the other the attribute of the displayed character. The coordinate system begins in the upper left of the screen at 1,1, and values are positive down and to the right. Both Turbo C and QuickC default to a text mode on starting. The lower right corner of the screen would be location 25, 80 (in row, column format).

In the *graphics mode* the screen displays data as *pixels*, or tiny dots. The number of horizontal and vertical pixels available on a particular display depends on the adapter card that is used (CGA, EGA, VGA, etc.). The coordinate system begins at the upper left of the screen, and values are positive down and to the right. The origin is 0,0, and the pixel in the lower right of an EGA screen would be at 639, 349 (in x, y format—the reverse of text format). Turbo C and QuickC both contain functions to select graphics modes.

The monochrome adapter defaults to mode 7; the EGA to mode 3.

A summary of the various graphics modes on PC, XT, AT, and PS/2 compatibles is shown in table 13.2. Notice that each mode has a resolution, a range of adapter support, and a certain number of colors available. The normal default mode for a monochrome monitor is 7. The

Table 13.2 Video Modes Available

	Mode	Rows	Cols	Boards	Character Resolution		Colors
Text Modes	0,1	25	40	CGA	8 × 8	320 × 200	16
				EGA	8 × 14	320 × 350	16/64
				MCGA	8 × 16	320 × 400	16/262K
				VGA	9 × 16	360 × 400	16/262K
	2,3	25	80	CGA	8 × 8	640 × 200	16
				EGA	8 × 14	640 × 350	16/64
				MCGA	8 × 16	640 × 400	16/262K
				VGA	9 × 16	720 × 400	16/262K
	7	25	80	MDA	9 × 14	720 × 350	Monochrome
				EGA	9 × 14	720 × 350	Monochrome
				VGA	9 × 16	720 × 400	Monochrome

	Mode	Resolution	Boards	Colors
Graphics Modes	4,5	320 × 200	CGA	4
			EGA	4/64
			MCGA	4/262K
			VGA	4/262K
	6	640 × 200	CGA	2
			EGA	2/64
			MCGA	2/262K
			VGA	2/262K
	13	320 × 200	EGA	16/64
			VGA	16/262K
	14	640 × 200	EGA	16/64
			VGA	16/262K
	15	640 × 350	EGA	Monochrome
			VGA	Monochrome
	16	640 × 350	EGA	16/64
			VGA	16/262K
	17	640 × 480	MCGA	2/262K
			VGA	2/262K
	18	640 × 480	VGA	16/262K
	19	320 × 200	MCGA	256/262K
			VGA	256/262K

normal default text mode for an EGA monitor is 3. Modes 15 and 16 support the Enhanced EGA adapter (see "Adapters" in a later section) with the ability to support 350 pixels vertically. These two modes require the use of an Enhanced Color Display that supports at least 350 lines.

Resolution

The higher the number of pixels, the better the resolution.

Graphic images on the screen are drawn with pixels. In a text mode the characters are sent to the screen as characters, but the monitor still converts each character to a pixel image. In general, the higher the number of pixels, the better the quality, or resolution, of the displayed image. The higher the number of horizontal or vertical pixels, the higher the amount of memory needed to store the image.

Color

Characters are displayed in a foreground color against a background color.

Characters and graphic images are displayed in a *foreground* color. The remainder of the screen is displayed in a *background* color. A single background color applies to the entire screen, whereas the foreground color can change by pixel (in graphics mode) or by cell (in text mode).

Some graphics modes permit the display of more foreground colors than others. The more colors that are available, the more memory required for the image. If the resolution is lower, you will have more colors available for the same amount of image memory.

Table 13.2 shows two foreground color numbers for many modes and adapters. In some modes a group of foreground colors can be stored as a palette, and you can choose a particular palette. At any given time, you have a single palette. For example, in mode 16 an EGA can display 64 colors, but only 16 at a time. You can choose any of four palettes and then choose from the 16 colors of that palette. The first figure shows the colors per palette; the second is the total number of colors available. The new VGA, for example, has a total of 262,144 colors available, but you can select only 256 at a time.

Adapters

The display adapter in your computer determines which modes are currently available for display.

The adapter in your computer system determines which modes are available for your programs. Table 13.3 shows the adapter standards currently available.

Many adapters will support multiple modes, often with automatic switching between modes. The monitor that you use with the adapter must support the desired mode. An analog monitor is required for MCGA and VGA modes. A digital monitor is required for all other modes.

Table 13.3 *Adapter Standards*

Adapter	Mode
Monochrome	Text modes only
Hercules	Text and high-resolution graphics modes in monochrome
CGA	Low-resolution color
EGA	High-resolution color
Extended EGA	Enhanced EGA (640 × 480 EGA)
MCGA	High-resolution with extended color support
VGA	High-resolution with extended color support

Paging

Some modes support the display of multiple pages.

Some modes (such as the EGA mode 13) support multiple pages. Images can be created on separate pages and the monitor switched quickly from one page to another. This is faster than redrawing an image on the same page and is a good alternative if you must switch between only a few images at a time and the mode support.

Note | In using multiple pages, make sure that there is adequate resolution at the mode you are using. More pages generally means less memory per page, or lower resolution per page.

Text Graphics: Using Graphics with the ANSI Driver

The simplest graphics method uses the ANSI driver supplied with MS-DOS to clear the screen and position the cursor.

One method of creating graphics is to use ANSI output commands. This is a screen-control standard defined by the American National Standards Institute and is supported by an IBM (or Microsoft) driver supplied with DOS called *ANSI.SYS*. To use this method, the ANSI driver must be installed as part of DOS by adding the following line in the CONFIG.SYS file:

```
device=ANSI.SYS
```

Once the ANSI driver is installed and the system booted with the new CONFIG.SYS file, you have effectively added a new option to your computer. The driver permits you to send commands to the display to clear it, control the cursor, and do other useful features.

This driver is also supported by IBM-compatible computers as well as by some computers that are not IBM-compatible, but the installation instructions may differ. Once installed, however, you can use the text graphics techniques of this section, and you can use these techniques with almost any C compiler as long as the display supports the ANSI standard.

How the Driver Works

The driver is essentially an extension of DOS that sits in memory and intercepts any output to the display. In monitoring the screen output, it is looking for special codes that identify commands for the ANSI driver. Once it finds one of these character groups, it removes them from the output character string and then acts on the command.

The commands are identified by a special 2-byte prefix code. The first byte is an escape character; the second is a left bracket. Following these 2 bytes are some bytes that identify the command itself, for example:

```
printf("\033[2J");
```

This command will clear the screen. The **\033** prefix is the escape character. The left bracket follows, and finally the **2J** that identifies the command (clear screen).

This same technique permits you to control the cursor. For example, to move the cursor to row 10 and column 15 you could use

```
printf("\033[%d;%dH",10,15);
```

To use these commands, the easiest method is to add the commands as an *include* file to your program. The following program is a graphics *include* file for an ANSI graphics driver.

```
#define CLR_SCREEN puts("\033[2J") /* clear screen */
#define CLR_LINE puts("\033[K") /* clear to end of line */
#define CUR_MOVE(r,c) printf("\033[%d;%dH",r,c) /* move to
    r, c */
#define CUR_UP(x) printf("\033[%dA",x) /* move cursor up x
    rows */
#define CUR_DOWN(x) printf("\033[%dB",x) /* move cursor down
    x rows */
#define CUR_RIGHT(x) printf("\033[%dC",x) /* move cursor
    right x spaces */
#define CUR_LEFT(x) printf("\033[%dD",x) /* move cursor left
    x spaces */
#define CUR_SAVE puts("\033[s") /* save cursor position */
#define CUR_RESTORE puts("\033[u") /* restore cursor
    position */
```

Using this file, you could execute the previous example as:

```
MOV_CURSOR(10,15);
```

Pros and Cons

Using text graphics offers the advantage of portability with hardware and C compilers, and is a good alternative if you need to do only simple graphics. Using text graphics does have some disadvantages, however. It is a slow method of generating graphics, frustratingly slow for most programs. For a quick clearing of the screen it is fine, but for drawing figures on a slower-type PC this method is not recommended. This method also requires the installation of the ANSI driver. Without the driver installed, the command codes will be displayed on the screen but the cursor will not do anything. Finally, graphics support is limited to that supplied by the ANSI driver, which is relatively weak.

The Extended Graphics Set

You can use the IBM extended character set with the ANSI driver to do text graphics.

For output and text graphics, IBM provides an extension to the standard ASCII codes. The computer represents symbols for display (characters) as numeric values in memory. The American Standard Code for Information Interchange (ASCII) defines which numbers are used for which characters. IBM extended this definition to include a wide variety of graphics characters. This extension is listed in appendix B. For example, to print the upper left corner of a double-line box you could use

```
printchar('╔');
```

or

```
puts("\xC9");
```

The ASCII code for this graphic is 201. To use the *printchar( )* function and enter the code from the keyboard (which doesn't have this graphics symbol) when creating your source program, use this procedure: put the keyboard in numeric mode, hold down the Alt key, and type 201 on the numeric keyboard. Release the Alt key (do not press Enter), and the graphic should be displayed in your program listing. Using the backslash form with *puts( )* eliminates this extra work.

These graphics are not always supported in IBM-compatible computers, and they may not print on your printer. They may not work with some C output routines. You may also discover that your editor will not support the entry of the Alt characters. The internal Turbo C and QuickC editors do support the entry of Alt characters.

An Example

Now let's look at a simple example showing how these codes are used:

```c
/* Procedure to draw a frame */

#include <stdio.h>
#define CUR_MOV(row,col) printf("\033[2J[%d;%dH",row, col)
#define CLR_SCREEN printf("\033[2J")
main()
{
        int lc,rc,tr,br,i;
        char *msg;

        msg = "MAILING LIST PROGRAM" ;

        /* find the coordinates for the frame */
        lc = ((80 - strlen(msg))/2 -3;
        rc = 80 - lc;
        tr = 8;
        br = 12;

        /* clear screen */
        CLR_SCREEN;

        /* output frame, then add message */
        frame(lc,rc,tr,br);
        CUR_MOV(tr+2,lc+4);
        printf("%s\n\n\n\n",msg);
        delay(1000);
}
frame(leftcol,rightcol,toprow,bottomrow)
int leftcol,rightcol;
int toprow,bottomrow;

{
        int vline, hline;

        /* display four corners */
        CUR_MOV(toprow,leftcol);
        puts("\xC9"); /* ASCII 201 */
        CUR_MOV(toprow,rightcol);
        puts("\xBB"); /* ASCII 187 */
        CUR_MOV(bottomrow,leftcol);
        puts("\xC8"); /* ASCII 200 */
        CUR_MOV(bottomrow,rightcol);
```

```
        puts("\xBC"); /* ASCII 188 */

        /* display vertical edges */
        for (vline=toprow+1;vline<=bottomrow-1;++vline) {
              CUR_MOV(vline,leftcol);
              puts("\xBA"); /* ASCII 186 */
              CUR_MOV(vline,rightcol);
              puts("\xBA");
        }

        /* display horizontal edges */
        for (hline=leftcol+1;hline<=rightcol-1;++hline) {
              CUR_MOV(toprow,hline);
              puts("\xCD"); /* ASCII 205 */
              CUR_MOV(bottomrow,hline);
              puts("\xCD"); /* ASCII 205 */
        }

}


/* DELAY function */
delay(n)
unsigned int n;
{
        unsigned int i,j;
        for (i=1; i<=n; ++i) {
              for (j=1; j <=n; ++j);
        }
}
```

This is a simple example that clears the screen and then puts a double-line frame around a message. You could use these routines in any program, and they are very portable. Try this program to get a feeling for the speed of this type of text graphics on your computer.

Using the Special C Graphics Functions

Both Turbo C and QuickC provide a library with an extensive list of graphics functions.

Both Turbo C and QuickC include a collection of text and graphics routines for doing everything from simply clearing the screen to animation. Turbo C supports CGA, EGA, VGA, and Hercules modes. QuickC supports all of these except the Hercules monitor. These modes are fast and efficient, and are the preferred method of graphics mode operations with C unless language portability is necessary. In addition, using the internal C graphics functions means that your program will work with whatever graphics video mode the user is using.

In both Turbo C and QuickC, the environmental compiler (QC with QuickC, TC with Turbo C), the source code, and the executable code all reside in memory together. The library for the graphics functions is too large to fit into memory with them. To use the Turbo C environmental compiler, you must specify the graphics library as a part of a project file. The graphics functions that are needed are then read from the graphics library on the disk at link time and do not have to share the memory space with the compiler.

Remember that in both cases the library functions are not portable; that is, the source program cannot be compiled on other compilers. The only exception is that all of the QuickC graphics functions can be compiled with the Microsoft version 5.0 (or higher) C compiler.

Note | Do not try to mix libraries between the two compilers. For example, the Turbo C graphics library is larger, but don't try to use it with QuickC to take advantage of QuickC's internal debugger. The graphics libraries are not portable to other compilers.

Introduction to the Graphics Routines

The graphics libraries with both Turbo C and QuickC have certain common characteristics: a setup routine, a closing routine, the use of a graphics *include* file, pixel addressing, and a logical coordinate system.

Setup and Closing Functions

With either compiler, you must set up the graphics environment before you can draw with the graphics functions. Once finished, you must restore the text mode.

The *setup( )* function must do two things: (1) set which video mode to use for the graphics and (2) get the data for that mode and store it in a data structure for program access. The data for the desired mode is stored in a global data structure and is accessible from your program as external variables. Sometimes, *setup( )* may set other default conditions, such as a fill color, origin, or the cursor display state (ON or OFF).

The *setup( )* routine is not provided with QuickC or Turbo C. You must write it yourself. Once you write the *setup( )* routine, you can save it and use it with each program you write that requires graphics.

The closing routine has as its primary purpose the resetting of the video to the default mode. The closing routine should be done just before exiting the program. It should be called on a normal exit or on any type of error exit.

To use the graphics functions with a QuickC or Turbo C program, you must follow a basic program structure (figure 13.1). There are three steps:

1 | Set up for graphics operation.

2 | Execute the body of your program.

3 | Restore the terminal to its default mode.

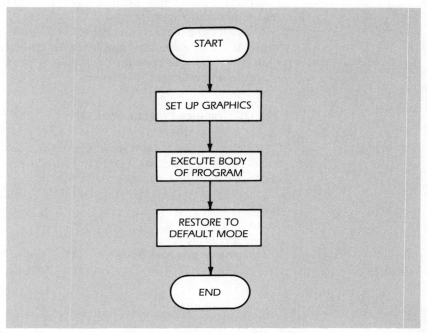

Figure 13.1 The structure of a C graphics program

The *include* File

In using the graphics functions, you must specify the *include* file that contains the defines, structures, and external variables for the graphics functions. For QuickC this file is *graph.h*; for Turbo C it is *graphics.h*.

Pixel Addressing and Coordinate Systems

The graphics functions always use pixel addressing.

Most of the graphics library functions for the graphics modes use pixel values as arguments. A pixel is the smallest available display unit on a screen. A typical EGA system uses a display of 640 pixels in each horizontal line and 350 pixels in each vertical line. For example, to go to the center of the EGA screen, you would specify location 319, 174 (the origin is 0, 0). Each point on the screen is identified by a unique set of coordinates.

QuickC and Turbo C support two coordinate systems: a physical and a logical. The concept of the logical coordinate system varies between the two compilers, and later examples will clarify this.

The QC Graphics

QuickC includes an internal library of over 40 graphics functions. The functions are fast and support EGA, VGA, and CGA modes. The Hercules mode is not supported.

With QuickC you can access the graphics library in either of two ways. You can use a program list with QuickC, or you can include a QuickC library that contains the graphics functions to be used with the /l option when QuickC is started.

The QC Graphics Program Structure

To use the graphics functions in QuickC, you must write two functions to add to your program. The first, *setup( )*, sets up your program. The second, *cleanup( )*, restores the terminal:

```
main()
{
     setup();
     <main program body>
     .
     :
     .

     cleanup();
}
```

Note | These functions are not supplied with QuickC. You must write them yourself, but once written they can be part of any graphics program that you write.

Now let's look at each function.

The *setup( )* Function

In its simplest form, you could write a *setup( )* function as

```
#include <graph.h>
struct videoconfig config;
void  setup()
{
     extern struct videoconfig config;
     _setvideomode(_ERESCOLOR);
     _getvideoconfig(&config);
}
```

Both _setvideomode() and _getvideoconfig are functions that are part of the QuickC graphics library. This setup routine switches the screen to high-resolution color (EGA) mode and then puts the information about this mode in a data structure named config.

If you haven't yet, take the time to print the *graph.h* file with QuickC and look at the data in it. You'll see the various arguments for _setvideomode() defined:

```
/* Arguments to _setvideomode() */
#define _DEFAULTMODE -1    /* restore to default mode */
#define _TEXTBW40     0     /* 40 x 25 text, 16 grey */
#define _TEXTC40      1     /* 40 x 25 text, 16/8 color */
#define _TEXTBW80     2     /* 80 x 25 text, 16 grey */
#define _TEXTC80      3     /* 80 x 25 text, 16/8 color */
#define _MRES4COLOR   4     /* 320 x 200, 4 color */
#define _MRESNOCOLOR  5     /* 320 x 200, 4 grey */
#define _HRESBW       6     /* 640 x 200, BW */
#define _TEXTMONO     7     /* 80 x 25 text, BW */
#define _MRES16COLOR  13 /* 320 x 200, 16 color */
#define _HRES16COLOR  14 /* 640 x 200, 16 color */
#define _ERESNOCOLOR  15 /* 640 x 350, BW */
#define _ERESCOLOR    16 /* 640 x 350, 4 or 16 color */
#define _VRES2COLOR   17 /* 640 x 480, BW */
#define _VRES16COLOR  18 /* 640 x 480, 16 color */
#define _MRES256COLOR 19 /* 320 x 200, 256 color */
```

Also in the *graph.h* file you will find the data structure videoconfig defined:

```
short far _setvideomode(short);
struct videoconfig
    {
    short numxpixels; /* number of pixels on X axis */
    short numypixels; /* number of pixels on Y axis */
    short numtextcols; /* number of text columns available
        */
    short numtextrows; /* number of text rows available */
    short numcolors; /* number of actual colors */
    short bitsperpixel; /* number of bits per pixel */
    short numvideopages; /* number of available video
        pages */
    };
```

This setup strategy in setting a mode permits the number of *x* and *y* pixels, as well as the number of rows and columns for that mode, to be available to your program as external variables.

Now let's improve our *setup( )* program by adding some default settings and permitting the function to be used with several modes:

The QuickC setup function that you write must set the desired video mode and provide the mode information to a data structure.

```c
#include <graph.h>
#include <stdio.h>
struct videoconfig config;
void  setup()
{
        extern struct videoconfig config;

        int set_mode(void);

        if (!set_mode())
                {
                printf("This video mode not supported.\n");
                exit(1);
                }
        _getvideoconfig(&config);
        _setcolor(5);
        _setlogorg(config.numxpixels / 2 - 1,
                config.numypixels / 2 - 1);

}
int set_mode()
{
        if(_setvideomode(_ERESCOLOR))
                return(_ERESCOLOR);
        if (_setvideomode(_HRES16COLOR))
                return(_HRES16COLOR);
        if (_setvideomode(_HRESBW))
                return(_HRESBW);
        else
                return(0);
}
```

This permits the program to scan, starting from the EGA mode, for a mode that the executing hardware will support. If no mode is found, the program exits with the message "This video mode is not supported." You can add to this set_mode() list as many options as you wish (including VGA), but the order is important. The scan should start at the highest resolutions (with color) first. Create a good copy of *setup( )* and use it with all your programs.

This *setup( )* routine also has two other statements that you may wish to use. The first, _setcolor(), sets the default fill color for closed objects such as rectangles and ellipses. The purpose of the second statement, _setlogorg(), will be discussed later in the section "The Coordinate Systems."

The *cleanup( )* Function

The *cleanup( )* function's primary purpose is to reset the video to the default mode. The function is very simple:

```
#include <graph.h>
struct videoconfig config;
void cleanup()
{
      _clearscreen(0);
      _setvideomode(_DEFAULTMODE);
}
```

This function clears the screen and resets the video to the mode it was in before the program started.

Writing Text

You can use the QuickC graphics routines to write text to a specified screen location.

You can use graphics routines to write text to the display. Use the two internal QuickC functions *_settextposition( )* and *_outtext( )*. The first function positions the cursor; the second writes the text at the cursor position. For example, to output a message on the last line of the screen, you could use

```
extern videoconfig config;
      .
      .
      .
_settextposition(config.numtextrows,1);
_outtext("Press <CR> to continue...");
```

You can also write your own function to output text at a specified position:

```
#include <graph.h>
#include <stdio.h>
int set_mode(void);
struct videoconfig config;
main()
{
      extern struct videoconfig config;

      void setup(void), cleanup(void);
      void graphout(char[],int,int);

      char msg[80];
```

```
        setup();
        strcpy(msg,"Press any key to continue");
        graphout(msg,config.numtextrows,1);
        getche();
        cleanup();

}
void graphout(msg,row,col)
char *msg[];
int row,col;
{
        extern struct videoconfig config;
        static char buffer[0]= '\0';

        _settextposition(row,col); /* set cursor position */
        strcpy(buffer,msg);
        _outtext(buffer); /* output the text */
}
```

The *_settextposition( )* function arguments refer to the actual row and column on the display, not to any pixel location values. You can, however, make this function mode independent by using the variables of the `config` structure and the technique of this example.

Notice also that the use of the *_outtext( )* routine does not affect the use of any input routines. Input routines, which support the keyboard, are not related to any graphics routines.

Physical and Logical Coordinate Systems

In the default mode, QuickC draws by using a physical coordinate system.

QuickC uses both a physical and a logical coordinate system. When the graphics mode is entered, the system assumes that the origin is in the upper left corner of the screen, and the coordinate values increase going down or to the right; that is, there are no negative coordinate values. This is the default coordinate system, and is referred to as the *physical coordinate system*.

The statement

```
_moveto(319,174);
```

moves the cursor to pixel row 174 and pixel column 319, the center of an EGA display. You can make this statement generic for any type of display supported by using

```
struct videoconfig.config;
_moveto(config.numxpixels/2-1,config.numypixels/2-1);
```

Tip | In using graphics functions, use the `config` variables as much as possible to keep your program independent of the display mode.

QuickC supports a logical coordinate system with an origin shifted from the physical coordinate system.

With the *logical coordinate system*, you can change the origin of your coordinate system to anywhere on the screen by using the *_setlogorg( )* function. You can then, for example, set the origin at the middle of the screen and have both positive and negative coordinate values. Here is an example in which the *setup( )* function has been modified to set the logical origin to the middle of the screen. As before, the program draws a line from the middle of the screen to the lower right:

```
#include <graph.h>
#include <stdio.h>
int set_mode(void);
struct videoconfig config;
main()
{
        extern struct videoconfig config;
        int color;
        void setup(void), cleanup(void);

        setup();
        _moveto(0,0);
        _lineto(config.numxpixels/2 - 1,config.numypixels/2 -
                1);
        getche();
        cleanup();

}
void   setup()
{
        extern struct videoconfig config;

        int set_mode(void)

        int xorigin, yorigin;

        if (!set_mode())
                {
                printf("This video mode not supported.\n");
                exit(1);
                }
        _getvideoconfig(&config);
        xorigin = config.numxpixels/2 - 1;
        yorigin = config.numypixels/2 - 1;
        _setlogorg(xorigin,yorigin);
```

```
}
int set_mode()
{
        if(_setvideomode(_ERESCOLOR))
                return(_ERESCOLOR);
        if (_setvideomode(_HRES16COLOR))
                return(_HRES16COLOR);
        if (_setvideomode(_HRESBW))
                return(_HRESBW);
        else
                return(0);
}
void cleanup()
{
        extern struct videoconfig config;
        _settextposition(config.numtextrows, 1);
        _outtext("Hit <CR> to continue...");
        getchar();
        _clearscreen(0);
        _setvideomode(_DEFAULTMODE);
}
```

Setting the Color

You can set the foreground color in QuickC with the _setcolor( ) function. Text color is set with the _settextcolor( ) function.

The colors of shapes, pixels, and lines drawn with the graphics functions are set with the _setcolor( ) function. For example,

```
_setcolor(1);
_moveto(0,0);
_lineto(config.numxpixels/2 - 1,config.numypixels/2 - 1);
```

on the EGA screen draws the line as dark blue. You will find an example of setting colors for shapes in the section "Drawing Shapes." Note that the _setcolor( ) function also sets the foreground color for pixels. Table 13.4 shows the actual color codes for an EGA display.

> **Tip** | Use the _setcolor( ) function in your setup( ) function to set a default color for your graphics. If a default is not set, the default color will be bright white.

Using the _settextcolor( ) function, you can set the colors for any text displayed with the _outtext( ) function:

```
_settextcolor(1);
_outtext("This will be in dark blue.");
```

Table 13.4 EGA Color Codes

Code	Color	Code	Color
0	black	8	dark gray
1	dark blue	9	light blue
2	green	10	light green
3	cyan	11	light cyan
4	red	12	light red
5	magenta	13	light magenta
6	brown	14	yellow
7	light gray	15	bright white

Controlling the Cursor Display

The cursor display can be turned off or on.

Use QuickC's internal _*displaycursor( )* function to turn the cursor display on or off. In the default mode, the cursor will be off:

```
_settextposition(15,1);
_outtext("Continue? ");
_settextposition(15,11);
_displaycursor(_GCURSORON);
in = getche();
_displaycursor(_GCURSOROFF);
```

The **_GCURSORON** and **_GCURSOROFF** argument values are defined in *graphic.h*.

Drawing Lines

In the previous examples a line was drawn with QuickC. The _*moveto( )* function is used to move the cursor to the starting position; then the _*lineto( )* function is used to draw the actual line.

The type of line is determined by the _*setlinestyle( )* function. The general form is

```
_setlinestyle(mask)
```

where **mask** is a 16-bit template used to determine the pixel pattern of the line. The default mask is **0xFFFF**, which displays a solid line. To set up a dashed line, for example, the mask would be **0xAAAA** and the statement would be

```
_setlinestyle(0xAAAA);
```

Drawing Shapes

QuickC has an extensive library for drawing lines and shapes.

You can use graphics functions to create shapes. Here is a list of the available functions and the corresponding shape drawn by each.

Function	Shape
_rectangle( )	rectangle
_ellipse( )	ellipse
_arc( )	arc
_pie( )	pie

As an example, let's write a program to draw a rectangle. The general form of the _rectangle function is

```
_rectangle(control,x1,y1,x2,y2)
```

where,

control	= The fill flag
x1,y1	= Upper left corner in pixel coordinates
x2,y2	= Lower right corner in pixel coordinates

For control, you can use either of the following, which are defined in graph.h:

_GFILLINTERIOR	Fill rectangle with current color from last _setcolor( ).
_GBORDER	Do not fill rectangle.

The rectangle is drawn with the current line style.

Let's draw a rectangle that covers the center fourth of the screen in dark green:

```
#include <graph.h>
#include <stdio.h>
#define GREEN 2;
int set_mode(void);
struct videoconfig config;
main()
{
    extern struct videoconfig config;

    void setup(void), cleanup(void);
```

```
     setup();

     /* set color to green */
     _setcolor(GREEN);
     xorigin = config.numxpixels/2 - 1;
     yorigin = config.numypixels/2 - 1;

     /* set logical coordinates */
     _setlogorg(xorigin,yorigin);

     /* draw rectangle and fill */
     _rectangle(_GFILLINTERIOR,-xorigin/2,-yorigin/2,
          xorigin/2, yorigin/2);
     _settextposition(config.numtextrows,1);
     getche();
     cleanup();
}
```

If the first argument of _rectangle() is changed to _GBORDER, the rectangle will have a solid green border with an interior that is the same as the background.

To draw rectangles in various colors, the entire program becomes

```
#include <graph.h>
#include <stdio.h>
#define TRUE 1
int set_mode(void);
struct videoconfig config;
main()
{
     extern struct videoconfig config;

     void setup(void), cleanup(void);

     int no;
     char noa[9];

     setup();
     do   {
          _clearscreen(0);
          _settextposition(1,1);
          _outtext("Please enter a color number: ");
          fgets(noa,9,stdin);
          no = atoi(noa);
          _setcolor(no);
          _settextcolor(no);
          x = config.numxpixels / 2 - 1;
```

```
                    y = config.numypixels / 2 - 1;
                    _rectangle(_GFILLINTERIOR,-x/2,-y/2,x/2, y/2);
                    _settextposition(config.numtextrows,1);
                    _outtext("Press any key to continue");
                    getche();
               } while (no > 0);
          cleanup();


}
void  setup()
{
     extern struct videoconfig config;
     int set_mode();

     if (!set_mode())
               {
               printf("This video mode not supported.\n");
               exit(0);
               }
     _getvideoconfig(&config);
     _setcolor(5);
     _setlogorg(config.numxpixels / 2 - 1,
               config.numypixels / 2 - 1);


}
int set_mode()
{
     if (_setvideomode(_VRESCOLOR))
          return(_VRESCOLOR);
     if(_setvideomode(_ERESCOLOR))
          return(_ERESCOLOR);
     if (_setvideomode(_HRES16COLOR))
          return(_HRES16COLOR);
     if (_setvideomode(_HRESBW))
          return(_HRESBW);
     else
          return(0);
}
void cleanup()
{
     extern struct videoconfig config;
     _settextposition(config.numtextrows, 1);
     _outtext("Hit <CR> to continue...");
     getchar();
     _clearscreen(0);
     _setvideomode(_DEFAULTMODE);
}
```

The Turbo C Graphics

Turbo C provides over 70 functions for graphics support. The following sections will explain the basic concepts of Turbo C graphics programming and illustrate the use of particular functions.

Display Modes

Using Turbo C functions, you can set your screen to either a text or a graphics mode. In the text mode, output is to a rectangular area on the display screen called a *window*. In the graphics mode, output is to a portion of the window called a *viewport*.

In text mode Turbo C permits you to define a logical window of a specified size on the display.

In text mode the window defaults to the entire screen. You can use the *window( )* function to define a smaller window:

```
window(left,top,right,bottom)
```

The first two arguments define the upper left corner of the window; the second two define the lower right corner. The upper left of the window is considered the origin for text output.

In graphics mode the viewport is set with the *setviewport( )* function:

```
setviewport(left,top,right,bottom,OFF);
```

where the first two coordinates specify the upper left corner of the viewport and the second two the lower right corner. The last argument controls the clip flag, which will be explained later.

The viewport acts as a virtual screen for output, and the rest of the window is untouched. The logical origin is 0,0 in the upper left corner of the viewport, and values increase down and to the right. The default viewport is the entire window. Coordinates are always relative to the viewport origin.

Setting Up for Graphics

Turbo C permits you to set a particular graphics mode or to default to a graphics mode supported by your display adapter.

As with QuickC, you must set up for graphics mode and then restore the system before exiting the program. For Turbo C the general program is

```
#include <graphics.h>

struct videoconfig
    {
    int       GraphicDriver;
    int       GraphMode;
```

```
        int         MaxX, MaxY;
        int         MaxColors;
        double      AspectRatio;
        struct      palettetype palette;
        };
struct videoconfig config;

main()
{

    void setup(void);

    setup();
    .
    .
    .
    closegraph();
}

void setup()
{
    extern struct videoconfig config;

    int ErrorCode, xasp, yasp;

    config.GraphicDriver = DETECT; /* auto-detect mode */
    initgraph(&config.GraphicDriver,&config.GraphMode,"
        ");
    ErrorCode = graphresult();
    if (ErrorCode != grOk)
        {
        printf(" Graphic Initialize Error: %s\n",
            grapherrormsg(ErrorCode));
        exit(1);
        }
    config.MaxX = getmaxx();
    config.MaxY = getmaxy(); /* get screen size for this
        mode */
    config.MaxColors = getmaxcolor()+1; /* get max # of
        colors */
    getpalette(&config.palette);
    getaspectratio( &xasp, &yasp);
    config.AspectRatio = (double) xasp / (double) yasp;
    return;
}
```

Notice that *setup( )* uses the *initgraph( )* function to initialize for a

With Turbo C you must define your own structure for holding information about the current graphics mode.

graphics mode. In this example an auto-detect is specified, and *initgraph( )* calls the Turbo C *detectgraph( )* function to automatically select a graphics driver and mode. Then the *initgraph( )* function sets the mode and loads the proper graphics driver from disk. The *initgraph( )* function also resets all the graphics settings (position, color, palette, viewport, etc.) to their default values. Setting `config.GraphicDriver` to `DETECT` (0) requests an auto-detect mode. To force a graphics mode, use the following values for `config.GraphicDriver`:

CGA	1
MCGA	2
EGA	3
EGA64	4
EGAMONO	5
RESERVED	6
HERCMONO	7
ATT400	8
VGA	9
PC3270	10

As with QuickC, a structure should be set up to hold the global data pertaining to the graphics mode. Unlike a QuickC structure, this structure should be part of your program and is not part of the graphics *include* file. The *setup( )* routine should read the configuration data and store it to the structure.

You do not need to write any special closing routine, since you need only call the graphics function *closegraph( )* to restore the system.

Physical and Logical Coordinate Systems

The physical *window* is defined by the coordinates of the current screen mode. For example, with a monochrome monitor the window is 80 units wide and 25 units high. For an EGA system the physical window is 640 units wide and 350 units high.

Turbo C permits you to define a logical viewport for writing the output.

The actual graphics output, however, is to only a portion of this window. This portion is called the *viewport*. As an example, look at the following program:

```
main()
{

        struct viewporttype viewinfo;
        int h, w;
        void setup(void);
```

```
void changetextstyle(int, int, int);

setup();
getviewsettings(&viewinfo);
h = (viewinfo.bottom - viewinfo.top)/2;
w = (viewinfo.right - viewinfo.left)/2;
setviewport(w,h,viewinfo.right,viewinfo.bottom,OFF);
getviewsettings(&viewinfo);
closegraph();
}
```

This example sets the origin at the middle of the screen, at location 0,0. The *getviewsettings( )* function retrieves information about the current viewport (the *viewinfo* structure is part of *graphics.h*). The *setviewport( )* function sets the viewport to the right lower quarter of the screen. The arguments define the four corners of the new viewport as

```
setviewport(left,top,right,bottom,clipflag)
```

The last argument defines whether any image outside of the viewport is clipped. If ON, text written by the *outtext( )* and *outtextxy( )* functions is truncated at the viewport boundaries. If OFF, bit-mapped output is thrown away if any part extends beyond the viewport, and stroked output is truncated at the viewport boundary.

Writing Text

In text mode the following functions support text output support. These are part of the normal C library and are portable to other compilers:

Function	Purpose
cprintf( )	Write formatted output to screen
cputs( )	Write string output to screen
putch( )	Write a single character to the screen

Here is an example with the *cprintf( )* function:

```
    .
    .
    .
fgets(name,80,stdin);
cprintf("The name is ", name);
    .
    .
    .
```

In addition, here is a partial list of available cursor, screen, and text control functions for text modes:

Function	Purpose
clrscr( )	Clear screen
gotoxy( )	Position cursor
textcolor( )	Set foreground color
textbackground( )	Set background color
textattr( )	Set text attributes
textmode( )	Set screen to text mode
window( )	Define logical window
highvideo( )	Set text to high intensity
lowvideo( )	Set text to low intensity
normvideo( )	Set text to normal intensity

In the graphics mode, text can be written in several fonts and styles.

With graphics modes, Turbo C provides several internal text fonts and font sizes for greater flexibility in text output. As an example, here is a text output program (the *setup( )* routine is the same as in previous examples):

```
#include <graphics.h>

struct videoconfig
    {
    int     GraphicDriver;
    int     GraphMode;
    int     MaxX, MaxY;
    int     MaxColors;
    double  AspectRatio;
    struct  palettetype palette;
    };
struct videoconfig config;

main()
{

    struct viewporttype viewinfo;
    int h, w;
    void setup(void);
    void changetextstyle(int, int, int);
    int gprintf(int *w, int *h, char *fmt);

    setup();
    getviewsettings(&viewinfo);
```

```
        changetextstyle(TRIPLEX_FONT,HORIZ_DIR, 3);
        settextjustify(CENTER_TEXT,CENTER_TEXT);
        h = (viewinfo.bottom - viewinfo.top)/2;
        w = (viewinfo.right - viewinfo.left)/2;
        gprintf(&w, &h, "The best way to predict the");
        gprintf("future is to invent it.");
        changetextstyle(DEFAULT_FONT,HORIZ_DIR,1);
        gprintf(&w, &h, "Alan Kay");
        getche();
        closegraph();
}


/* utility routine to change text style */
void changetextstyle(font, direction, charsize)
int font, direction, charsize;
{
        int ErrorCode;

        graphresult(); /* clear all error codes */
        settextstyle(font, direction, charsize);
        ErrorCode = graphresult();
        if (ErrorCode != grOk)
                {
                closegraph();
                printf("Graphic font loading error: %s\n",
                        grapherrormsg(ErrorCode));
                exit(1);
                }
        return;
}


/* utility routine for formatted graphics output */
int gprintf(int *xloc, int *yloc, char *fmt)
{
        char str[160]; /* buffer for string */
        int no;

        strcpy(str,fmt); /* put string to buffer */
        outtextxy(*xloc, *yloc, str); /* output the text */
        *yloc += textheight("X") + 2; /* bump to next line */
        return;
}
```

In the preceding example the actual output text was written with a
gprint( ) function, which is supplied by the user. The general form is

```
gprintf(x_origin, y_origin, text string)
```

The text style is set by using the Turbo C *changetextstyle( )* function with the following form:

```
changetextstyle(font, direction, charsize)
```

where *font* has these permissible values:

Font Name	Description	Value
DEFAULT_FONT	8 × 8 bit-mapped font	0
TRIPLEX_FONT	Stroked triplex font	1
SMALL_FONT	Stroked small font	2
SANSSERIF_FONT	Stroked sanserif font	3
GOTHIC_FONT	Stroked gothic font	4

and *direction* has these permissible values:

Direction	Description	Value
HORIZ_DIR	Left to right	0
VERT_DIR	Bottom to top	1
LEFT_TEXT	Horizontal	0
CENTER_TEXT	Horizontal and vertical	1
RIGHT_TEXT	Horizontal	2
BOTTOM_TEXT	Vertical	0
TOP_TEXT	Vertical	2

The `charsize` value is a multiplier for the 8 × 8 pixel display. A value of 1 is normal; that is, an 8 × 8 font is mapped to an 8 × 8 pixel value on the screen.

The Turbo C *settextjustify( )* function sets the horizontal and vertical justification. In this case both are centered, so the first line of text will be centered horizontally and vertically.

Setting Colors

The foreground color of graphic objects is defined with the *setcolor( )* function.

The colors of graphic objects can be defined with the *setcolor( )* function. The values for the colors are the same as for the corresponding QuickC function (see table 13.4).

```
main()
{
    :
    :
    setcolor(RED);
```

:
:

}

You can set the background color by using the *setbkcolor( )* function.

Note | The *defines* for the color definitions are in the *graphics.h* file. With Turbo C, you do not need to define them yourself.

Drawing Lines

Turbo C provides the two line-drawing functions *line( )* and *lineto( )*. The function *line(x1,y1,x2,y2)* draws a line from *x1,y1* to *x2,y2*; the function *lineto(x,y)* draws a line from the current position to *x,y*.

In the following example the viewport is set to the lower right quarter of the screen, and the line is drawn from the upper left to the lower right of the viewport.

```
#include <graphics.h>

struct videoconfig
      {
      int         GraphicDriver;
      int         GraphMode;
      int         MaxX, MaxY;
      int         MaxColors;
      double      AspectRatio;
      struct      palettetype palette;
      };
struct videoconfig config;

main()
{

      void setup(void);
      void changetextstyle(int, int, int);

      struct viewporttype viewinfo;
      int h, w;

      setup();
      getviewsettings(&viewinfo);
      changetextstyle(TRIPLEX_FONT,HORIZ_DIR, 3);
      settextjustify(CENTER_TEXT,CENTER_TEXT);
      h = (viewinfo.bottom - viewinfo.top)/2;
      w = (viewinfo.right - viewinfo.left)/2;
```

```
        setcolor(RED);
        setviewport(w,h,viewinfo.right,viewinfo.bottom,1);
        getviewsettings(&viewinfo);
        line(0,0, viewinfo.right, viewinfo.bottom);
        getche();
        closegraph();
}
void setup()
{
        extern struct videoconfig config;

        int ErrorCode, xasp, yasp;

        config.GraphicDriver = DETECT; /* auto-detect mode */
        initgraph(&config.GraphicDriver,&config.GraphMode,"
                ");
        ErrorCode = graphresult();
        if (ErrorCode != grOk)
                {
                printf("Graphic Initialize Error: %s\n",
                        grapherrormsg(ErrorCode));
                exit(1);
                }
        config.MaxX = getmaxx();
        config.MaxY = getmaxy(); /* get screen size for this
                mode */
        config.MaxColors = getmaxcolor()+1; /* get max # of
                colors */
        getpalette(&config.palette);
        getaspectratio( &xasp, &yasp);
        config.AspectRatio = (double) xasp / (double) yasp;
        return;
}


/* utility routine to change text style */
void changetextstyle(font, direction, charsize)
int font, direction, charsize;
{
        int ErrorCode;

        graphresult(); /* clear all error codes */
        settextstyle(font, direction, charsize);
        ErrorCode = graphresult();
        if (ErrorCode != grOk)
                {
                closegraph();
                printf("Graphic font loading error: %s\n",
```

```
                    grapherrormsg(ErrorCode));
            exit(1);
            }
        return;
}
```

Drawing Objects

Lines and shapes can be drawn with functions in the Turbo C graphics library.

Turbo C provides a large number of functions for drawing circles, rectangles, arcs, and other shapes. Here are a few of them:

Function	Shape
arc( )	Arc
circle( )	Circle
drawpoly( )	Polygon
ellipse( )	Ellipse
rectangle( )	Rectangle

The following functions draw *filled* objects:

Function	Shape
bar( )	Filled rectangle
bar3d( )	Three-dimensional bar
fillpoly( )	Filled polygon
pieslice( )	Filled pie slice

The next program draws a blue rectangular frame on the screen:

```
/* RECT.C - draws a rectangular frame */

#include <graphics.h>

struct videoconfig
    {
    int        GraphicDriver;
    int        GraphMode;
    int        MaxX, MaxY;
    int        MaxColors;
    double     AspectRatio;
    struct     palettetype palette;
    };
struct videoconfig config;

main()
```

```
{

      int left,top,right,bottom;

      void setup(void);

      setup();
      left = config.MaxX/4;
      top = config.MaxY/4;
      right = config.MaxX - config.MaxX/4;
      bottom = config.MaxY - config.MaxY/4;
      setcolor(BLUE);
      rectangle(left, top, right, bottom);
      getche();
      closegraph();
}
```

The function arguments define the four corners of the rectangle. The left edge of the rectangle is one-fourth of the screen from the left edge. The top edge is one-fourth of the distance from the top of the screen.

Similarly, the *bar( )* function draws a filled rectangle of the current fill pattern:

```
/* BAR.C - draws a rectangular filled frame */

#include <graphics.h>

struct videoconfig
      {
      int         GraphicDriver;
      int         GraphMode;
      int         MaxX, MaxY;
      int         MaxColors;
      double      AspectRatio;
      struct      palettetype palette;
      };
struct videoconfig config;

main()
{

      int left,top,right,bottom;

      void setup(void);

      setup();
      left = config.MaxX/4;
```

```
        top = config.MaxY/4;
        right = config.MaxX - config.MaxX/4;
        bottom = config.MaxY - config.MaxY/4;
        setcolor(BLUE);
        bar(left, top, right, bottom);
        getche();
        closegraph();
}
```

The fill pattern can be changed with the Turbo C *setfillpattern( )* function. The general form is

```
setfillpattern(upattern,color)
```

where the *upattern* values are the following:

Pattern	Description	Value
EMPTY_FILL	Fill with background color	0
SOLID_FILL	Solid fill	1
LINE_FILL	Fill with ————	2
LTSLASH_FILL	Fill with ////	3
SLASH_FILL	Fill with //// (thick)	4
BKSLASH_FILL	Fill with \\\\	5
LTBKSLASH_FILL	Fill with \\\\ (thick)	6
HATCH_FILL	Fill with light hatch	7
XHATCH_FILL	Fill with heavy hatch	8
INTERLEAVE_FILL	Fill with interleaving lines	9
WIDEDOT_FILL	Wide dot fill	10
CLOSEDOT_FILL	Close dot fill	11
USER_FILL	User-defined fill	12

With Turbo C you can also make 3-D objects. The following program creates a 3-D rectangle on the screen. The outline will be in dark blue, and the fill is red:

```
/* BAR3D.C - draws a 3-D rectangle */

#include <graphics.h>

struct videoconfig
        {
        int        GraphicDriver;
        int        GraphMode;
```

```
          int         MaxX, MaxY;
          int         MaxColors;
          double      AspectRatio;
          struct      palettetype palette;
          };
struct videoconfig config;

main()
{

     int left,top,right,bottom;

     void setup(void);

     setup();
     left = config.MaxX/4;
     top = config.MaxY/4;
     right = config.MaxX - config.MaxX/4;
     bottom = config.MaxY - config.MaxY/4;
     setcolor(BLUE);
     setfillstyle(SOLID_FILL,RED);
     bar3d(left, top, right, bottom,(right-left)/4,1);
     getche();
     closegraph();
}
```

The *bar3d( )* function has two additional arguments. The fifth argument defines the depth of the projection in pixels, and the last argument defines whether the top of the rectangle is also projected. The normal depth is one-fourth of the width of the box.

Controlling the Cursor Display

Turbo C contains no functions for turning the cursor display on and off.

Turbo C, unlike QuickC, contains no functions for controlling the cursor display. Turbo C does, however, support a pseudo-assembly code. The following program is written in assembly code and will control the cursor display:

```
(c) 1988 by Michael Maurice
#include <stdio.h>
#include <dos.h> /* needed for "geninterrupt" */

#if 0 /* a little documentation */
CurOnOff passed argument:
OFF = 0, ON != 0      Written 2-2-1988
#endif
```

```
void
CurOnOff(int arg) /* the cursor on-off routine */
{
        _BX = arg; /* save the argument for later */
        _AH = 0x03; /* get cursor location, shape */
      geninterrupt(0x10); /* video interrupt */
                                /* on return */
                        /* info in DX is not needed */
                        /* CX contains info to be used */
    if (_BX != 0)      /* turn -- ON -- */
    {
      _CH &= 0xDF; /* be sure bit 5 off */
    } else { /* turn -- OFF -- */
      _CH &= 0x0F; /* clear top 4 bits */
      _CH |= 0x20; /* turn on 5 bit */
    }
    _AH = 0x01; /* set cursor shape */
    geninterrupt(0x10); /* video interrupt */
}

main() /* a test program */
{
      CurOnOff(0); getch(); /* turn off */
      CurOnOff(1); getch(); /* turn on */
      CurOnOff(0); getch(); /* turn off */
      CurOnOff(1); return; /* leave on, back to DOS */
}
```

Other Graphics Methods

You can draw graphics by using the *int86( )* function in the BIOS services, or you can write directly to the memory locations containing the graphic image to be displayed.

Besides the two graphics methods already discussed (text graphics and an internal graphics library), there are two more methods of creating graphics: the *int86( )* function and the direct mode.

Using the *int86( )* Function

You can use the *int86( )* function to create graphics. The *int86( )* function permits you to load values directly to registers and then activate a software interrupt. Like any method involving the BIOS services, it is slow. It does, however, provide far more flexibility than the ANSI driver and has good portability to other C compilers. Some examples using this technique can be found in *Advanced C Primer++* by Stephen Prata (Howard W. Sams, 1986). The next chapter will also look briefly at the *int86( )* function.

Direct Mode

The fourth method for graphics is to write the image directly to the memory location from which it is displayed. (On the PC, XT, AT, and PS/2, the video image displayed on the monitor is not stored in the monitor but in a reserved portion of memory above the 640K that programs and data normally use.) Text images are stored starting at location A0000, and graphic images starting at B0000. The amount of memory required depends on the mode. The trick for direct mode and fast displays (which is method four) is to write the image directly to that memory area, which bypasses the BIOS services. It is then available for display immediately. This method will work on most DOS systems, but it is not supported by the DOS developers (Microsoft and IBM). Programs using this type of I/O will not work properly under multitasking systems such as Windows or OS/2. Some examples using this method can be found in *Turbo C Programming for the IBM* by Robert Lafore (Howard W. Sams, 1987).

Review

This chapter has introduced the four methods of supporting graphics with Turbo C or QuickC. It has presented the basics of text and graphics modes and the differences between the modes. It has provided you with opportunities for extensive experience with the graphics functions supplied with your Turbo C or QuickC (or perhaps both).

Quiz for Chapter 13

1 | The resolution of a graphics mode refers to:
    a | The number of pixels per byte of storage
    b | The clarity of the displayed image
    c | The number of colors per pixel
    d | The number of pixels in the display

2 | Which of the following graphics modes has the highest color resolution?
    a | Monochrome
    b | CGA
    c | EGA
    d | Hercules

3 | What are the two easiest methods to use for graphics output?
    a | Direct, graphics functions
    b | Text graphics, direct
    c | Text graphics, graphics functions
    d | Graphics functions, direct

4 | How many colors can an EGA display at one time:
    a | 64
    b | 16
    c | 8
    d | 2

5 | How many text modes are available on an IBM PC compatible?
    a | 3
    b | 4
    c | 5
    d | 1

6 | Where is the default origin for a graphics display?
    a | Center of the screen
    b | 0, 0
    c | 1, 1
    d | Lower left of the screen

7 | What is the total number of pixels on an EGA screen?
    a | 640
    b | 350
    c | 224,000
    d | 64,000

8 | What must be installed to use text graphics?
    a | ASCII.SYS
    b | ANSI.SYS
    c | The graphics library
    d | DOS 3.1 or later version

9 | When using graphics functions, where is the variable data for the current mode stored?
   a | In a data structure
   b | In an array
   c | In the function using the data as local variables
   d | In the data segment

10 | What should always be done before returning from the program?
   a | Clear the screen.
   b | Set the screen to text mode.
   c | Display a prompt and wait for user input.
   d | Restore the screen to the default mode.

11 | Why should you use the `videoconfig` variables (such as `numtext-row`) in your program as much as possible instead of your own variables?
   a | To make the program portable with other compilers
   b | To minimize memory space requirements
   c | To keep your program independent of the mode type of the system
   d | To improve the readability of the program

12 | The color of the text on the screen is
   a | The background color
   b | The foreground color
   c | Always white
   d | The default text color

13 | Where are the color definitions kept?
   a | As *defines* in a QuickC program, and in the *graphics.h* file of a Turbo C program
   b | As *defines* in QuickC or Turbo C program
   c | As *defines* in a Turbo C program, and in the *graph.h* file of a QuickC program
   d | In the graphics *include* file

14 | Where is the structure defined for keeping data about the current mode?
   a | As part of the program in a QuickC program, and in the *graphics.h* file of a Turbo C program
   b | As part of the program in QuickC or Turbo C
   c | As part of the program in a Turbo C program, and in the *graph.h* file of a QuickC program
   d | In the graphics *include* file

15 | What is the fastest graphics method?
   a | Using graphics functions
   b | Direct
   c | Using text graphics
   d | Using the *int86( )* function

14 | Using BIOS Services

About This Chapter

There are some things that you will want to do in C that cannot be accomplished with the conventional standard library, such as using the mouse, interfacing with a modem, or accessing special areas of the hard disk (for example, to change the name of a subdirectory). C provides a method of accessing almost any feature supported by the operating system through the use of low-level BIOS service functions. This chapter will show you how these functions can be used.

Introduction to BIOS Service Functions

The C BIOS functions permit you to access almost any feature of your computer.

It should be emphasized that the BIOS service functions are *low-level*, even more so than the unbuffered file functions of chapter 12. The BIOS service functions provide access to the real power of the processing system, permitting you to do many things that you can't do with other functions. Using them doesn't take much memory space in the program, and they are generally faster than alternative approaches in a program. At the same time, because these routines are low-level, they don't provide much protection if something goes wrong, and it is up to you, the programmer, to provide whatever protection is necessary. You also lose portability to other C languages, since other languages may, even if they include these functions, support them in a different way. Finally, they are not as easy to use as most functions and can cause serious problems if used incorrectly, such as scrambling a disk sector.

This chapter will look at two examples of using the low-level BIOS services: a simple C program to obtain disk directory information and a mouse interface routine.

The BIOS Services

The BIOS services of the computer provide a programming interface that is independent of the hardware.

Microsoft and IBM, in developing the PC-compatible DOS operating system, tried to create a programming interface for all languages that was independent of the hardware on which the operating system was functioning. This programming interface, known as the BIOS services, is standard for all systems using MS-DOS or PC-DOS. Any program written for one of these computers should run on any other with no changes, as long as the program is interfaced to the hardware through the BIOS service routines (figure 14.1).

BIOS is an acronym for *Basic Input Output System*. This collection of routines is part of DOS and is very hardware-specific. Using the routines, you can interface with just about anything: the video, keyboard, disk drive, printer, etc. Many of these routines are stored in the computer ROM, but others are in ROMs on adapter cards (such as an EGA card) or in SYS files loaded from the CONFIG.SYS file when the system is started (such as a RAMdisk interface).

Programs can use these BIOS routines directly, but Microsoft and IBM advise programmers to avoid this. Although technical information on these routines is readily available, neither IBM nor Microsoft provides support BIOS interfacing at this level. The routines are fast, but somewhat hardware-dependent. You also can't expect much error-checking support. As an example, the screen image on a PC-compatible is stored in a well-defined area of memory. A program can go into this area and, with dazzling speed, change the screen image to produce graphics. However, the program will face serious portability problems with other hardware systems that are using the numerous graphics modes available.

As an alternative, Microsoft and IBM provide a software "shell" between the BIOS and the application program called the *BIOS services*. These routines provide more hardware-independence and better control of errors. They provide a well-defined consistency in how the registers, flags, stack, and memory are used. There is some loss of speed, but with the faster personal computers this is not as important. The BIOS service routines output to, or drive, the BIOS routines. The input to the BIOS services is a well-defined programming interface that is the subject of this chapter. The BIOS services routines are supported by

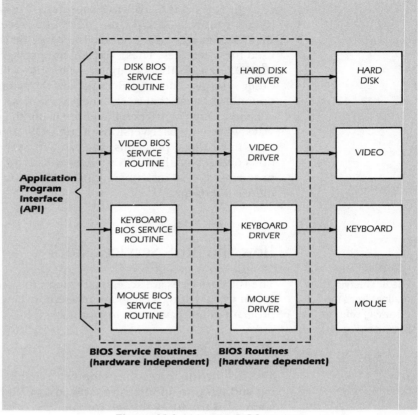

Figure 14.1 Using the BIOS services

Microsoft and IBM, and are part of the DOS operating system (table 14.1).

Table 14-1 Low-Level BIOS Functions versus High-Level Functions

Low-Level	High-Level
Access to almost any DOS feature	Limited access to DOS features
Poor portability to other C languages	Excellent portability to other C languages
Can be slow	Variable in speed
Uses small amount of program code	Uses large amounts of program code
Very limited error checking	Good error checking
Unbuffered	Buffered

In the C high-level I/O routines of the earlier chapters, the C library routines (*fgets( )*, *putchar( )*, etc.) were created by using the BIOS service routines. Even the low-level file I/O routines of chapter 12 used these services. These services are provided as a hidden file called IBMIO.COM on IBM computers. This file will have another name on other systems. These services remain the same for each version of the operating system; that is, each new version is a superset of the previous versions. Once a program is written using the BIOS services, it will always work with later versions of the DOS operating system.

In writing C programs, you can bypass the high-level library functions and access the BIOS services directly. This is useful for modem programs, special disk operations (such as a file unerase program), and mouse interfacing.

How the BIOS Services Work

The BIOS services routines work through the use of software interrupts.

The BIOS services are accessed through the use of software interrupts. If you were writing a program in assembly language, for example, your program might have as an instruction:

```
INT 10H
```

This instruction forces the computer to temporarily stop what it is doing and jump to an interrupt table in low memory. This table has the address of the BIOS service routine that is to be activated. The computer then switches to that address, and the execution continues. When the service routine ends, execution control is returned to your program at the point where it left off.

This DOS design strategy is very clever. It permits the service routines to be modified, moved about in memory, or even replaced by an enterprising programmer, without affecting any program that uses the routine.

The resident program concept is one method in which programmers have taken advantage of this flexibility. Programs such as Prokey, Sidekick, and Hotshot modify the interrupt table in low memory so that a keyboard interrupt switches to the resident program before the normal interrupt processor. In effect, the resident program becomes a filter for a certain keystroke combination, defined as the ''hot key,'' that activates the resident program.

The BIOS services could have been designed so that they operate from one interrupt code; instead they are broken into several subject categories. This design requires a separate interrupt handler for each group. Each of the handlers can be edited or replaced without affecting the others. For example, you can do any video operations (and write your own graphics routines) through interrupt 10H, which controls the video services. To add a new video display mode, it is necessary only to change this driver.

Twelve of the BIOS services are grouped together as the ROM-BIOS services and are divided into five groups (table 14.2). Half of the twelve support specific peripheral devices. Of the remainder, two return the equipment status, one is for the clock, one is for printing the screen, and two support BASICA.

Table 14.2 ROM-BIOS Service Routines

	Interrupt Number		Use
	DEC	HEX	
Peripheral Device Services	16	10	Video display services
	19	13	Diskette services
	20	14	Communication services
	21	15	Cassette services
	22	16	Keyboard services
	23	17	Printer services
Equipment Status Services	17	11	Equipment list service
	18	12	Memory size service
Time and Date Service	26	1A	Time and date service
Print-Screen Service	5	5	Print-screen service
Special Services	24	18	Activate ROM-BASIC
	25	19	Activate bootstrap

Each of these services, in turn, has subservices. For example, the video service routine has sixteen subservices that do everything from setting the video mode or cursor position to defining the size of the cursor.

Data is passed to or from the BIOS services routines using the registers.

For each of the services, the basic programming technique is to pass data to the service routine by putting the data in the computer's registers. Data from the function is returned to the program through these same registers. The use of these registers for each service routine is well defined in Peter Norton's *Programmer's Guide to the IBM PC* (Microsoft Press, 1985). A brief overview of the use of each register for the 8088 microprocessor is shown in table 14.3.

Table 14.3 *Register Listing for the 8088*

	Register	Description
Scratch-Pad Registers	AX	Accumulator
	BX	Base
	CX	Count
	DX	Data
Segment Registers	CS	Code segment
	DS	Data segment
	SS	Stack segment
	ES	Extra segment
Offset Registers	IP	Instruction pointers
	SP	Stack pointer
	BP	Base pointer
	SI	Source index
	DT	Destination index
Flag Registers	Flag register	

Each register has a designation of *X*, *L*, or *H*. The X suffix designates the entire 16 bits of the register; the L suffix, the lower 8 bits; and the H suffix, the higher 8 bits, for example:

AX Entire 16 bits of A register

AL Lower half of A register

AH Upper half of A register

The general rule is that the scratch-pad registers are used for passing data to or from a service routine. The subservice number is passed to the service in the A register.

Other BIOS Services

In addition to the ROM BIOS services, there are several other interrupt services available. Two of these are the DOS services and the mouse services.

DOS Services

The DOS services are controlled from a set of nine interrupts. Table 14.4 lists the interrupt numbers and their uses.

Table 14.4 The DOS Interrupt Services

Interrupt Number HEX	Use
20	Terminate a program
21	Execute a DOS function
22	Terminate address
23	Break address
24	Critical error-handler address
25	Absolute disk read
26	Absolute disk write
27	Terminate and stay resident
2F	Print spool control (DOS-3)

Of these, perhaps the most important is interrupt 21H, which provides such an extensive set of subservices that it has become the real workhorse of most programming. The subservice functions of interrupt 21H are listed in table 14.5. The function number, as the subservice number, is passed to the service in the AX register.

Table 14.5 DOS Functions for Interrupt 21

Function Number DEC	HEX	Use
0	0	Terminate
1	1	Keyboard input with echo
2	2	Display output
3	3	Serial input
4	4	Serial output
5	5	Printer output
6	6	Direct keyboard/display I/O
7	7	Direct keyboard input w/o echo
8	8	Keyboard input w/o echo

Table 14.5 (Cont.)

Function Number		Use
DEC	HEX	
9	9	Display string
10	A	Buffered keyboard input
11	B	Check keyboard input status
12	C	Clear keyboard and do function
13	D	Reset disk
14	E	Select current drive
15	F	Open file
16	10	Close file
17	11	Search for first matching file
18	12	Search for next matching file
19	13	Delete file
20	14	Read sequential file record
21	15	Write sequential file record
22	16	Create file
23	17	Rename file
24	18	(not available)
25	19	Report current drive
26	1A	Set disk transfer area
27	1B	Get FAT information, current drive
28	1C	Get FAT information, any drive
33	21	Read random file record
34	22	Write random file record
35	23	Get file size
36	24	Set random record field
37	25	Set interrupt vector
38	26	Create program sector
39	27	Read random file records
40	28	Write random file records
41	29	Parse filename
42	2A	Get date
43	2B	Set date
44	2C	Get time
45	2D	Set time

Table 14.5 (Cont.)

	Function Number		Use
	DEC	HEX	
	46	2E	Set disk write verification
DOS 2.00	47	2F	Get DTA address
Additions	48	30	Get DOS version number
	49	31	Terminate and stay resident (advanced)
	51	33	Get/set Ctrl-Break
	53	35	Get interrupt vector
	54	36	Get disk free space
	56	38	Get country-dependent information
	57	39	MKDIR (make directory)
	58	3A	RMDIR (remove directory)
	59	3B	CHDIR (change directory)
	60	3C	Create file
	61	3D	Open file
	62	3E	Close file handle
	63	3F	Read from file or device
	64	40	Write to file or device
	65	41	Delete file
	66	42	Move file pointer
	67	43	Get/set file attributes
	68	44	I/O control for devices
	69	45	Duplicate file handle
	70	46	Force handle duplication
	71	47	Get current directory
	72	48	Allocate memory
	73	49	Free allocated memory
	74	4A	Modify allocated memory block
	75	4B	Load and execute program
	76	4C	Terminate process
	77	4D	Get return code of subprogram
	78	4E	Start file search
	79	4F	Continue file search

Table 14.5 (Cont.)

	Function Number		Use
	DEC	HEX	
	84	54	Get verify state
	86	56	Rename file
	87	57	Get/set file date and time
DOS 3.00 Additions	89	59	Get extended error code
	90	5A	Create temporary file
	91	5B	Create new file
	92	5C	Lock/unlock file access
	98	62	Get PSP address

Now let's look at an example of a program using this service. The example will be simple, since our purpose is only to illustrate the basic principle. The example program will display the free space and the total space on the designated drive (A = 1).

```c
#include <stdio.h>
#include <dos.h>
#define DISK_IO   0x021
union REGS inregs,outregs;
main()
{
     char drivea[3];
     float free_space,total_space;

     printf("Enter drive Number: ");
     fgets(drivea,sizeof(drivea),stdin);
     inregs.h.ah = 0x36;
     inregs.h.dl = atoi(drivea);
     int86(DISK_IO,&inregs,&outregs);
     printf("%d %d %d %d\n",
          outregs.x.ax,outregs.x.bx,outregs.x.cx,
               outregs.x.dx);
     free_space = 1.0 * outregs.x.bx * outregs.x.cx *
          outregs.x.ax;
     total_space = 1.0 * outregs.x.dx * outregs.x.cx *
          outregs.x.ax;
          printf("%f %f",free_space,total_space);
}
```

The *int86( )* function permits the user to access the BIOS service routines.

The program uses the *int86( )* function to pass information to and from the BIOS services. This technique permits access to all the scratch-pad registers. The general form is

int86(*interrupt_no, in_registers, out_registers*)

The interrupt number, *interrupt_no*, is passed as an integer. The register data is passed in a structure, which is defined in *dos.h*. For this reason, the *dos.h* file must be included with this function. It defines the structure used for the *int86()*, *in_registers()*, and *out_registers* arguments:

```
/* Word registers */

struct WORDREGS {
      unsigned int ax;
      unsigned int bx;
      unsigned int cx;
      unsigned int dx;
      unsigned int si;
      unsigned int di;
      unsigned int cflag;
      };

struct BYTEREGS {
      unsigned char al, ah;
      unsigned char bl, bh;
      unsigned char cl, ch;
      unsigned char dl, dh;
      };

union REGS {
      struct WORDREGS x;
      struct BYTEREGS h;
      };
```

This union (in *dos.h*) permits the register variables to be used as either 16-bit words or 8-bit bytes in the program. The entire input to the A register, for example, becomes inregs.x.ax. The lower half of this register is inregs.h.al.

If you need to use only the DOS functions (interrupt 21H) and only the A and D registers, the *bdos( )* function is simpler:

bdos(*function_no,dosdx,dosax*)

where the first argument is the function number, *dosdx* is the D register, and *dosax* is the A register.

C also provides several special-purpose BIOS functions. Using these can simplify your work, though in many cases you sacrifice portability.

Using the Mouse

The BIOS service routines for the mouse are defined in a MOUSE.SYS file that is installed as part of DOS. To install MOUSE.SYS, use the following line in the CONFIG.SYS file read at bootup:

```
device = MOUSE.SYS
```

This service is driven from interrupt 33H with the subservices shown in table 14.6.

Table 14.6 Mouse Subservices

Subservice Number	Use
0	Initialize mouse
1	Show mouse cursor (arrow)
2	Hide cursor
3	Get mouse position and button status
4	Set mouse cursor
5	Get button press information
6	Get button release information
7	Set minimum and maximum horizontal position
8	Set minimum and maximum vertical position
9	Set graphics cursor block
10	Set text cursor
11	Read mouse motion counters
12	Set user-defined subroutine input mask
13	Light pen emulation mode on
14	Light pen emulation mode off
15	Set mickey/pixel ratio

Here is a simple QuickC program using the mouse:

```c
#include <stdio.h>
#include <graph.h>
#include <dos.h>
#define MOUSE_IO 0x033
#define INITIALIZE 0
#define SHOW_CURSOR 1
#define GET_INFO 3
#define TRUE 1
int set_mode(void);
struct videoconfig config;
union REGS inregs,outregs;
main()
{
     extern struct videoconfig config;
     int x, y;
     int color;
     void setup(), cleanup();
     unsigned int button,row,col;

     setup();
     _setcolor(1);
     inregs.x.ax = INITIALIZE;
     int86(MOUSE_IO,&inregs,&outregs);
     inregs.x.ax = SHOW_CURSOR;
     int86(MOUSE_IO,&inregs,&outregs);

     /* get current position */
     inregs.x.ax = GET_INFO;
     int86(MOUSE_IO,&inregs,&outregs);
     button = outregs.x.bx;
     col = outregs.x.cx;
     row = outregs.x.dx;
     _moveto(row,col);
     while (TRUE)
          {
          inregs.x.ax = GET_INFO;
          int86(MOUSE_IO,&inregs,&outregs);
          button = outregs.x.bx;
          col = outregs.x.cx;
          row = outregs.x.dx;
          if (button==1)
               _moveto(col,row);
          if (button==2)
               _lineto(col,row);
          if (button==3)
               {
               cleanup();
```

```
                        exit(0);
                    }
                }
        getche();
        cleanup();

}
```

The basic principle is the same as in the previous section: the *int86( )* function sets and reads the registers. Holding down button 1 and moving the mouse moves the starting position for drawing. Holding button 2 down while dragging the mouse draws in the color determined by _*setcolor( )*. Button 3 (holding down both mouse buttons) exits the program. This program can be easily modified for Turbo C.

In trying the program, note its speed on your computer. This gives you an idea of the speed problem in using the BIOS services. Moving the mouse too fast can result in some pixels not being displayed.

Review

Using the methods described in this chapter, you have access to almost any feature of your computer system. The 10H interrupt, for example, gives you access to another graphics display method. Remember that the BIOS services may not be as fast as you would like for some applications (such as drawing graphics), but you do gain access to almost any feature of your computer with a program that is very portable to other IBM-PC compatibles.

Quiz for Chapter 14

1 | What does the acronym BIOS stand for?
    a | Binary Input/Output System
    b | Basic Input Output Services
    c | Basic Input Output System
    d | Binary Input Output Services

2 | What is one characteristic of the BIOS service routines?
    a | They are very fast.
    b | They are supported by Microsoft and IBM, the DOS suppliers.
    c | They are easy to use.
    d | They are part of the C library.

3 | What is one advantage of using the BIOS service routines over the standard C library?
    a | You can access system features that are not accessible through the C library routines.
    b | The program will execute faster.
    c | The program is more portable to other compilers.
    d | Development time is faster.

4 | What is the interrupt for DOS services?
    a | 0x10
    b | 0x21
    c | 0x12
    d | None of the above

5 | Where are the BIOS service routines for the mouse defined?
    a | As part of the DOS supplied with your computer
    b | In the C library
    c | In a file defined in CONFIG.SYS
    d | On the mouse adapter card in a ROM

6 | Where are the BIOS services for the hard disk defined?
    a | As part of the DOS files supplied for your computer
    b | In the C library
    c | In a file defined by CONFIG.SYS
    d | On the mouse adapter card in a ROM

7 | What information is passed to the *int86( )* function?
    a | The interrupt number and register input values
    b | The interrupt number
    c | Register input values
    d | BIOS service name

8 | What is a disadvantage of using the BIOS services?
    a | They are very slow.

b | They are more difficult to use than programming with the standard C library functions.

c | They provide no error or buffer support.

d | All of the above

9 | What is an advantage of using the BIOS services?

a | You gain access to almost every feature of the system.

b | You have more control over input and output.

c | Programs can be shorter.

d | All of the above

10 | How many registers are in the 8088?

a | 12

b | 13

c | 14

d | 18

15 | Introduction to Structured Development

About This Chapter

Designing a large computer program is just as complex as designing a bridge, a building, or an automobile. You would not purposely begin the construction of anything so complex without careful advance planning. Writing a computer program without careful planning would be like sending a construction crew to construct a building without first giving them a plan from which to work.

In this chapter we'll look at some of the basic issues of designing and testing programs. The principles described apply to any complex system such as a general ledger, job-costing system, inventory control system, etc.

The Importance of Planning

Several years ago I received a request to develop a job-costing system for a well-known company that prepared media advertising for many clients. The company had a program that had been developed by someone without a lot of programming experience. Although the program used a very popular high-level language, it didn't work and didn't do what the company needed. They wanted me to get everything working.

My first action was to request the plans for the system they were currently using. What were the goals? What did the programs they had do? How did the programs relate to each other? What was the database structure? I discovered that the original goals had never been clearly defined and that there were no comprehensive plans. The company suggested that I list the programs and work backward, doing what programmers call "reverse engineering." However, working backward to study a program that didn't meet the needs would have not solved the problem.

The final result was to begin anew, defining what really needed to be done in clear, objective goals, carefully working through the design, and then doing the programming again. A lot of money and time could have been avoided had this structured design been done the first time.

This chapter will look at two alternatives to resolving this type of problem: structured design and rapid prototyping. It will introduce the principles of structured design as applied to a mailing list program.

The Five Steps

In the context of programming, a *system* is a collection of programs and data acting as a unit.

Any *system* is a set of components that acts as a whole. In the context of designing a software system, we could say that a system is an integrated collection of programs and data that acts as a unit. The purpose of this system is to process information. The output is generally in the form of reports, labels, or display screens. In other cases the system may be called upon to perform a specific action, such as activating traffic signals, sounding an alarm, or activating a robot for the assembly of a product. The input to the system is normally data supplied by the user, but it could also be data from sensors or another computer. Systems use feedback to ensure that the goals are met; that is, some of the output is fed back to the input and becomes part of the input data.

The five steps for developing a system are: analysis, design, programming, implementation, and maintenance.

The process of developing a system can be seen as five steps: analysis, design, programming, implementation, and maintenance (figure 15.1). Figure 15.1 seems to imply that the development is a linear process in time, beginning with the analysis and concluding with the maintenance. In reality, this is true to only a limited extent. Although the ideal development goal is to complete each step before moving to the next, in most applications there is a considerable amount of backtracking and redesign. The development process itself is a systematic process, and feedback is constantly used to ensure that the development goals are being met.

For each phase of development, there are many tools and techniques available. For many applications the most cost-effective approach is that of structured development.

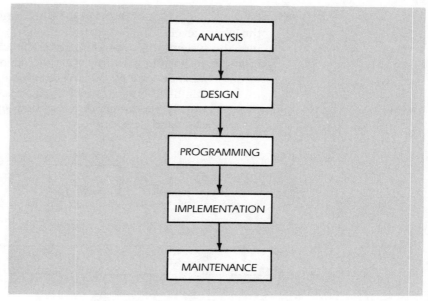

Figure 15.1 Developing a system

Structured Development

A structured system implies modularity, with the modules in a defined hierarchy.

The word *structured* here is a general term that can be applied to any of the five phases. Structured development implies two aspects:

1 | *Modularity*—the system involves a collection of smaller modules. For example, the automobile is really a collection of smaller systems or modules: the cooling system, the electrical system, the drive system, the braking system. Engineers view all of these very complex systems as a collection of modules, which are in turn collections of small modules. Each module has less complexity than the whole. For example, the ignition system is part of the electrical system. When repairing a car, the first objective is to identify the smaller system (or module) that is causing the problem. This localizes the problem and reduces diagnostic time.

2 | *Hierarchical*—there is an order or relationship between the modules. The order is top-down. In program design, for example, we start at the top with the design of the main program, or control program. What should be the objective of this program? From this we can define which modules or programs will be needed at the next level to support the main objective. Once this is done, we can define the modules and functions at the next level. What should

be the objective of each of these? This continues until we reach the lowest level of the program (figure 15.2). No matter how complex the system, this procedure generally leads to a solution. For example, in starting we know what the main module is supposed to do. That is defined by our overall global objectives. This can then be "chunked out" to small objectives, which are less complex. Eventually we can get down to very small modules that are easy to design and develop.

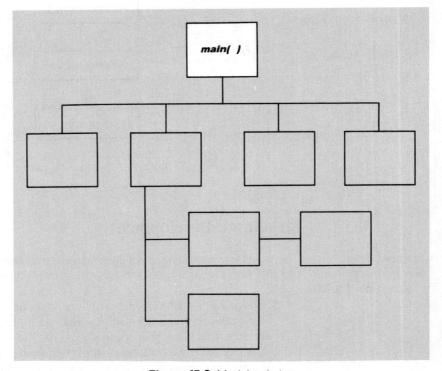

Figure 15.2 Modular design

Structured techniques can be applied to each of the five steps involved in developing a system. We will now look at each step in light of structured techniques.

Structured Analysis

The analysis phase defines the problem, and the result is a specification sheet and the data flow diagrams.

The objective during the analysis step is to study the problem in detail before beginning the design. The analysis should yield a goal as well as subgoals for the individual modules. The goals should be documentable in clear, objective terms so that the system performance can later be measured against these goals. From this, specifications can be created and a cost-analysis made. There should also be feedback at this level to ensure that the specifications are accurate.

The analysis cycle may involve surveys. Generally, two types of surveys are involved: management and user. The *management survey* should involve the people who will be using the data from the program. What type of data do they need to make decisions? What type of data do they already have? Too much data is as bad as too little. Are graphics or charts needed? What type? What financial resources and time frames are available for solving the problem? What hardware and software resources are already available? If reports or charts are currently being used, do they contain missing or unnecessary data?

The *user survey* involves those who will be entering the data to the computer, using the program directly, and capturing the output for the management. What type of software interface do they need for maximum productivity? If a computer program is being used now, what are the current data entry problems?

The user survey provides a good chance to identify present problems in how the data is obtained, entered, and processed. For example, in one company a receptionist answered the phone and, in addition, entered data to the computer between phone calls and also welcomed visitors. Such a three-way job description could seriously impair the accuracy of the data being entered as well as frustrate the user. It would have been better to rotate the responsibility, having someone else at the front desk for the hour or so a day it took the user to enter the day's data.

The result of the analysis phase is generally two items: a specification sheet and the data flow diagrams.

The Specification Sheet

The analysis phase should define the specifications for the primary system, the submodules, and, if possible, the lower-level modules below the submodules. Specifications are the starting point for the design and programming. You may wish to backtrack and modify them later, but they should be specific and detailed. You cannot hold the programmers accountable for something that isn't in the specifications. For example, you might start with a single line for the street address. Later (during programming) you discover some new members coming in that need two lines for the street address. Then you'll have to backtrack to square one and decide whether the cost involved justifies the need to modify the specification. In making the original specifications, you could have saved some time by putting in a note to the effect that it should be easy to change the field specifications at a later time. You would also need to specify what this "later time" meant (before or after you start adding addresses to the file?). Adding this note, however, could increase the design cost.

The Data Flow Diagram

The data flow diagram is a graph of related functions and files showing all interfaces.

Another output of the analysis phase is the current data flow diagram. This *data flow diagram* (DFD) is a graph of related functions and files showing the interfaces between all the system components. It is called a bubble diagram by some developers because in the diagram each component is represented by a bubble. The DFD shows only how the data flows and does not illustrate the control of this data.

The data flow diagram is then converted to a logical diagram. The bubbles will now contain verb phrases ("Edit address," "List addresses"). Between the bubbles the lines will contain the objective of that phase ("new address," "labels, printouts"). An example is shown in figure 15.3.

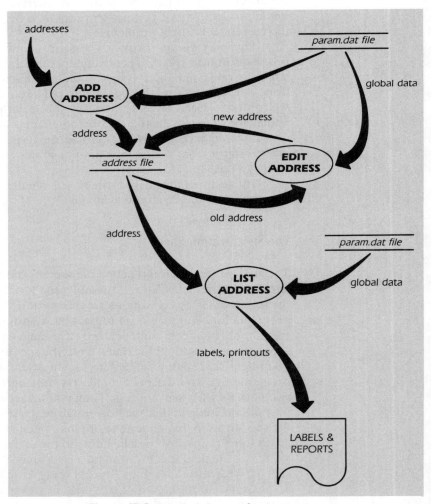

Figure 15.3 *A logical diagram for the new system*

The Data Dictionary

The *data dictionary* is a set of definitions for the data flows, data elements, files, databases, and processes.

The data flow diagram is a valuable communications tool for the programmer as well as for the managers and users of the system. A parallel document, the *data dictionary*, is a set of definitions for the data flows, data elements, files, databases, and processes on the DFD. It is the glossary for the DFD.

For more information on the process of structured analysis, see *Structured Analysis and System Specification* by Tom De Marco (Prentice-Hall, 1979).

Structured Design

In the design phase, the specifications and data flow diagrams are translated to a plan for implementing the proposal.

The purpose of the design step is to transform the specifications and data flow diagram into a plan for implementing the proposal. *Structured design* implies conquering the complexity of the system by using partitioning and hierarchical organization.

Structured design uses two tools to accomplish its purpose: a structure chart and pseudocode.

The Structure Chart

The *structure chart* shows the partitioning of the system design into modules and their hierarchical relationship.

The *structure chart* is a graphics tool that shows the partitioning of the system in modules. It is created from the DFD. The modules are rectangles in this diagram, and the lines between the modules show the flow of data.

Each rectangle in the structure chart solves one well-defined piece of the problem. It can be specified separately with its inputs and outputs. Each box has a single function. Each box should be as independent as possible.

Figure 15.4 shows the partial structure chart for a mailing list program. Notice that the structure chart has a hierarchy, which can be of several levels.

At the top level is a single module, the main menu module. This, in turn, can call any of five main modules:

Module	Use
mailadd	Adds an address
mailedit	Edits an address
maildsp	Displays an address
maildel	Deletes an address
mailrpt	Reports an address
mailmisc	Indexes, controls parameters

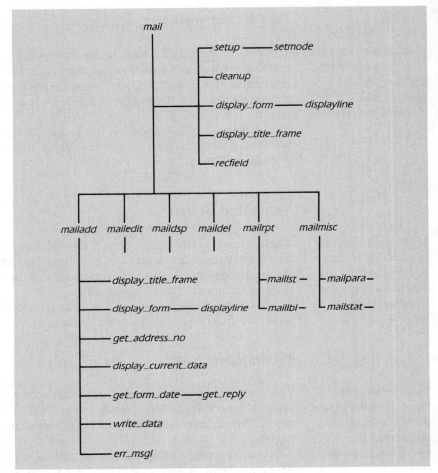

Figure 15.4 Partial structure chart

Notice even at this level that each module has a single well-defined function. Some of these modules have another level. For example, the *mailrpt* module can call either of two modules: one for listing labels, another for listing the directory.

This modular concept has several advantages:

- Modules are easy to construct. Each can be specified independently of the others.

- Modules are easy to test. If the system has any problem, it is easily localized to the specific box that is causing the problem.

- Modification is easy. You can replace an entire module without changing the rest of the system.

Pseudocode

After the structure chart has been prepared, the basic outline of the program code is created by using simple English sentences. This outline is not computer-language–specific. A sample of the *pseudocode* (English-like language) for the mailing list program is shown in figure 15.5.

```
Get Global Data From Parameter File
Validate Password
Turn on Graphics
Do While OPTION<> QUIT
        Clear Screen
        Display Title Screen
        Display Option Menu
        Enter Option
        Call Option Module
Enddo
Return Screen to Default
```

Figure 15.5 The pseudocode for the main module

Structured Programming

The program is written as a set of related modules.

By now you've had some experience with programming, but what exactly is structured programming? *Structured programming* simply means following the rules of modularization that have already been described. As a general rule you will work top-down, writing the menu program first and then the next level modules. In some cases, however, you may work bottom-up, dropping down to write low-level modules. To summarize:

1 | The programs, modules, and functions are designed as independent entities. Each is specified and written as an independent unit.

2 | The modules have a hierarchical relationship to each other.

3 | Each module performs a single function.

4 | Each module has a single entry point and a single exit point. You cannot "Goto" any particular point in the module, nor can you branch to another point based on a variable value.

5 | Common modules are stored as functions and used by multiple programs.

6 | Decision control is accomplished with *if . . . else*, *while*, and *do . . . while*. You cannot use *gotos*.

7 | Indentation can be used with all decision controls.

8 | Data is passed to functions as arguments. Data is returned using arguments or return values. The use of global variables should be kept to a minimum.

9 | Modules should be documented.

10 | Data structures should be supported to permit the user to group like data in hierarchical relationships. Function arguments should be kept to a minimum, and structures or arrays used to pass like data to a function should be kept as a single argument.

Whatever language is used for structured programming, it will need to support all the features just described. C is specifically designed for structured programming, and it supports all of these features.

Programming involves four steps:

Programming involves design, entry of the code, compiling, editing, and finally debugging.

- Designing the program

- Entering the program

- Compiling and editing the program

- Debugging the program

Structured programming generally reduces the time needed to complete all of the steps. Turbo C and QuickC are faster and easier to use than most compilers, since they support an internal developmental environment that enables the design, editing, compiling, and debugging to be completed faster.

Structured Implementation

Structured implementation is the implementation of programs one module at a time. For example, once the main menu program and *mail-add* module are ready, the users can begin adding addresses while the remaining programs are being written.

At a more general level, structured implementation is often not as important as another aspect of implementation—parallel testing. For any complex system, both the new system and the old system should be used until there is a high degree of security about the new system. For example, if you are using a new computer program to implement a general ledger system, the older manual system or the old computer program should be used with the new program for several periods. The reports should be compared for errors or discrepancies. This should be done even if the new program is a well-proven commercial product.

Structured Maintenance

Structured maintenance is the use of top-down techniques to resolve problems in the system. If your automobile is not working properly, the mechanic begins by localizing the problem to the cooling system, fuel delivery system, electrical system, emissions control system or another system. The mechanic works in a top-down fashion, from the general to the specific.

In the same way, software diagnostic procedures work top-down, from the general to the specific. The primary goal is to isolate the function involved as quickly as possible.

Documentation

Documentation is a dynamic process that is done at each step.

Documentation is not something that is done when the work is completed and there's time and money left. Documentation should be done at each step. It is the "baton" in the relay race that is passed to those working on the next step. If you have to backtrack to a previous step, update the documentation and then move forward again.

Rapid Prototyping

In some cases it is difficult or impossible to define the modules explicitly from the start and to work through the complete design before programming.

Rapid prototyping is an alternative development method that can be used when the procedure for solving the problem cannot be defined objectively.

An example of this might be a diagnostic medical system. In this case the goal might be specific, with a defined small group of diseases as conclusions and another collection of symptoms as the input data. The relationship of the symptoms to the conclusions, however, may not be clearly known or the research knowledge may be changing frequently. In this case the structured approach would not meet the needs, and another alternative would be necessary.

One frequently used alternative is what is known as *rapid prototyping* or step-wise refinement. In this case a small system is created that does a limited part of what the user desires. The user begins with this system and then makes suggestions for refinement. These suggestions are then implemented. Gradually, the system becomes more complex and useful. Program code that becomes repetitive is broken off as modules, and new statements are added that permit the inclusion of new features.

Preliminary System Design Goals

The system should give the user positive feelings. It should be easy to use (while perhaps supporting complex functions), predictable (it shouldn't work one way today and another way tomorrow), fast (it should keep up with the user), and reliable (the results should always be correct).

The designer must consider the environment in which the system will be used.

The designer should also keep in mind the environment in which the system will be used. Here are some general environment categories:

Home/Entertainment

Business/Office

Industrial/Military/Commercial

Life-Critical

Exploratory/Expert/AI

Scientific/Engineering

The environment and the experience of the user determine the vocabulary of the screens, the level of functionality to be supported, the reliability of the program, the degree of protection from invalid program entries, the program complexity (size, cost, development time), and the help level that must be supported. In short, the developer must always keep the user in mind.

There may also be personal or physical constraints on the program design. A disabled person having the use of only one hand may prefer a mouse to a keyboard. Thus, a mouse interface may be required. Displays that use color can be difficult for a color-blind person to use if the colors are set to the wrong values. If you are writing a program for commercial distribution, all of these constraints and more must be taken into account.

One of the best starting points is to examine similar products that are well-designed. The type of application is not as important for this study as the method in which the product is designed and the user interface. The basic menu structure of Lotus 1-2-3, for example, has been copied into other products, such as the Paradox database manager.

Review

This chapter has covered the following important points:

1 | The two primary methods for system development are structured development and rapid prototyping.

2 | A system is developed in five steps: analysis, design, programming, implementation, and maintenance.

3 | Structured development implies modularity and hierarchy.

4 | The analysis step defines the specifications and data flow diagrams.

5 | The design step translates the specifications and data flow diagrams into a plan for solving the problem.

6 | The programming step creates the executable program.

7 | The implementation step enables the program to do productive work.

8 | The maintenance step modifies and fixes the program, as necessary, to meet current objectives.

9 | Programming involves design, writing and entering the code, compiling and editing, and debugging.

10 | Structured programming involves creating the system as a set of interrelated modules, with a defined specification and function for each.

11 | Rapid prototyping is an alternative development method that can be used when the procedure for solving the problem cannot be clearly defined. It involves creating a small model that is a subset of the final system and then gradually evolving the model into a larger system that meets the desired specifications.

12 | The programmer should always be sensitive to the environment in which the system will be used and who the user will be.

Quiz for Chapter 15

1 | What method of program development is generally used when the problem-solving procedure is known?

    a | Rapid prototyping

    b | Structured

    c | Modular

    d | Modeless

2 | What does the term *hierarchical* imply?

    a | Modular

    b | Top-down order

    c | Modular, with top-down order

    d | One procedure is in control of the program

3 | Which of the following is not one of the five steps in developing a system?

    a | Programming

    b | Design

    c | Analysis

    d | Editing the program

4 | What is the purpose of the design phase?

    a | To transform the specifications for the system into a plan for implementing the system

    b | To determine what is being done now to solve the problem

    c | To write the system specifications

    d | To find out what the managers and users need

5 | What is the purpose of the analysis phase?

    a | To write the pseudocode for the system

    b | To write the system specifications and data flow diagrams

    c | To transform the specifications for the system into a plan for implementing the system

    d | To write the data dictionary

6 | What is an advantage of modular programming?

    a | The program is easier to debug.

    b | Development time is generally less.

    c | Pieces of the program can be used in other programs.

    d | All of the above

7 | What is a feature of structured programming?

    a | Programs, modules, and functions are all designed as independent entities.

    b | The modules have a hierarchical relationship.

    c | Each module performs a single function.

    d | All of the above

8 | What type of application would not lend itself to structured programming?
    a | General ledger
    b | Spreadsheet
    c | Word processor
    d | Expert system

9 | What type of development technique is not supported by C?
    a | Structured design
    b | Rapid prototyping
    c | Step-wise refinement
    d | C supports all of the above.

10 | Which of the following is not considered part of the programming phase?
    a | Debugging
    b | Program maintenance
    c | Editing the program
    d | Compiling the program

A Turbo C and QuickC Comparison

Table A *Comparison of Turbo C and QuickC Specifications*

		Turbo C (Ver. 1.5)	QuickC (Ver. 1.0)
System Characteristics	Minimum memory required	384K	448K
	Maximum module code size	64K	64K
	Maximum program code size	640K	640K
	Full EGA support	yes	yes
	Mouse support	no	yes
Programming Environment	Full screen editor	yes	yes
	Maximum source code size	64K	64K
	Maximum characters/line	248	255
	WordStar command support	yes	yes
	Find & replace	yes	yes
	Block operations	yes	yes
	Insert/overtype mode	yes	yes
	Context-sensitive help	yes	yes

Table A (Cont.)

		Turbo C (Ver. 1.5)	QuickC (Ver. 1.0)
Compiler Features	Passes	1	1
	Errors/pass permitted	26 or more	26
	Compile & run in memory	yes	yes
	Compile rate (lines/min)	>7000	10,000
	Command-line compile option	yes	yes
	Math coprocessor support	yes	yes
	Floating point emulator	yes	yes
	Optimization	yes	limited
	Conditional compile	yes	yes
	Interlanguage calling	yes	yes
	ANSI compatible	yes	no*
	Support in-line assembly?	yes	no
Debugging Features	Trace debugging	no	yes
	Breakpoints	no	yes
	Watch variables/expressions	no	yes
	Single-step	no	yes
	Edit and continue	no	yes
	Codeview support	no	no
Runtime Library	Library manager	yes	yes
	User-creatable libraries	yes	yes
	XENIX compatible	no	yes
	UNIX compatible	no	yes
	include files supplied	27	40
	Library routines included	454	488
Graphics Support	Graphics functions	68	41
	Auto-detect adapter	yes	no
	Hercules support (code)	yes	no
	CGA support	yes	yes
	EGA support	yes	yes
	VGA support	yes	yes
	AT&T 6300	yes	no

Table A (Cont.)

		Turbo C (Ver. 1.5)	QuickC (Ver. 1.0)
Utilities	Linker	yes	yes
	Library manager	yes	yes
	Assembler	no**	optional
	Make	yes	yes
	Disassembler	no	no
Code Output	.OBJ files	yes	yes
	.EXE files	yes	yes
	ROMable	no	no
	.OBJ files LINK-compatible	yes	yes
Models	Tiny (.COM)	yes	no
	Small	yes	yes***
	Medium	yes	yes
	Compact	yes	yes***
	Large	yes	yes***
	Huge	yes	no
	Mixed	yes	no
Source Code	Library	optional	optional
	Start-up	yes	yes

*QuickC does not include some ANSI standard precompiler directives. It accepts, but does not use, the **volatile** keyword. *(Since there is little optimization, the need for the keyword is nonexistent.) Some predefined macros, such as* `_TIME_` *and* `_DATE_`*, are not supported.*

**Supports an in-line pseudo-assembly code.

***Supported by QuickC externally to environment only.

Notes on Turbo C and QuickC

Comparing compilers for speed is difficult because most compilers recognize the standard benchmarks and generate special optimized code. Here, however, are some general notes:

- *Turbo C* has excellent compiling speed, good execution speed, and outstanding floating-point performance. Turbo C has a slow display (such as the *print( )* function), and dynamic memory allocation is slow. The graphics support is outstanding and fast. The execution code is very intelligent, and the compiler is an optimizing compiler. Turbo C is weak on debugging support (there is none in version 1.5).

- *QuickC* has good compiling speed, produces excellent code, and has excellent debugging support. QuickC has very little optimization and lacks some ANSI standard features (see table A). Graphics support is weaker than Turbo C. On-line help support is better than Turbo C.

B | ASCII Character Set

Table B ASCII Character Set

	Decimal	Key	Hexadecimal	Octal	Escape Sequence	Name
Nonprinting ASCII Characters	0	^@	'\x00'	'\000'		NULL
	1	^A	'\x01'	'\001'		SOTT
	2	^B	'\x02'	'\002'		STX
	3	^C	'\x03'	'\003'		ETY
	4	^D	'\x04'	'\004'		EOT
	5	^E	'\x05'	'\005'		ENQ
	6	^F	'\x06'	'\006'		ACK
	7	^G	'\x07'	'\007'		BELL
	8	^H	'\x08'	'\010'	'\b'	BKSPC
	9	^I	'\x09'	'\011'	'\t'	HZTAB
	10	^J	'\x0a'	'\012'	'\n'	NEWLN
	11	^K	'\x0b'	'\013'	'\v'	VTAB
	12	^L	'\x0c'	'\014'	'\f '	FF
	13	^M	'\x0d'	'\015'	'\r'	CR

Table B (Cont.)

	Decimal	Key	Hexadecimal	Octal	Escape Sequence	Name
Nonprinting ASCII Characters	14	^N	'\x0e'	'\016'		SO
	15	^O	'\x0f'	'\017'		SI
	16	^P	'\x10'	'\020'		DLE
	17	^Q	'\x11'	'\021'		DC1
	18	^R	'\x12'	'\022'		DC2
	19	^S	'\x13'	'\023'		DC3
	20	^T	'\x14'	'\024'		DC4
	21	^U	'\x15'	'\025'		NAK
	22	^V	'\x16'	'\026'		SYN
	23	^W	'\x17'	'\027'		ETB
	24	^X	'\x18'	'\030'		CAN
	25	^Y	'\x19'	'\031'		EM
	26	^Z	'\x1a'	'\032'		SUB
	27	ESC	'\x1b'	'\033'		ES C
	28		'\x1c'	'\034'		FS
	29		'\x1d'	'\035'		GS
	30		'\x1e'	'\036'		RS
	31		'\x1f'	'\037'		US

	Decimal	Key	Hexadecimal	Octal
Printing ASCII Characters	32	(Space)	'\x20'	'\040'
	33	!	'\x21'	'\041'
	34	"	'\x22'	'\042'
	35	#	'\x23'	'\043'
	36	$	'\x24'	'\044'
	37	%	'\x25'	'\045'
	38	&	'\x26'	'\046'
	39	'	'\x27'	'\047'
	40	(	'\x28'	'\050'
	41	)	'\x29'	'\051'
	42	*	'\x2a'	'\052'
	43	+	'\x2b'	'\053'
	44	,	'\x2c'	'\054'

Table B (Cont.)

	Decimal	Key	Hexadecimal	Octal
Printing ASCII Characters	45	–	'\x2d'	'\055'
	46	.	'\x2e'	'\056'
	47	/	'\x2f'	'\057'
	48	0	'\x30'	'\060'
	49	1	'\x31'	'\061'
	50	2	'\x32'	'\062'
	51	3	'\x33'	'\063'
	52	4	'\x34'	'\064'
	53	5	'\x35'	'\065'
	54	6	'\x36'	'\066'
	55	7	'\x37'	'\067'
	56	8	'\x38'	'\070'
	57	9	'\x39'	'\071'
	58	:	'\x3a'	'\072'
	59	;	'\x3b'	'\073'
	60	<	'\x3c'	'\074'
	61	=	'\x3d'	'\075'
	62	>	'\x3e'	'\076'
	63	?	'\x3f'	'\077'
	64	@	'\x40'	'\100'
	65	A	'\x41'	'\101'
	66	B	'\x42'	'\102'
	67	C	'\x43'	'\103'
	68	D	'\x44'	'\104'
	69	E	'\x45'	'\105'
	70	F	'\x46'	'\106'
	71	G	'\x47'	'\107'
	72	H	'\x48'	'\110'
	73	I	'\x49'	'\111'
	74	J	'\x4a'	'\112'
	75	K	'\x4b'	'\113'
	76	L	'\x4c'	'\114'
	77	M	'\x4d'	'\115'
	78	N	'\x4e'	'\116'

Table B (Cont.)

	Decimal	Key	Hexadecimal	Octal
Printing ASCII Characters	79	O	'\x4f'	'\117'
	80	P	'\x50'	'\120'
	81	Q	'\x51'	'\121'
	82	R	'\x52'	'\122'
	83	S	'\x53'	'\123'
	84	T	'\x54'	'\124'
	85	U	'\x55'	'\125'
	86	V	'\x56'	'\126'
	87	W	'\x57'	'\127'
	88	X	'\x58'	'\130'
	89	Y	'\x59'	'\131'
	90	Z	'\x5a'	'\132'
	91	[	'\x5b'	'\133'
	92	\	'\x5c'	'\134'
	93	]	'\x5d'	'\135'
	94	^	'\x5e'	'\136'
	95	_	'\x5f'	'\137'
	96	`	'\x60'	'\140'
	97	a	'\x61'	'\141'
	98	b	'\x62'	'\142'
	99	c	'\x63'	'\143'
	100	d	'\x64'	'\144'
	101	e	'\x65'	'\145'
	102	f	'\x66'	'\146'
	103	g	'\x67'	'\147'
	104	h	'\x68'	'\150'
	105	i	'\x69'	'\151'
	106	j	'\x6a'	'\152'
	107	k	'\x6b'	'\153'
	108	l	'\x6c'	'\154'
	109	m	'\x6d'	'\155'
	110	n	'\x6e'	'\156'
	111	o	'\x6f'	'\157'
	112	p	'\x70'	'\160'

Table B (Cont.)

	Decimal	Key	Hexadecimal	Octal
Printing ASCII Characters	113	q	'\x71'	'\161'
	114	r	'\x72'	'\162'
	115	s	'\x73'	'\163'
	116	t	'\x74'	'\164'
	117	u	'\x75'	'\165'
	118	v	'\x76'	'\166'
	119	w	'\x77'	'\167'
	120	x	'\x78'	'\170'
	121	y	'\x79'	'\171'
	122	z	'\x7a'	'\172'
	123	{	'\x7b'	'\173'
	124	—	'\x7c'	'\174'
	125	}	'\x7d'	'\175'
	126	~	'\x7e'	'\176'
	127	DEL	'\x7f'	'\177'

	IBM Graphic	Dec	Hex	IBM Graphic	Dec	Hex
Extended ASCII Set	Ç	128	80	Å	143	8F
	ü	129	81	É	144	90
	é	130	82	æ	145	91
	â	131	83	Æ	146	92
	ä	132	84	ô	147	93
	à	133	85	ö	148	94
	å	134	86	ò	149	95
	ç	135	87	û	150	96
	ê	136	88	ù	151	97
	ë	137	89	ÿ	152	98
	è	138	8A	Ö	153	99
	ï	139	8B	Ü	154	9A
	î	140	8C	¢	155	9B
	ì	141	8D	£	156	9C
	Ä	142	8E	¥	157	9D

Table B (Cont.)

	IBM Graphic	Dec	Hex	IBM Graphic	Dec	Hex
Extended ASCII Set	P_t	158	9E	└	192	C0
	f	159	9F	┴	193	C1
	á	160	A0	┬	194	C2
	í	161	A1	├	195	C3
	ó	162	A2	─	196	C4
	ú	163	A3	┼	197	C5
	ñ	164	A4	╞	198	C6
	Ñ	165	A5	╟	199	C7
	ª	166	A6	╚	200	C8
	º	167	A7	╔	201	C9
	¿	168	A8	╩	202	CA
	⌐	169	A9	╦	203	CB
	¬	170	AA	╠	204	CC
	½	171	AB	═	205	CD
	¼	172	AC	╬	206	CE
	¡	173	AD	╧	207	CF
	«	174	AE	╨	208	D0
	»	175	AF	╤	209	D1
	░	176	B0	╥	210	D2
	▒	177	B1	╙	211	D3
	▓	178	B2	╘	212	D4
	│	179	B3	╒	213	D5
	┤	180	B4	╓	214	D6
	╡	181	B5	╫	215	D7
	╢	182	B6	╪	216	D8
	╖	183	B7	┘	217	D9
	╕	184	B8	┌	218	DA
	╣	185	B9	█	219	DB
	║	186	BA	▄	220	DC
	╗	187	BB	▌	221	DD
	╝	188	BC	▐	222	DE
	╜	189	BD	▀	223	DF
	╛	190	BE	α	224	E0
	┐	191	BF	β	225	E1

Table B (Cont.)

	IBM Graphic	Dec	Hex	IBM Graphic	Dec	Hex
Extended ASCII Set	Γ	226	E2	$\pm$	241	F1
	π	227	E3	$\geq$	242	F2
	Σ	228	E4	$\leq$	243	F3
	σ	229	E5	$\lceil$	244	F4
	μ	230	E6	$\rfloor$	245	F5
	τ	231	E7	$\div$	246	F6
	Φ	232	E8	$\approx$	247	F7
	Θ	233	E9	$\circ$	248	F8
	Ω	234	EA	$\cdot$	249	F9
	δ	235	EB	$\cdot$	250	FA
	∞	236	EC	$\sqrt{}$	251	FB
	φ	237	ED	η	252	FC
	ϵ	238	EE	^{2}	253	FD
	$\cap$	239	EF	$\blacksquare$	254	FE
	$\equiv$	240	F0	(blank)	255	FF

C | C Operators

The following table lists C's operators, in descending order of precedence. The L (for left-to-right) or R (for right-to-left) after the precedence number indicates the grouping order of the operator.

Table C The C Operators

Precedence	Type	Operator	Name
15L	Primary	( )	Parentheses
		[ ]	Subscript
		–>	Arrow
		.	Dot
14R	Unary	!	Logical NOT
		~	Bitwise NOT
		++	Increment
		––	Decrement
		–	Negative
		(type)	Cast
		*	Indirection

Table C (Cont.)

Precedence	Type	Operator	Name
		&	Address of
		sizeof	Size of
13L	Arithmetic	*	Multiplication
		/	Division
		%	Remainder (modules)
12L	Arithmetic	+	Addition
		−	Subtraction
11L	Bitwise	<<	Left shift
		>>	Right shift
10L	Relational	>	Greater than
		>=	Greater than or equal to
		<	Less than
		<=	Less than or equal to
9L	Relational	==	Equal to
		!=	Not equal to
8L	Bitwise	&	Bitwise AND
7L	Bitwise	^	Exclusive OR (XOR)
6L	Bitwise	−	Bitwise OR
5L	Logical	&&	Logical AND
4L	Logical	——	Logical OR
3R	Conditional	?:	Then, else
2R	Assignment	=	Assignment
2R	Assignment	+=, /= (see note below)	Shorthand assignment
1L	Sequence	,	Comma

This is not the complete list of assignment shorthand operators.

D | C Data Types

Fundamental Types and Type Specifiers

char	int	typedef *name*
const	long	union
double	short	unsigned
enum	signed	void
float	struct	volatile

E | C Keywords

Keywords

auto	extern	short
break	float	sizeof
case	for	static
char	goto	struct
continue	if	switch
default	int	typedef
do	long	union
double	register	unsigned
else	return	while

Implementation-Dependent Keywords

asm*	huge	_cs*
cdecl	interrupt*	_ds*
far	near	_es*
fortran	pascal	_ss*

*Turbo C only.

ANSI Extension to Kernighan and Ritchie

| const | signed | volatile |
| enum | void | |

Appendix **F** | # Tips for C Users

The following are some tips and guidelines for developing programs in C.

1 | In declaring integer variables, the *int* type is preferred over the *short*. For most compilers, the *int* type is the most efficient. An even better alternative is to define your own type as

```
typedef COUNT int;
```

and use this in your program. You can then switch all integer declarations, if necessary, by editing a single statement.

2 | Use the *scanf( )* function only for machine-readable input. Do not use *scanf( )* for user input through the keyboard. With most compilers, the *scanf( )* function has unusual and undefined side effects with certain types of input.

3 | If possible, use *fgets( )* for user input. It is the preferred input function for user input. The C *gets( )* function will not check for input buffer overflow. Loading a long string to a local variable can corrupt the local variable stack on overflow. The *fgets( )* does a check and avoids this overflow problem. However, you must allow two extra buffer bytes for the line-feed character and null.

4 | Avoid the use of the *char* type to hold single characters or small

numbers. The *int* type is considered more efficient with most compilers.

5 | Don't confuse the equality operator (==) with the assignment operator (=). The assignment operator is used to change the value of the variable to the left of the operator. The equality operator is used to check for equality.

6 | Avoid floating point comparisons. Use integers when testing for equality.

7 | Don't confuse the backslash with the forward slash. The backslash is used for directory names and escape characters. The forward slash is used for compiler options, comments, and division.

8 | Pointers are one of the most confusing issues for beginning C programmers, since pointers are not supported in most other languages. Initialize pointers to null. Don't assign a value to an address contained by a pointer without assigning an address to the pointer, for example:

```
/* Don't do this */

main()
{
        int *ptr;
        *ptr = 5;
        printf("%d",*ptr);
}
```

Ignoring this restriction may still allow the program to work, since the value will be stored at an arbitrary and random address; but if the random address is in the middle of your code, you could create a strange effect.

9 | Always be sure to include the break statement at the end of each case block in your switch structures. If you fail to do this, all case statements after the matching case will be executed.

10 | An array starts at 0, not 1. In declaring an array, the value in the brackets is the total number of elements; that is,

```
char msg[10];
```

stores 10 characters, not 11. The first element is msg[0].

11 | The general form of the *for* statement is

```
for(i=0; i < END_VALUE; i++)
        list[i]= 0;
```

where the first expression is the initializing statement, the second the control, and the third the step.

12 | In naming variables, choose names that are significant within the context of your program. Don't start a name with an underscore, since names starting with an underscore are reserved for system use.

13 | In declaring strings that will be used for input with the *scanf( )* function, use arrays instead of pointer variables.

14 | Keep expressions simple. If necessary, use macros and multiple statements to simplify expressions.

15 | Keep the scope of your variables as small as possible. Pass values and addresses by using arguments and return values, not by using global variables. This keeps your functions portable and you can use them in other programs. It also simplifies debugging.

16 | Don't use the same variable name for two different variables. If `square` is used as an auto variable in the main program, don't use the same name for an auto variable in a function.

17 | Don't initialize a variable unless necessary. For example, it is not necessary to initialize a *for . . . else* loop counter because the *for . . . else* construct initializes the counter.

```
int ctr = 0;

for (ctr = 1; ctr <=10; ++ctr)
```

18 | Always use the *extern* keyword for external referencing, even when the function immediately follows the declaration. It improves the readability of the program.

19 | In declaring a static or global array, you can omit the value for the array size if you initialize it:

```
static char msg[] = "Hello out there";
```

This saves you from having to count the characters.

20 | Use register variables for loop counters to improve the execution speed of the program.

21 | Avoid superseding a declaration. Do not redeclare a variable that you have already declared. *Note*: The *extern* keyword does not redeclare a variable, but only references a variable already declared.

22 | Avoid overloading, or trying to minimize, variables by using a variable name for multiple purposes.

23 | Keep declarations at the beginning of the block in which they are used.

24 | References to external variables in a function should precede local declarations.

25 | When using large constants, parameterize the constant to improve portability to other machines or compilers. For example, notice how **MAXNEGINT** is used here:

```
#define MAXSIZE 20
#define MAXNEGINT 0100000
main()
{
        static int values[MAXSIZE];
        int index = 0, size, max = MAXNEGINT;
        char inputa[10];

        do {
                printf("Please enter a number: ");
                fgets(inputa,10,stdin);
                values[index] = atoi(inputa);
                }
        while (values[index++] != 0);
        size = index - 1;
        for (index=0; index < size; index++)
                if (values[index]>max)
                        max = values[index];
        printf("The maximum value is %d\n", max);
}
```

The following form for the same declaration would be poor style:

```
int index = 0, size, max = -32768;
```

26 | Declare all globals in one place, and that should be in the *include* file. In this file, a comment statement should label them as globals. For example, suppose you wrote the previous example as

```
{
short number, square, cube, quad;
main()
        extern int number, square, cube, quad;
/* Don't do it this way */
        :
        :
```

The variables are declared globally as *short* and are then accessed within the function, using the *extern* keyword as *int*. The results are unpredictable and will vary with the compiler. Declaring all globals in one place minimizes this. See chapter 9 for an even better idea.

27 | Arrays of class *automatic* are created out of stack space and are not cleared to zero on starting. For this reason, you should always ini-

tialize any *automatic* class arrays. Arrays that are declared *static* or *external* are cleared by the C run-time start-up code.

28 | Avoid using *long* type when *int* will do. Cast if necessary. For example,

```
width = (w1+2) * config.numxpixels / config.numtextcols;
```

will not work. The value of `(w1+2)` could be as high as 82 and `config.numxpixels` as high as 640. The product exceeds the range for an *int* type. You could solve this by typing everything *long*, but a better method is to cast:

```
width = (int) (((long) (w1+2)) * (long)
config.numxpixels / (long) config.numtextcols);
```

29 | Use high-level file I/O instead of low-level unless you have a specific need to use low-level file I/O.

On Portability

When you are porting code between C implementations, keep in mind the following:

1 | Keep macros to eight or fewer arguments.

2 | Keep text strings to 512 or fewer characters.

3 | You may get different error messages, depending on how rigorously the compiler checks the code. For example, QuickC will compile

```
#define FALSE 0
#define FALSE 0
```

without an error message about the variable being defined twice. Another compiler might give an error message.

On Optimization

QuickC, unlike Microsoft C version 5.0 and Turbo C, is not an optimizing compiler. If the optimization option is selected on compiling, QuickC generates 80286 code and does some constant folding, but that's about it.

Some programmers try clever tricks to hand-optimize their code, such as using deeply nested expressions to eliminate lines of code. This may or may not provide any real optimization. The same number of code lines may be generated or, even worse, the compiler may not accept the complex statement.

G | Resources

The following resources are recommended for C programmers:

Books

Harbison, Samuel P., and Guy L. Steele, Jr. | *C: A Reference Manual.* 2nd ed. Englewood Cliffs, NJ: Prentice-Hall, 1987.

This should be considered the primary reference manual for C programming definitions, techniques, and style. No programmer should be without a copy.

Lafore, Robert | *Microsoft C Programming for the IBM.* Indianapolis, IN: Howard W. Sams, 1987.

This is a good tutorial for the C language with extensive examples.

Prata, Stephen | *Advanced C Primer++.* Indianapolis, IN: Howard W. Sams, 1986.

This is a good overview of more advanced C techniques, including the use of the *int86( )* function for graphics displays.

Townsend, Carl | *QuickC Programming for the IBM.* Indianapolis, IN: Howard W. Sams, 1988.

This contains a mailing list program in QuickC, illustrating basic programming principles and the techniques of structured programming.

Waite, Mitchell, Stephen Prata and Donald Martin | *C Primer Plus*. Indianapolis, IN: Howard W. Sams, 1987.

This is a good tutorial for the C language with extensive examples.

Tools

Many commercial products are available to C programmers, including code libraries, debuggers, and utilities. The following are intended only as a sample.

Database Management

FairCom (4006 West Broadway, Columbia, MO 65203) markets c-tree and r-tree. The c-tree product is an ISAM indexing system for managing relational database files. Records can be fixed or variable in length. The r-tree product is a report generator using script files to control the report format. The system is not a database manager, but rather a set of library routines to enable programmers to write custom database managers. Considerable programming expertise in C is required. The system does provide a level of support for Windows (see the next section). A d-tree product is also in development for supporting high-level database system design.

Windows

Microsoft markets a Software Development Kit for developing programs for its Windows environment. The SDK currently supports certain implementations of C and Pascal language. It does not support either Turbo C or QuickC, since special compiler options, start-up code, and linking are required. You can, however, develop a basic program model in QuickC and then convert it to the Windows environment by using Microsoft C version 5.0 or later. For more information see *Windows Programming* by Carl Townsend (Howard W. Sams, 1988).

Utilities

The C language, as already mentioned, is weak on input and output functions, particularly for graphics displays. Various manufacturers make utility toolkits that extend the basic support. Of particular interest is Creative Programming's Vitamin-C product (Box 112079, Carrollton, TX 75011-2097). This utility provides functions for text graphics support such as writing or entering text at a cursor location and text-mode window creation. Vitamin-C also provides input functions for validating input and receiving keyboard input against a defined template. You can also create help files that are accessible with the F1 key.

Glossary

Algorithm | A set of steps for solving a problem.

Array | A data structure in which all the elements are the same type.

BIOS | An acronym for Basic Input Output System. BIOS is a collection of hardware-specific drivers for peripherals.

BIOS services | DOS-supported software routines that are used for interfacing programs with the user's hardware. The DOS routines are independent of the user's hardware, making programs using them system independent. The output of the BIOS services drives the BIOS routines.

Block | Statements grouped together with enclosing braces and executed as a unit.

Buffer | A set of continuous memory locations that are used to temporarily store a collection of related data.

Compiler | A program that converts one language to another, generally from a high-level to a machine-level language. The output of the compiler is an object code.

Conditional structure | A program structure in which the program chooses one of several groups of statements to execute based on the value of a control expression. C supports the *if . . . else* and *switch* conditional structures.

Control expression | Any expression that evaluates to zero or nonzero and that is used to determine whether a statement is executed or to determine the order of statement execution.

Data-driven language | A language that supports programming in which a problem is defined in terms of objects and the relationships between the objects.

Declarations | Statements in a C program that associate identifiers with C objects such as variables, functions, or types.

Direct mode | A fast method of creating graphics by bypassing the DOS routines and writing directly into memory at the locations from which the image is displayed.

Directives | *See* **Preprocessor directives.**

Executable code | A binary code file that can be executed directly.

Expression | Any combination of operands and operators.

Files | Named sections of storage on a floppy disk, hard disk, tape, or other storage device.

Function | A procedure that relates a dependent variable to one or more independent variables or performs a single, specified action.

Global variables | Variables available to all functions and modules of a program.

Iteration structure | A program structure that permits the program to execute a group of statements a specified number of times based on a certain condition. C supports the *while, do . . . while*, and *for* iteration structures.

Linker | A program that converts the object code produced by a compiler to an executable form, converting relative addresses to absolute and resolving references to library routines.

Machine language | A computer language that uses the internal binary codes of the computer's processor.

Macro | A defined substitution in a C program.

Object code | The machine-language code produced by a compiler. The code contains relative (rather than absolute) memory locations for instructions and variable data and must be linked with library routines and other code before it is executable.

Operator | The "verb" in a C statement. The operator defines actions to be performed on one or more operands.

Origin | The starting point on the display for writing text or drawing graphics. For a text mode, the origin is in the upper left at 1, 1. For a graphics mode, the origin is in the upper left at 0, 0.

Pixel | The smallest addressable unit on a graphics display. An EGA display is 640 pixels wide by 350 pixels high.

Preprocessor directives | Instructions placed at the beginning of the program that contain instructions for the compiler.

Procedural language | A high-level language that is designed to support programming in which a series of steps is followed to get the desired output from a specified input.

Recursion | The process of defining an operation in terms of itself. An example is the factorial function, which calls itself during execution.

Stack | A local memory area that functions in a last-in first-out mode. Automatic variables are stored in the stack.

Statement | An expression followed by a semicolon.

Storage class | An attribute of a C variable that defines its scope (availability to other functions) and the length of time the variable remains in memory. The default storage class is automatic.

Text graphics | A method of creating a graphics display by sending ASCII codes to the display.

Type | A set of values in a C program and a set of operations on those values. For example, the *int* is an integer type that supports addition, subtraction, multiplication, division, the modulo operation, and assignments.

Answers to Quizzes

1 | 1-C, 2-D, 3-C, 4-D, 5-C, 6-A, 7-D, 8-C, 9-A, 10-C, 11-C, 12-C, 13-C, 14-D, 15-D

2 | 1-C, 2-A, 3-C, 4-B, 5-A, 6-C, 7-D, 8-C, 9-B, 10-A, 11-A, 12-C, 13-C, 14-C, 15-A

3 | 1-B, 2-B, 3-C, 4-B, 5-B, 6-B, 7-A, 8-B, 9-D, 10-B, 11-C, 12-D, 13-C, 14-B, 15-D

4 | 1-A, 2-B, 3-A, 4-C, 5-B, 6-B, 7-D, 8-C, 9-D, 10-D, 11-B, 12-A, 13-D, 14-C, 15-B

5 | 1-D, 2-D, 3-D, 4-C, 5-B, 6-A, 7-B, 8-A, 9-D, 10-A, 11-C, 12-D, 13-A, 14-A, 15-C

6 | 1-D, 2-C, 3-B, 4-A, 5-A, 6-B, 7-B, 8-A, 9-A, 10-B, 11-A, 12-C, 13-D, 14-C, 15-B

7 | 1-C, 2-B, 3-D, 4-A, 5-D, 6-B, 7-D, 8-B, 9-C, 10-B, 11-B, 12-A, 13-B, 14-B, 15-B

8 | 1-C, 2-B, 3-D, 4-C, 5-A, 6-B, 7-B, 8-C, 9-B, 10-B, 11-A, 12-D, 13-D, 14-B, 15-A

9 | 1-D, 2-A, 3-C, 4-D, 5-C, 6-C, 7-C, 8-B, 9-B, 10-D, 11-D, 12-D, 13-B, 14-D, 15-D

10 | 1-B, 2-C, 3-D, 4-A, 5-A, 6-C, 7-C, 8-B, 9-A, 10-B, 11-C, 12-C, 13-D, 14-D, 15-A

11 | 1-D, 2-D, 3-C, 4-D, 5-D, 6-D, 7-D, 8-D, 9-C, 10-C, 11-A, 12-C, 13-A, 14-D, 15-A

12 | 1-C, 2-B, 3-B, 4-B, 5-C, 6-B, 7-C, 8-D, 9-A, 10-A, 11-A, 12-A, 13-B, 14-C, 15-B

13 | 1-D, 2-C, 3-C, 4-B, 5-C, 6-B, 7-C, 8-B, 9-A, 10-D, 11-C, 12-B, 13-A, 14-C, 15-B

14 | 1-C, 2-B, 3-A, 4-B, 5-C, 6-A, 7-A, 8-D, 9-D, 10-C

15 | 1-B, 2-C, 3-D, 4-A, 5-B, 6-D, 7-D, 8-D, 9-D, 10-B

Index

A

The Waite Group's
Inside the AMIGA® with C, Second Edition
John Berry

Everyone who has recently upgraded their AMIGA computer system, or is thinking about doing it, needs this revised edition of *Inside the AMIGA with C*. The book covers the AmigaDOS™ operating system in greater detail, and is compatible with the new AmigaDOS 1.2. Paying particular attention to the AMIGA 500, the book presents special AMIGA graphics features including sprites, Genlock, and blitter objects, with updated information on Intuition™

Like the original book, code listings in each chapter are carefully constructed both as practical routines and as instructional examples for beginning to intermediate C programmers. The new edition features several new programs that demonstrate the use of color palettes and registers and a software toolkit that contains a library of C routines to create and manage screens, windows, input from gadgets, and control graphics.

Topics covered include:

- The AMIGA Programming Environment
- Using Intuition
- Process Control and AmigaDOS
- Drawing in Intuition
- Animating the Sprites
- Programming Sound
- Artificial Speech
- Programming with Disk Files

400 Pages, 7½ x 9¾, Softbound
ISBN: 0-672-22625-1
No. 22625, $24.95

C++ Programming Guide for the IBM®
John Berry and Mitchell Waite, The Waite Group

C++ Programming Guide for the IBM is a complete guide and tutorial to the C++ language specifically adapted to the IBM PC family.

Aimed at developers and students, it teaches the use of object-oriented programming skills and introduces the major features of the language with explanations followed by practical examples. It builds three professional libraries—cEntry, cGraphics, and cWindows—which enable programmers and developers to find shortcuts to the often cumbersome programming process.

Topics covered include:

- How the C++ Translator Works
- New C++ Syntax
- The C++ Stream h. Library
- The Inline Functions
- What the New C++ Pointers Offer
- Memory Allocation Functions
- Void Type Pointer to Generic Object
- New C++ Structured Data Type Versus the Old
- Private and Public Structures
- Hiding the Implementation
- Access by Non-member Functions
- Constructors and Destructors
- Overloading Functions and Operators

400 Pages, 7½ x 9¾, Softbound
ISBN: 0-672-22619-7
No. 22619, $24.95

Microsoft® C Bible
Nabajyoti Barkakati, The Waite Group

Microsoft C Bible provides a thorough description of the 370 functions of the Microsoft C library, complete with practical, real-world MS-DOS-based examples for each function. Library routines are broken down into functional categories with an intermediate-level tutorial followed by the functions and examples.

Included are two "quick-start" tutorials, complete ANSI prototypes for each function, extensive program examples, and handy jump tables to help enhance learning.

Topics covered include:

- Overview of the C Language
- Microsoft C 5.0 Compiler Features and Options
- Process Control
- Variable Length Argument Lists
- Memory Allocation and Management
- Buffer Manipulation
- Data Conversion Routines
- Math Routines
- Character Classification and Conversion
- String Comparison and Manipulation
- Searching and Sorting
- Time Routines
- File and Directory Manipulation
- Input and Output Routines
- System Calls
- Graphics Modes, Coordinates, and Attributes
- Drawing and Animation
- Combining Graphics and Text

824 Pages, 7½ x 9¾, Softbound
ISBN: 0-672-22620-0
No. 22620, $24.95

Turbo C Developer's Library
Edward R. Rought and Thomas D. Hoops

Designed for the programmer and applications developer, this book contains a wealth of information to eliminate the dreary task of creating all the background routines that make up a high-quality professional application. It is a comprehensive collection of high-performance routines created by applications developers. The routines allow the reader to concentrate on what the application will accomplish rather than on the tools needed to create it.

This complete set of procedures and functions includes routines for menu management, data base development, data entry, printing, and many other areas that are used daily in applications development.

Topics covered include:

- Introduction
- How to Use the Libraries
- How to Use the Routine Descriptions
- Hardware and Software Configurations
- Main Library Routines
- Btrieve® File System Routines
- Novell Networking Routines
- Sample Applications and Utilities
- Appendices: Cross References, Keyboard Scan Code Table, Bibliography

450 Pages, 7½ x 9¾, Softbound
ISBN: 0-672-22642-1
No. 22642, $24.95

Visit your local book retailer, use the order form provided, or call 800-428-SAMS.